IMAGINING URBAN FUTURES

IMAGINING URBAN FUTURES

CITIES IN SCIENCE FICTION AND WHAT WE MIGHT LEARN FROM THEM

CARL ABBOTT

WESLEYAN UNIVERSITY PRESS | MIDDLETOWN, CONNECTICUT

Wesleyan University Press
Middletown CT 06459
www.wesleyan.edu/wespress
© 2016 Carl Abbott

Manufactured in the United States of America
Designed by April Leidig
Typeset in Whitman by Copperline Book Services

Hardcover ISBN: 978-0-8195-7671-2
Ebook ISBN: 978-0-8195-7672-9

Library of Congress Cataloging-in-Publication Data
available upon request.

5 4 3 2 1

CONTENTS

ACKNOWLEDGMENTS

I like cities large and small—a good thing, since I've been studying and writing about their history for over forty years—while recognizing the challenges that urbanization and urban life can present. In a previous book called *Frontiers Past and Future: Science Fiction and the American West*, I explored the ways in which American science fiction has adapted the different narratives that we have used to understand the English-speaking conquest and settlement of North America. This book is the complement and companion piece, an exploration of ways in which science fiction utilizes the stories that we tell about the mature societies and cultures that cities embody.

I have received feedback from the Chicago Urban History Seminar held at the Chicago Historical Society. The Alternate Realities reading group at Portland State University, organized by Annabelle Dolidon and including Tony Wolk and Grace Dillon, has helped me think about different ways to approach speculative fiction. I also received welcome comments and advice from science fiction scholars Carol McGuirk and Rob Latham, historian Robert Fishman, and an outside reader for the Wesleyan University Press. A portion of the introduction appeared in the online journal *Deletions* and a portion of chapter 3 in the online magazine *Clarkesworld*.

IMAGINING URBAN FUTURES

Winner of an Academy Award for special effects, the 1951 film *When Worlds
Collide* is one of the most striking early examples of the disaster movie in
which an external force lays low the cities of the Earth, in this case leaving
only a handful of earthlings to escape in a highly streamlined rocket ship.
Courtesy Paramount Pictures / Photofest © Paramount Pictures.

INTRODUCTION

Nothing says trouble like a city smashed to smithereens on screen. Meteors and earthquakes, tsunamis and glaciers, earthly monsters and alien invaders—moviegoers might think that the only thing science fiction does with cities is demolish them with big-budget special effects. Giant waves crash over New York in *Deluge* (1933) and *When Worlds Collide* (1951), an asteroid pulverizes it in *Deep Impact* (1998), and ice crushes it in *The Day after Tomorrow* (2004). Everyone knows that the star of *Godzilla: King of Monsters* (1956) has it in for Tokyo. Los Angeles takes hits in *Earthquake* (1974) and *Independence Day* (1996), whose flying saucer bad guys also take out New York, Washington, and Paris, itself soon reobliterated in *Armageddon* (1998). Not to be outdone, screenwriters for *2012* (2009) devised a planetary cataclysm to eradicate Los Angeles, Washington, Rome, and every other city lower than Tibet.

Look again and the picture is far more interesting. Cities certainly perish on the science fiction screen and page, but they also grow, thrive, and decline in complex and intriguing ways. Hit the science fiction section at your local library or used bookstore for the pure pleasure of browsing the covers. Among the exotic planetscapes, cosmic vistas, and battling starships are cities seen from above and below, from near and afar. Cities soar in the distant view of foregrounded heroes and shelter beneath transparent domes like gigantic snow globes. Tiny humans and all manner of other creatures clog street corners and thread their way among the intricate towers, tunnels, sky bridges, wiring, and plumbing of the coming metropolis. Artists bathe their visions with the patina of fantasy or the shimmer of high tech.

We—the majority of humankind—already live in an urban world and share an urban future. Cities are home to a majority of our planet's population, and they are gaining a greater edge over the countryside with each passing year. Sometime in the first decade of the present century, so far as demographers can calculate, more than half of humankind became city people. I wouldn't bet on the exact date, but the world crossed the fifty–fifty threshold between city life and rural life in 2008, according to the United Nations Department of Economic and Social Affairs. China passed the same milestone at the end of 2011, with an official count of 691 million city dwellers. By the end of the century, the worldwide ratio of city to country is likely to be three to one or even four to one, the balance already reached in Western Europe and North America.

Since our mundane future will be so decidedly urban, it is no surprise that the science fiction imagination has generated cities by the bucketful. Cities are background and setting for stories on and off future Earth, often assumed as a natural part of coming society. They are sometimes an active part of the plot, places whose characteristics are essential to a story's contests and conflicts. At times they become actors in their own right, intervening and shaping as well as framing the action. The future, the native land of science fiction, will be an urban future for all foreseeable generations. It's like a syllogism:

Science fiction is about the future.
The human future will be urban.
Therefore, science fiction should be about urban futures.

Voyage outward from Earth. Settlers on the moon will likely live in underground cities—at least that's what Larry Niven and Allen Steele propose. Martian pioneers will start off in domed cities and then transition to surface cities as terraforming takes effect—at least as Kim Stanley Robinson has projected that planet's future. On Venus cities will float in the thick atmosphere, says Pamela Sargent. Intrepid extraterrestrial homesteaders may hope to make new lives under new skies and stars, but they will need cities and towns to supply their tools and market their crops—at least that is how Robert Heinlein envisioned the future on Ganymede. And sometimes creative imaginations have run wild to fashion implausible superfantastic cities that are built into miles-deep canyon sides, that pierce the stratosphere like huge stalagmites, that raft together on the deep sea, that span huge chasms on vast platforms, that englobe entire planets, and that even disassemble and reassemble themselves to creep across the landscape.

Waive your berth on the next interstellar departure and you may still find yourself in the future of a present-day city. We can experience the effects of climate change on Boston and Washington and economic stagnation on Los Angeles and Detroit. We can navigate an imagined megacity—super-high-rise Chicago or cybernetic Tokyo or hypertrophied Shanghai. We can choose among dozens of different Londons and New Yorks and explore the rise of the Global South in future Bangkoks, Saigons, and Istanbuls where a few social or technological tweaks can lead to fascinatingly different cities.

What is a city, by the way? With lots of small variations, historians and archaeologists agree that cities are *big, long lasting, densely developed,* and *full of difference*—different types of people, jobs, neighborhoods, and economic activities.[1] They are also *points of exchange* that influence people outside their boundaries. People come to cities to trade goods, services, ideas, and their own labor. More than anything else, a city is a device for making connections. It is a system for creating innovation and change, because the best way for any of us to come up with a new idea is to bring us in contact with strangers and their strange opinions. This is what Samuel R. Delany has in mind when he writes that "cities are fun precisely because they encourage encounters across class lines" and other social strata of race and sexuality. Putting it more concretely, says Delany, "There must be places where Capulets can regularly meet Montagues and fall in love."[2]

Deeper in time behind the last two centuries of exploding industrial urbanization are six thousand years when humans independently invented cities at least six times in what are now Egypt, Iraq, China,

India-Pakistan, Mexico-Guatemala, and Peru. In fits and starts, as king-doms and empires flourished and fell, urban society spread gradually into different corners of the world—to Londinium and Angkor and Tim-buktu and Cahokia and Cuzco. Some cities have been so useful as to be invented and then reinvented multiple times, as with the Romes of Hadrian, the Medici popes, Mussolini, and Federico Fellini. Cities are a natural part of human society past and present . . . so it is not surprising that they are part of our near and far futures.

So, sure, science fiction is about rocket ships and weird aliens and strange new worlds. It is about technologies possible and impossible—genetic engineering, cloning, robotics, artificial intelligence, nanotech-nology . . . and warp drives and time travel. Cities do not often appear as a category on these common lists of science fiction subject matter, but they are ubiquitous nevertheless. Some future cities function as effort-lessly as glitchless software. Others are dystopian disaster zones.

Science fiction cities sometimes work as familiarizing frames, serving up useful expectations for readers and viewers. Indeed, SF often employs cities as backgrounds and settings that function in much the same way that cities do today (just as Star Fleet functions in the Star Trek universe as a familiar naval bureaucracy). Peter Hamilton's city of Memu Bay in his space thriller *Fallen Dragon* (2001) would be totally familiar to a res-ident of Zurich or Milwaukee. C. J. Cherryh's city of Reseune in *Cyteen* (1988) and *Regenesis* (2009) is the research center for an empire based on cloning, with all the new social dynamics that implies, but the place itself is not all that different from an American or Indian science-park district found in Palo Alto or Bangalore. The planetary capital to which it reports has hotels and public buildings, streets and back alleys, airport and commercial waterfront—it could just as well be Seattle or Chicago.

Melissa Scott in *Burning Bright* (1993) similarly serves up a city that is far more familiar than strange. The plot intertwines interstellar political and commercial intrigue with the adventures of a space pilot who takes shore leave in the city of Burning Bright to practice her skills as the designer of computer-based role-playing games. The city itself sounds like fun, but it is one where Scott's readers could easily find their way around. It has elite neighborhoods and poorer neighborhoods, upscale shopping streets, warehouse districts, down-market bars, and a colorful waterfront. Residents get about on foot, with water buses on a canal system, and with helicabs. Just like home, the main streets are brightly illuminated but the side streets dimly lit with "pool[s] of light that marked each intersection to the brief edge of almost-dark where the first light ended and the next did not quite reach" (112). We're far, far away from Earth, but not far at all from the noir ambiance of 1940s Los Angeles.

There is some resistance to an urban approach to science fiction. Anti-urbanism is an easy reflex for anyone raised within Anglo-American culture, with its long-standing reverence for Arcadian scenes and rural society. Clifford Simak's *City* (1952) presents a society that happily evolves beyond the need for urban places. Ursula Le Guin's *The Eye of the Heron* (1978) presents a recently settled planet divided between a rural society that values hard work, peace, and gender equality and a city that is a nascent Nineveh—masculine, rigid, corrupt, exploitative, and cruel. Only by escaping the city and joining with the People of Peace can Luz Marina Falco realize her personhood. Or here, from *City of Ruins* (2011), are words that Kristine Kathryn Rusch puts into the mouth of Boss, the kickass woman who is the continuing protagonist in a series of novels about space exploration, time travel, and galactic politics:

> I travel to Vaycehn reluctantly. I don't like cities. I never have. Cities are as opposite from the things I love as anything can get.
>
> First, they exist planetside, and I try never to go planetside.
>
> Second, they are filled with people, and I prefer to spend most of my time alone.
>
> Third, cities have little to explore, and what small amount of unknown territory there is has something built on top of it or beside it.
>
> The history of a city is known, and there is no danger. (7)

Rusch seems to be channeling critic Gary K. Wolfe, who has argued that cities are basically antithetical to the science fiction imagination. Cities, he suggests, represent confinement, limitations on possibility, the known rather than the unknown. They are stasis rather than change, contrary to the science fiction spirit of adventure and discovery.[3] This position goes beyond a simple negative evaluation of city life (cities as jungles, cities as sources of eco-catastrophe) to a larger position that, in effect, cities are useful only to serve the spaceports that allow authors to launch their stories into unfamiliar territory. It is another version of space as frontier, with cities standing in for the jump-off points for the Oregon Trail. In *The Martian Chronicles* (1950), Ray Bradbury began his story "The Settlement" with emigrant families waiting to embark for Mars from Independence, Missouri.

I argue the contrary—that cities can be front and center as vividly imagined worlds whose characteristics play active roles that help to structure the arc of the story, forcing and constraining the choices that the characters make. For earthly cities, the Los Angeles of Octavia Butler in *Parable of the Sower* (1993) and the Bangkok of Paolo Bacigalupi in *The Windup Girl* (2009) fill the bill. Their state of physical and social decay is an essential driver for their developing plots. On an imagined world, New Crobuzon is as much a force in China Miéville's novels as London was for Charles Dickens. Cities are sentient actors in John Shirley's *City Come A-Walkin'* (1980), Greg Bear's *Strength of Stones* (1988), and Carrie Richerson's "The City in Morning" (1999).

There are thousands of science fiction cities—as many or more than the number of actual cities of twenty-first-century Earth. My solution to this abundance is to identify common ways in which we imagine the urban future in a wide and eclectic range of books, films, and television rather than dwelling on a few noteworthy examples, although familiar places like Arthur C. Clarke's Diaspar and Isaac Asimov's Trantor will make their appearance. No matter how varied the specific twists and locations, science fiction writers imagine future and alternative cities in several distinct ways—as machines, for example, or as prisons, or, sometimes, as places just a little bit different from those of today. The field supplies a shared repertoire of city types that writers can use for background or develop for their own purposes.

As we think about the multiple cities of science fiction, it is useful to consider additional syllogisms that suggest two basic and inclusive ways that the field approaches cities. One strand derives from the technological/design imagination and its ability to think up cities whose form and function express new technical possibilities. The second comes from the desire to consider future social and cultural systems that find their most developed and conflicted forms in cities. Together the physical and social imaginations create the two big clusters of city types explored in the following chapters.

Science fiction is about the implications of new technologies.
Cities are the most complex of technological artifacts.
Therefore, science fiction is [often] about the physical and
    technological possibilities of city making.

Science fiction tries to explore the future of human society.
Cities are the central organizing system for human society.
Therefore, SF is [often] about the complexities of living in future cities.

The first syllogism reaches back to early efforts to imagine the shape of ideal places, both fantastical schemes like Tommaso Campanella's *City of the Sun* (1602) and bureaucratic prescriptions like the Laws of the Indies that the Spanish crown promulgated as a guide to laying out colonial cities in the Americas. The impulse continued in the proposals of early industrial-era reformers like Robert Owen and Charles Fourier, who were engrossed with schemes for social betterment through remaking the physical structure of settlements. These were the "utopian socialists" whom Friedrich Engels pointedly criticized for ignoring the primacy of economic relationships that truly determined spatial patterns. In practice, early Western utopias imitated the everyday communities of the time. The City of the Sun was an idealized Renaissance city. Fourier's phalanstery and the idealized scheme for Owen's Harmony colony in Indiana resembled the factory/dormitory complexes of textile towns like Lowell, Massachusetts.[4]

About 150 years ago, new technologies of transportation—horizontal railways and self-powered automobiles, vertical elevators—allowed the design imagination to expand and soar. Facing ever-growing industrial cities, design visionaries began to explore a fundamental choice: Should the metropolis deconcentrate or centralize more effectively—should it grow outward or upward? In the first group we can count Frederick Law Olmsted, Horace Cleveland, and other landscape architects who wanted to reduce urban densities by building parks and open space into the urban fabric. Ebenezer Howard proposed "Garden Cities of To-morrow" (his 1902 book title) as a way to deconcentrate London. Frank Lloyd Wright's scheme for Broadacre City preceded the General Motors Futurama exhibit at the New York World's Fair, with its model of a freeway nation in miniature, by only seven years. The opposite impulse was to envision megastructures that extrapolated the first-generation skyscrapers of New York and Chicago. The Swiss-French architect Le Corbusier proposed clusters of towers in a park linked into a single entity by underground passages. Paolo Soleri envisioned vast self-contained cities for hundreds of thousands of residents with quirky names like "3-D Jersey" and "Novanoah."[5]

Pictures are powerful, and the visual punch of creative design has made it a rich source for science fiction. As Bruce Sterling has noted, genre science fiction emerged in tandem with the art deco extravaganzas of "century of progress" expositions in Chicago (1933–34), New York (1939–40), and San Francisco (1939–40), which provided the visual vocabulary that artists like Frank R. Paul transmuted into pulp magazine covers.[6] Garden cities, Corbusian towers, and arcologies have all come with compelling diagrams and drawings that easily capture eyes and imaginations—especially Soleri's drawings in the oversized *Arcology: The City in the Image of Man*.[7] Architects continue to relish chances to show their imaginations and drawing skills, as with *eVolo* magazine's decade-long imaginary skyscraper competition.[8] The fantastic cities of comics, anime, and video games extend the same tradition of science fiction as a visual medium.

Behind many of the classic diagrams and drawings, however, are social visions that link to the second syllogism. Ebenezer Howard wanted to find a route toward a socialist society via land reform inspired by the theories of Henry George in *Progress and Poverty* (1879), with Garden

Cities as the tool rather than the end point. The first edition of his book in 1899 summarized his goal with its title *To-morrow: A Peaceful Path to Real Reform*, and he regretted the distracting diagrams he had published as thought experiments. With an approach completely opposite that of his contemporary Howard, the eccentric entrepreneur King Camp Gillette in 1894 proposed consolidating the entire American population in a single vast metropolis in western New York State to counter the chaos of individualism.[9] Le Corbusier and Soleri both claimed the environmental goal of freeing land from urban encroachment by concentrating people within limited building footprints. Recurring proposals for lineal cities stretched along transportation lines have aimed at economic efficiency and social equality—a sort of urbanist manifestation of collectivist principles.

Even design utopians thus recognize that the social dimension is primary in the process of urban growth, despite the seductions of the visual. Cities are vast physical objects because they are machines for making connections among thousands and millions of individuals. They are human life support systems with distinct metabolisms. They collect, process, and distribute goods and information in the complex economy of production and consumption. They bring individuals together to facilitate the routines of everyday life. In *The Gold Coast* (1988), Kim Stanley Robinson interweaves all three connective functions. He highlights the freeway system as the support structure for future Orange County, California, critiques defense contractors as the economic drive wheel, and explores individual efforts to connect into communities through workplace, school, church, and social clique. The picture is not pretty, for the book is Robinson's version of California well along the wrong path of rampant capitalism, but the elements of connection are there.

Like Robinson, ecologists, economists, geographers, and sociologists all want to understand the costs and benefits of urban connectivity: Do cities run on poverty and immiseration as their necessary social and economic fuel, an assertion that goes back to Karl Marx? Do capitalist cities generate spatially structured inequality by their very nature, as geographer David Harvey argues, or do they provide the tools with which individuals build the capacities to improve their lives? How do the new contacts and interactions that they enable compare with the social worlds in alternative settings such as small towns and villages? Is community-without-propinquity—the development of interpersonal connections based on common interests rather than residential proximity —as rich as localized neighborhood communities?[10]

Anglo-American culture—the dominant seedbed of science fiction— assumes the negative about urban life more often and more easily than does continental culture.[11] It is easy to trace American antiurban thinking through intellectual traditions and popular culture.[12] When Thomas Jefferson compared cities to cancers and sores on the body politic, he set a tone that has resonated in American politics for two centuries ("Ford to City: Drop Dead" read the *New York Daily News* headline of October 29, 1975, after President Gerald Ford nixed a federal bailout for the bankrupt city).[13] Nineteenth-century fears of cities as cauldrons of social disorder and political chaos fueled the urban dystopias that appeared again and again in imagined futures of the late nineteenth and early twentieth centuries. Even in the twenty-first century, a majority of Americans hold to the ideal of small-town living over big-city life that is supposedly less satisfying, less authentic, less healthy, more dangerous, and more alienating.

The comprehensive findings of social science, however, are not so clear. City people in the United States have roughly the same density of social networks as small-town folks, just skewed away from kin and toward groups of common interest.[14] Even the slums and shantytowns of Latin America and South Asia are places of opportunity for the rural poor, with better health care, education, and job opportunities. In developing countries, city dwellers generally are more likely than their rural counterparts to say they are happy.[15] Cities are cultural incubators, technological innovators, and the places where reformers introduce and test progressive institutions. The city as creative milieu is a network of industries and universities, artists and entrepreneurs. It is easy to poke fun at Richard Florida's trendy idea of an urban creative class, but economists and urban planners can agree that certain metropolitan settings have a special ability to generate change.[16]

Science fiction, of course, always draws on the knowledge base available to its creators. Writers of hard SF take scientific advances from the pages of *Science*, *Nature*, *New Scientist*, or *Scientific American* and build stories on those foundations. Robert Heinlein argued decades ago that writers of science fiction are free to imagine the uncertain and unknown, but not to ignore the body of accepted knowledge. Writers who want to base stories on the effects of black holes or on genetic engineering need specific understanding of the relevant physics or biology. The producers of the SF epic film *Interstellar* (2014) won kudos from the science fiction community for consulting with astrophysicist Kip Thorne and utilizing wormholes "appropriately," whereas Star Trek warp drives don't merit the same respect. H. G. Wells was free in 1898 to populate Mars with spiderlike beings, given contemporary astronomy. If writers working in 2016 want to set some action on Pluto, however, they will have to pay attention to the findings from the New Horizons flyby in July 2015.

There is a difference, however, in the relationship of the natural sciences to hard SF when we move to the urban realm, where there are few firm answers to powerful questions. Someone writing cities into social science fiction has fewer reliable sources and fewer constraints than someone building a plausible planet according to the laws of physics. Novelists and scriptwriters who highlight cities are unlikely to consult Cal Tech professors, or even urban studies professors, but they do draw on the ideas and projects of designers, social scientists, and social utopians.

The design professions on their visionary edge are a free-for-all world of sometimes sober, sometimes audacious, and sometimes silly ideas that are an inviting grab bag for writers and artists. The stacked trailer towers in Ernest Cline's *Ready Player One* (2011) exaggerate the modular apartments of Le Corbusier's *unité d'habitation* in Marseilles. Geodesic domes are ubiquitous over future cities, imaginative projections of Buckminster Fuller's 1970s proposal for Old Man River City, a bundt-cake megastructure under a geodesic umbrella to replace troubled East St. Louis.[17]

Wright, Soleri, Fuller, and other ambitious and self-conscious planners and architects like Constantinos Doxiadis did not think of themselves as offering science fictions. Nevertheless, their versions of ideal cities—to be realized in the future—tilt toward the fantastic and provide jump-off points for writers as radically different as J. G. Ballard and Larry Niven.

The social sciences are even more uncertain ground. Dozens of stories have depended on John B. Calhoun's studies of overcrowded rats, but the application to people is much more tenuous than we popularly believe.[18] Social sciences are often ambiguous, uncertain, and roiled by competing political agendas and ideologies—just consider the five-hundred-year debate about the causes of poverty that started under the Tudors and shows no signs of resolution in the U.S. Congress or British Parliament. Writers can pick and choose between Jane Jacobs's celebration of Greenwich Village and Lewis Mumford's preference for Hudson River exurbia. They can attribute caste systems in a future city to capitalism, racism/speciesism, or genetic differences and find supporting experts and arguments. They can draw on Walter Benjamin's celebration of the variegated surface of big cities or Louis Wirth's analysis of the alienating effects of urban life, and neither is a wrong choice.

Nor do most writers feel much need to be explicit about their choices, for residents of an urbanizing world have internalized many assumptions about the nature of cities. As Nicola Griffith put it, "fiction generally embodies that which a culture knows to be true."[19] In a previous book, I argued that American science fiction has incorporated the common historical narratives of the American West. In some cases the frontier references are front and center, as in future homesteading stories about "the little house on the big planet," but in many others they are part of the background understanding that writers and readers share.[20] In this book I am making a parallel argument. We think we *know* that high-rise living is alienating, so neither Robert Silverberg nor J. G. Ballard has to justify dystopian assumptions. We *know* that multiethnic cities are both stimulating and intimidating, so China Miéville can easily project the same values on a multispecies city. In the chapters that follow, I will be looking at the explicit borrowing of ideas about cities and city life, but also at implicit parallels and broader assumptions that are the basis for imagined places. Novelists and screenwriters are creative artists, but they are also symbionts with the social sciences, with history, and with the design professions, drawing on their ideas and simultaneously enriching their conversations.

I write about cities as a historian and urban planner and about science fiction as both a reader and a critic, and think that it is not only fun but informative to explore the different types of SF cities. For this book I have identified eight generic science fiction cities that appear and reappear in different settings as variants on common themes and concerns. What I call types bear a close resemblance to what critic Brian Attebery has recently called science fiction "parabolas." Unlike some genre fiction like romances and westerns, where formulas nearly require certain plot elements and certain endings, science fiction is open-ended. Writers may start from a common premise or situation—galactic empires, generation starships—but science fiction readers relish the variations that can be developed from the same starting point as writers respond to each other's version. These departures never take us to the same place, just as the parabola is a curve that never returns to its starting point. Parabolas, write Attebery and Veronica Hollinger, are "combinations of meaningful setting, character, and action that lend themselves to endless redefinition and jazzlike improvisation."[21]

These types have developed in dialogue with the efforts of social reformers, social scientists, and designers to understand and improve cities. One of the goals of this book is to explore the variety and range of borrowings, influences, and interactions between SF and the ideas and practice of mundane urbanism and to embed science fiction in the body of urban theory and criticism. The loosely grouped set of cyberpunk writers from the 1980s and 1990s, for example, reflected critical urban theory around cities as communication systems and the effects of economic globalization. Samuel R. Delany has acknowledged that the Unlicensed Sector in *Trouble on Triton: An Ambiguous Heterotopia* (1976) is "a Jane Jacobs kind of thing" while drawing the subtitle from the work of Michel Foucault.

Each chapter will keep these questions in mind as it discusses ways in which writers, filmmakers, and visual artists have made use of these city types. What defines each type? What are some key examples? How do particular urban settings impact their stories? What do we gain in wonder, terror, and insight as we follow characters through different sorts of city? How do these cities reflect or exemplify our understanding of mundane cities in popular culture and formal social theory? The approach will be panoramic without being exhaustive, drawing examples from different media, from different science fiction eras, and from writers with very different sensibilities and politics. Chapters 5 and 6 are most closely grounded in the specific American experience of suburbanization and urban crisis, tracing a historical trajectory as writers in different decades respond to the changing world around them. The other chapters are structured synchronically as variations on a theme.

Taking off from design urbanism, the first three chapters explore different ways in which we envision future cities as physical objects—impressive, imposing, exciting, curious. "Techno City" deals with cities as containers for new technologies, from slideways to high-rise towers. The cities in "Machines for Breathing" become mega-machines in themselves, huge comprehensive artifacts that depend on sophisticated engineering to function. "Migratory Cities" are a variation on the self-contained cities of the previous chapters, carrying designer thought experiments to imaginative extremes in fictional form. Because these cities appear in narratives rather than in architectural portfolios and engineering specs, people in crisis and conflict drive the story line; but the physical container itself—whether space station city, migratory city, or some other variation—stirs readers' imaginations. C. J. Cherryh builds interesting characters and exciting situations to make *Downbelow Station* an exciting read, for example, but the central tension revolves around the fragility or survivability of the huge space-station city itself.

Chapters on "The Carceral City" and "Crabgrass Chaos" begin to shift focus to cities as social environments. The physical character of the city remains important—the city of refuge or city behind walls in the one chapter, the decaying suburban environment in the other. The pivots of the stories, however, are human responses to two types of confinement. Carceral cities are places where the physical barriers of ramparts and cavern walls produce psychological imprisonment that is integrated into the culture of everyday life—to be broken only by maverick misfits. The residents of feral suburbs, in contrast, live in places only a step from newspaper headlines. They are individually rebellious but imprisoned by the economic and social limitations of poverty, and their stories are dramas of stress and survival.

Chapter 6 deals with the variety of catastrophes that can threaten to undermine and destroy metropolitan life, and with the abandoned cities that result from disaster. Like the suburbs of "Crabgrass Chaos," the tottering cities discussed in "Soylent Green Is People!" are earthbound places of the near future. Over the decades, science fiction has explored a variety of crisis-and-collapse scenarios drawn from the social sciences and from societal fears of proletarian revolution, overpopulation, and overconsumption.[22] Cities intensify and concentrate problems and pressures to the point of social breakdown, planting the seeds of their own destruction. The result may be the abandoned cities that populate chapter 7 with stories of post-apocalyptic Earth and distant worlds where danger lurks among the ruins.

"Market and Mosaic" focuses on the city as a nexus of human activity—the city as social and economic community. Cities bring disparate individuals in contact with each other, sometimes through exchanges in the marketplace, sometimes through the interactions of communities and neighborhoods. By this point in the book, the city as megamachine no longer dominates the imaginative horizon. We come instead to a ground-level view of life on the streets and in the neighborhoods. This is where the science fiction city becomes most relevant to contemporary problems. Cordwainer Smith could model the social inequities of mid-twentieth-century America through the metaphor of fantastic cities, William Gibson can highlight the city as creative environment, and China Miéville can offer cities that reflect the real places in which we live and work.

Imagining Urban Futures thus moves in a broad arc from the physical city to the social city. Extrapolating current technologies, inventing new city types, and extending visionary ideas about urban form to their logical extremes can be fun, but the imagined cities remain thought experiments. They are limited by the practical constraints of materials science, energy consumption, and safety engineering. As Harry Harrison observed in *Bill, the Galactic Hero* (1965), world-spanning cities with populations in the tens of billions will have a major garbage disposal problem. Places can be interesting in themselves, but the most compelling stories are about the experience of living in specific places with distinct social relations, histories, and myths. My approach is congruent with the work of Michel de Certeau, who contrasts the totalizing view of a city from a skyscraper observation deck to the ways in which urbanites actually construct and experience city life as they inhabit the streets and buildings of the metropolis.[23] To twist a phrase that Mrs. Snedeker used to explain "synecdoche" to my seventh-grade class, the container of the physical city is much less interesting than the individuals who are the "thing contained."[24]

Writers like Samuel R. Delany, Molly Gloss, and Octavia Butler have used the possibilities and limitations of future cities to explore character under stress. Texts as different as *Blade Runner* and Paolo Bacigalupi's *The Windup Girl* reproduce and interrogate the social inequities of modern society. This embedded argument about cities as creative social milieux leads to my choice of Kim Stanley Robinson's "Science in the Capital" trilogy about political and scientific responses to global warming as the final example. It is science fiction that is earthbound, near future, politically engaged, and character driven, and which recognizes the large metropolis of Washington as a set of constantly shifting small communities. Even under stress, residents cooperate and public systems work—an implicit refutation of the libertarian survivalist scenarios common in much American science fiction.[25]

This exploration of science fiction and cities ends purposefully on the upbeat. I like cities large and small—a good thing, since I have been studying and writing about their history for over forty years. There are plenty of dystopian cities among my examples, but the book is structured around the *variety* of imagined city types rather than a contrast of rational utopias, critical utopias, and utterly bleak dystopias.[26] What makes cities attractive and exciting is that very variety. Urbanization and urban life present plenty of challenges, but cities are where ideas happen as their residents interact in a dazzling number of combinations. John Stuart Mill long ago recognized the importance of cities as centers of interaction: "It is hardly possible to overrate the value, in the present low state of human improvement, of placing human beings in contact with persons dissimilar to themselves, and with modes of thought and action unlike those with which they are familiar. . . . Such communication has always been, and is peculiarly in the present age, one of the primary sources of progress."[27] The thought experiments of science fiction cities, in all their disparate versions and types, embody and contribute to that dialogue. Avid viewers and readers of science fiction may well find that I have missed a telling example and left out their favorite city. By all means let me know so we can continue a conversation beyond the confines of this book.

CHAPTER ONE

TECHNO CITY; OR, DUDE, WHERE'S MY AIRCAR?

Joh Fredersen's eyes wandered over Metropolis, a restless roaring sea with a surf of light. In the flashes and waves, the Niagara falls of light, in the colour-play of revolving towers of light and brilliance, Metropolis seemed to have become transparent. The houses, dissected into cones and cubes by the moving scythes of the search-lights gleamed, towering up, hoveringly, light flowing down their flanks like rain.—Thea von Harbou, *Metropolis* (1927)

They glided down an electric staircase, and debouched on the walkway which bordered the north-bound five-mile-an-hour strip. After skirting a stairway trunk marked "Overpass to Southbound Road," they paused at the edge of the first strip. "Have you ever ridden a conveyor strip before?" Gaines inquired. "It's quite simple. Just remember to face against the motion of the strip as you get on." They threaded their way through homeward-bound throngs, passing from strip to strip.—Robert Heinlein, "The Roads Must Roll" (1940)

Commuting is going to be lots more fun in the future.

Where now we trudge wearily on crowded sidewalks, we'll ride cheerfully along on slideways. Now we squeeze into crowded, squeaky trains with old chewing gum under the seats, but soon we'll enjoy shiny silent subways that shoot passengers to their destinations with a pneumatic whoosh. We'll no longer need to time dangerous dashes across intersections crowded with heedless automobiles when soaring sky bridges connect nearly topless towers. Forget freeway traffic jams—airspeeders will lift us off the pavement as they careen along skylanes that interweave among the towers.

These images are familiar from paintings, movies, and other visualizations of future cities. Artists know that one of the best ways to give a touch of "authenticity" to a science fiction cityscape is to fill the skies with personal flying machines. Aircars figure in the early tongue-in-cheek SF film *Just Imagine* (1930), in *Blade Runner* (1982), where the cops tool around in VTOL Spinners, and *The Fifth Element* (1997), where Bruce Willis is an aircabbie. If viewers thought the car chase through the streets of San Francisco was exciting in *Bullitt* (1968), how about an airspeeder chase through the airways of Coruscant in *Star Wars Episode II: Attack of the Clones* (2002)?

Cities are vast and complex machines for moving things around, and science fiction often suggests that movement will be slicker in the future. The idea that air avenues and air boulevards might seriously supplement or supplant surface streets goes back a century plus, to balloon ascensions, blimps, and the first powered flight. A flying car maneuvering through skyscraper canyons is an instantly recognizable sign that we are in the world of the future, and one that is especially vivid for readers and moviegoers in mundane cities whose skies are clear except for distant jetliners, occasional TV station news copters, and new law enforcement drones. Nearly a century ago, Hugo Gernsback included an aeroflyer in *Ralph 124c 41+*, introducing a relatively straight ancestor of George Jetson's bubble-top aerocar. Predictions of personal flying vehicles were a post–World War II staple for *Popular Science, Popular Mechanics, Mechanix Illustrated,* and other hobby magazines that combined real science, exciting speculation, and home projects.[1] By the end of the twentieth century, the nostalgic lament that "It's 199- [or even 20--] and where's my aircar?" was a meme that infected syndicated columnist Gail Collins, the *Tonight Show,* and the comic strip *Calvin and Hobbes.*

Some parts of the science fiction future have already happened. We have personal communication devices and voice recognition software, much like what fourteen-year-old Arcadia Darell used to do her home-

The television series *Futurama* used science fiction clichés to satirize American society and popular culture. Among its most common features were aircars and air scooters, here ridden by Turanga Leela and Philip J. Fry. An aircar featured prominently in the show's opening credits, swerving through the skies of New New York and crashing into a giant video screen displaying the name of creator Matt Groening. Courtesy Fox Broadcasting / Photofest © & TM Fox Broadcasting.

work in Isaac Asimov's *Second Foundation* (1953). Smart phones do more tricks than Star Trek flip phone communicators. Imaging devices peer deep into the human body and send data to experts half a globe away, and we are working toward Dr. Leonard McCoy's medical tricoder. Entire libraries pop up on our screens in a few keystrokes. Twenty-first-century cities have elevated people movers and monorails (not very successful), intercity maglev trains, and even occasional subdivisions built around airstrips—if not a Cessna in every garage.

It is striking how easily aeroflyers fit into visions of urban futures. We don't need to imagine cities radically transformed, but rather places that function much as they do now, but with a bit more zip and pizzazz. Aircars will be taxis and commuter vehicles and family sedans. They'll chase criminals through the streets and engage in drag races. Because aircars are machines that instantly signal "future," they are also tempting targets for satire. Episodes of *Futurama* (1999–2013), the American cartoon series from *Simpsons* creator Matt Groening, opens with an aircar careening wildly through the high-rise canyons of New New York before crashing into an animated billboard showing snippets of twentieth-century cartoons. The world of New New York in the year 3000 includes hover cars, pneumatic tubes rather than wheeled vehicles, wiseass robots, and spaceships that take off directly from the roof of the Planet Express headquarters, all in the interest of lampooning American culture, *Star Trek*, and the whole idea of better living through mechanical devices.[2]

MODERN AND MODERNE

Aircars are a prime feature of Techno City, my term for the future metropolis stocked with straight-line *Popular Mechanics* projections that imagine technological innovations and experiments as the everyday future . . . and as everyday, nonrevolutionary parts of such futures.[3] Techno cities are places that work, where society and government have adopted and adapted to new technologies. Indeed, they often seem to work much the same way as the places where we already live. They have public and private transit and utility networks. They have hotels, shopping malls, government buildings, and neighborhoods. They have climate-controlled buildings with secure entry systems—now that retinal and fingerprint recognition locks are available in real time, perhaps it will be DNA recognition that opens the dilating door.

Techno City is often simply background for a story whose plot interest is elsewhere, an example of the framing technique that Robert Heinlein famously developed in the late 1930s and 1940s by inserting references to new technologies and customs into descriptive passages without offering elaborate explanations. These are obviously science fiction cities, reached by space travel or projected into the future—but their look and feel can be quite homey. They are like regular cities with enough new gizmos and spicing of technological change to signal that we are in a different time-place. Of course you get from one hotel floor to another with a bounce tube—how else would you do it? Of course newspaper pages turn themselves—hardly worth more than a passing nod of attention (especially since the pages of my daily paper now turn themselves on my iPad).

Here is an example from Heinlein's story "The Roads Must Roll," first published in *Astounding* in 1940 and widely anthologized as a Golden Age classic. The action takes place along the Diego-Reno roadtown, a vast moving highway that links the Los Angeles–Fresno–Stockton–Sacramento corridor. The "road" is a set of parallel moving slideways that step up from five miles per hour at the edge to a hundred miles per hour at the center. Using power from Solar Reception Screens, the United States has developed conveyor roads to save the nation from the unsustainable costs associated with maintaining 70 million automobiles (for perspective, the nonfictional United States actually had more than 250 million registered vehicles in the early twenty-first century). Solar-powered factories flank the roads and are flanked in turn by commercial districts, and then housing that is scattered over the surrounding rural landscape.

After this quick sketch, Heinlein drops his interest in the "city" part of roadcities. The plot involves a wildcat action by road maintenance technicians for the Stockton segment. Adherents of a radical worker ideology, they shut down the road, causing havoc among thousands of commuters. The federal officials who control the roads under the auspices of the military retake the Stockton office and quash the strike. The narrative choices met the expectations of *Astounding* readers, with attention to the physics of slideways, celebration of the disinterested engineer, and a slam at organized labor—a hot-button issue only five years after the organization of the CIO in 1935 and three years after the success of its controversial and technically illegal sit-in strike against General Motors.

Had he wished, Heinlein could have developed roadcities more fully. As early as 1882, Spanish designer Arturo Soria y Mata had proposed using railroads as the spine of what he called Cuidad Lineal, an idea that he illustrated with a scheme for a fifty-kilometer ring city around Madrid and a proposal for a linear city from Cádiz to St. Petersburg. The highly eccentric Edgar Chambliss advocated for a Roadtown from the 1910s to the 1930s, conceiving it as a row of Empire State Buildings laid end to end on top of an "endless basement" for service conduits. He got a friendly hearing from New Deal officials but no serious take-up.[4] Meanwhile, Soviet planner Nikolai Miliutin in the 1930s suggested decentralizing industry in exurban corridors sandwiched between roads and rail lines and flanked by housing; the result was to be industrial efficiency, easy commutes for workers, and elimination of invidious class distinctions between center and periphery—a sort of urban industrial version of King Arthur's round table. A decade later, Le Corbusier sketched a similar sort of linear industrial city (without acknowledging any predecessors).[5]

The idea resurfaced in the United States after World War II as automobiles began to draw tightly centered downtowns outward along highway corridors. Journalist Christopher Rand in 1965 suggested that Los Angeles had a spine rather than a heart, commenting that the Wilshire-Sunset axis rather than downtown functioned as the urban core. He was channeling architect Richard Neutra, who soon after arriving in Los Angeles from Europe sketched "Rush City Reframed," consisting of traffic corridors lined with slab high-rises—quite like the unfortunate Robert Taylor Homes that would march alongside Chicago's Dan Ryan Expressway from 1962 to 2007. The thought experiments have kept on coming, such as the Jersey Corridor Project of Princeton University architecture professors Michael Graves and Peter Eisenman, proposed in 1965 at the start of their high-profile careers. Living in what was beginning to emerge as the Princeton area Edge City, they suggested bowing to the inevitable by connecting Trenton to New Brunswick with two parallel megastructures sandwiching and surrounded by strips of green, since "a linear city is the city of the twentieth century."[6]

The urban ordinary is a pervasive foundation through Heinlein's work in the 1940s and 1950s. The protagonists in "The Roads Must Roll" stop for a meal at Jake's Steakhouse No. 4, which comes complete with crusty proprietress and two-inch slabs of beef. In *The Door into Summer,* written in 1956, he projected protagonist Daniel Boone Davis thirty years into his future from 1970 to 2000. Because Heinlein's interest was time travel paradoxes, he depicted a Los Angeles that still worked pretty much the same as the twentieth-century city, but with some new laws and customs. In *Double Star* (1956), guests in the Hotel Eisenhower do indeed use bounce tubes rather than elevators, but the hotel rooms are numbered by floors, just like twentieth-century hotel rooms.

The urban ordinary is also a powerful presence in films set on near-future Earth and Earthlike places, where the "shinier" parts of the contemporary cityscape stand in for cities to come. Jean-Luc Godard used the high-rise towers of the brand-new La Défense district of Paris to represent an extraterrestrial city in *Alphaville* (1965). Office buildings and shopping malls in Los Angeles and Washington, DC, are the 2054 future in *Minority Report* (2002). Contemporary Los Angeles plays the role of future cities in *In Time* (2011), and LA and Irvine office buildings stand in for the mid-twenty-first century in *Demolition Man* (1993). In *Total Recall* (1990), portions of Mexico City do duty as a city of 2084.

These cinematic choices show the lasting cultural resonance of the art moderne and streamlined styles of the mid-twentieth century. Chicago's Century of Progress Exposition in 1933 and the New York World's Fair of 1939 used similar architectural rhetoric to signify progress during the troubled times of the Great Depression. In the midst of postwar prosperity, the organizers of the Century 21 Exposition in Seattle in 1962 made the same choices—the Space Needle is a kissing cousin of New York's Trylon and Perisphere. The aesthetic road took one fork to the glistening aluminum-and-glass skyscrapers of the 1950s and 1960s, another to the exuberant atomic age/space age "googie" architecture of motels, bowling alleys, and drive-in restaurants. In Tulsa, Oklahoma, the Oral Roberts University campus from the 1960s echoes the cardboard Buzz Corey spaceport that I assembled on my bedroom floor in 1952.

The ability of the sleek side of twentieth-century design to represent the future has an uncomfortable implication. Embedded is an unspoken assumption that cities aren't changing all that much or that fast. The last

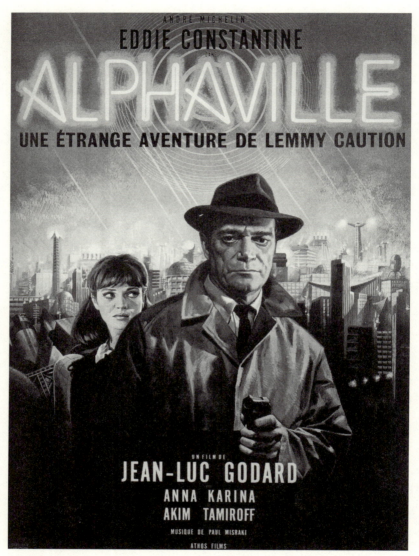

Jean-Luc Godard shot the science fiction film *Alphaville* in the modern buildings of Paris, but the advertising poster placed the main characters in front of a much more futuristic skyline. This is one of the most common designs for science fiction book covers and film advertising, used in movies as different as *Metropolis* and *Logan's Run*. Courtesy Janus Films / Photofest © Janus Films.

two generations, suggest several observers, have seen few innovations that have fundamentally changed the character of urban areas. Tyler Cowan has called it "the great stagnation," Peter Thiel has complained about "the end of the future," and Neal Stephenson about "innovation starvation."[7] Urban areas changed drastically from 1840 to 1940, but perhaps not so much since then. Most adults in the 2010s could be transported back to the 1940s and still get along—at least if their dads had made sure they learned how to drive a stick shift. Elevators no longer need operators for the mind-numbing work of opening doors and calling the floors, but they are still elevators. Traffic lights still cycle back and forth between red and green. I write on a two-year-old laptop, but I charge it with electricity from Columbia River dams and transmission lines that predate World War II. Even implementation of "big data" to create "smart cities" is being applied to old functions like better traffic-light cycles and more efficient siting of firehouses.

Perhaps the biggest disappointment of expectations has involved the impacts of electronic communication. The advent of personal computing and Internet connections in the 1980s spurred great expectations for urban decentralization. Soon, proclaimed the enthusiasts, crowded cities would be obsolete. Production workers would operate machinery by remote control, and professional workers would relocate to their favorite seacoast, mountain valley, or small town. Well, a bit of that has happened: radiologists can read X-ray results at a distance, college students can win big bucks with online poker, and soldiers can operate drones from consoles an ocean and continent away from their West Asian targets. Nevertheless, cities have continued to grow in both developed and developing nations. Superabundant flows of information turn out to favor greater *centralization* of decision making because on-site managers are less essential. The result has been the solidification of a global urban hierarchy topped by what sociologist Saskia Sassen calls global cities—New York, London, Tokyo, Paris, Hong Kong, and their ilk. Meanwhile, the centers of many old industrial cities like Birmingham (UK) or Chicago look just as good as or better than they did fifty years ago with the benefit of changing generational tastes and massive reinvestment.

SKYSCRAPER CITY

If real cities haven't lived up to techno-hype, the science fiction fixation on the sleekest of cityscapes to signal the future raises an interesting question about the technological city. The visual choices of film designers suggest, by and large, that the future will be not only shiny but also *tall*, a place where glass-and-steel towers frame urban airways through which the aircars weave. This is an imaginative leap, for cities over many millennia were far wider than they were high. Limited to five or six stories by construction technologies and the willingness of people to trudge up stairs, they draped over the landscape like slightly lumpy pancakes. Over the last 150 years, cities have been rethought and sometimes rebuilt in ways that prioritize height over breadth. Indeed, the vertical city of the real twenty-first century—Hong Kong, New York, Shanghai, Dubai—is itself a radical reimagining of traditional cities. In turn, science fiction has taken skyscraper districts as the most common jump-off for even bigger, higher, and denser cities of the future. For one example take Bruce Sterling's description of future Singapore in *Islands in the Net* (1988): "Nightmarishly vast spires whose bulging foundations covered whole city blocks. . . . Storey after storey rose silent and dreamlike, buildings so unspeakably huge that they lost all sense of weight; they hung above the earth like Euclidean thunderheads, their summits lost in sheets of steel-gray rain" (215).

The mechanically powered safety elevator, thanks to Mr. Otis, is one of the two great transportation inventions from the century of steam, along with track-and-vehicle combinations like railroads and streetcars. Combined with the development of steel-frame building construction, the elevator gave Paris the Eiffel Tower and New York and Chicago the first skyscrapers, helping to make the towering office building a visual clue and then cliché for visualizing the future.

The change was not instantaneous. It took time for an aesthetic keyed to seeing magnificence and power in great horizontally spread buildings to transform into the admiration of the vertical. In the nineteenth century, architects designed and developers filled new downtowns with "business blocks." Four- to six-story cubes and oblongs, they were meant to impress with their solidity. The best were magnificent structures like the Pension Office in Washington (now the National Building Museum) and Louis Sullivan's Auditorium Building in Chicago, a massive cube with a slender campanile tower that anchored Michigan Avenue. These were buildings that covered and held *ground*, defining their importance by lateral reach.

The new apartment blocks that housed the bourgeoisie of Vienna and Paris after 1870 were of the same architectural species. Four or five floors high, they extended in solid, never-ending rows along the avenues and boulevards. In the walkup city, the first floor above ground-floor shops was the prime location—the *piano nobile* for Italian town houses and palazzos, the *bel étage* in French apartments. Inverting the modern association of height and hierarchy, the top floor was despised for its cold and inconvenience, not valued for nice views, relegated to servants and starving artists.

The evolution of skyscrapers and a skyscraper aesthetic from this very different starting point is a story told time and again. From the 1890s to the 1930s the vertical gradually conquered the horizontal. The Metropolitan Life Building of 1909 was still a solid block with a now more substantial tower. The Woolworth Building, which took away the title of world's largest building in 1913, shifted the relative importance of base and tower. The big three that followed—the Chrysler Building, the Empire State Building, and the RCA Building—drew all their appeal from the vertical. In the nineteenth century, "skyline" had meant the natural horizon of country vistas. Only in the 1890s did writers commonly apply it to the horizon line of downtown buildings (the first such citation in the *Oxford English Dictionary* comes from George Bernard Shaw in 1896).

The high tower has endured as the symbol of modernity and urban importance. If New York and Chicago had skyscrapers, dozens of smaller cities wanted them too. Nebraska and North Dakota completed high-rise state capitols in the early 1930s. Los Angeles (1928) and Buffalo (1931) built high-rise city halls. Before the Great Depression hit, the Baltimore Trust Building reached thirty-four stories, Pittsburgh's Cathedral of

Learning reached forty, and the American Insurance Union tower in Columbus, Ohio, reached forty-six. "Des Moines is ever going forward," reported one of its newspapers. "With our new thirteen-story building and the new gilded dome of the Capitol, Des Moines towers above the other cities of the state like a lone cottonwood on the prairie."

It was an easy step from Des Moines to Zenith, the fictional amalgam of Cincinnati, Milwaukee, and Kansas City where Sinclair Lewis placed thoroughly modern real estate salesman George F. Babbitt in his 1922 novel. As the novel opens and Babbitt has yet to stir in his new Dutch colonial house in the new upscale suburb of Floral Heights, "the towers of Zenith aspired above the morning mist; austere towers of steel and cement and limestone, sturdy as cliffs and delicate as silver rods. They were neither citadels nor churches, but frankly and beautifully office-buildings." As Babbitt tells the Zenith Real Estate Board, their city is distinguished by "the Second National Tower, the second highest business building in any inland city in the entire country. When I add that we have an unparalleled number of miles of paved streets, bathrooms, vacuum cleaners, and all the other signs of civilization . . . then I give but a hint of the all round unlimited greatness of Zenith!"

With the aspiring constructions of Des Moines, Cleveland, and Zenith in the background, the last century has seen an imaginative three-way interaction between real buildings that have reached taller and taller, grandiose proposals from the drawing boards of ego-rich architects, and often beautifully rendered cityscapes from the easels of visionary (or hallucinatory) artists.

In the 1920s Le Corbusier—one of most self-confident of the design utopians who shaped twentieth-century ideas about cities—created a series of schemes for high-rise cities: a diorama and drawings for a "City for Three Millions" in 1922, the Ville Radieuse (Radiant City) in 1924, and in 1925 the Voisin Plan for central Paris, which would have carried modernity to a shocking logical extreme. Artists struggled to stay ahead of the curve when technological capacity grew and architects could let their minds out-roam the practical and politics (not even Baron Haussmann could have done that to Paris).

Meticulously constructed and articulated, the miniaturized city used for shooting the background for the 1930 film *Just Imagine* had a counterpart at the end of the decade at the New York World's Fair, where General Motors exhibited a scale model of a freeway-and-suburb metropolis of the future. Courtesy Fox / Photofest © Fox.

Artists struggled to stay ahead of the curve. The most prominent in the United States was New Yorker Hugh Ferriss, who staged a "Drawings of the Future City" exhibit in 1925 and followed with drawings for "Titan City," or New York from 1926 to 2026, exhibited at Wanamaker's department store. His drawings celebrated technological progress with ziggurat towers and sweeping searchlights illuminating urban canyons. The images can seem dark and foreboding, but General Electric and Goodyear advertisements adopted the same imagery, as did the miniaturized "Gotham" set for *Just Imagine*.

Rockefeller Center is a close steel and stone relative.[8] The Ferriss vision was echoed in the sets and backdrops for the silent movie classic *Metropolis* (1927), inspired by director Fritz Lang's first visit to New York, and anticipated the style of Batman's Gotham City.[9]

The backdrops for Fritz Lang's seminal film *Metropolis* reference thirty years of visionary depictions of New York and similar cities. Realistic skyscrapers rise next to fantasy architecture that recalls Pieter Brueghel's 1563 painting of the Tower of Babel, while traffic speeds across precarious elevated highways and railways and aircraft dodge through the concrete canyons. Courtesy UPA / Photofest © UFA.

Dial forward to 1956, when Frank Lloyd Wright proposed a mile-high skyscraper ("The Illinois")—four times the height of the Empire State Building. It would have climbed 528 stories, with fifteen thousand parking stalls and 150 helicopter parking slots. A half-century later, the world was catching up to both Wright and Bruce Sterling with stand-alone super-skyscrapers in Taipei, Kuala Lumpur, and most recently Dubai, where the Burj Khalifa soars more than a half mile high. Critic Witold Rybczynski draws direct parallels in engineering and design from "The Illinois" to the Burj Khalifa: use of reinforced concrete, a tapering silhouette, a tripod design, and "a treelike central core that rises the full height of the building to become a spire"—all in all a sort of stalagmite form to bring a touch of fantasy to the common corporate glass-and-metal box.[10]

(*Left*) This poster for *Metropolis* stresses the eerie and the fantastic, with the machine-human version of the heroine Maria backed by an abstracted skyline framed by the beams of searchlights. Courtesy UPA / Photofest © UFA.

(*Below*) This poster for the French release of *Metropolis* highlights the gigantic scale of the emerging megacity, multiplying the sort of stepback skyscrapers that filled Manhattan after the city's 1916 zoning ordinance. Courtesy UFA / Photofest © UFA.

In the real estate business, hype and high-rise go together: there are the real buildings we have just mentioned, ambitious but serious designs that don't quite get off the ground, and exuberant entries into design competitions by big names like Paul Rudolph, Paolo Soleri, and Rem Koolhaus that are little more than thought experiments in the style of architectural science fantasy. From there, it's an easy segue to artistic renditions of future cities. The difference: without needing even a cursory bow to engineering realities and financial possibilities, visual artists can assemble a thousand Burj-Khalifas into a single super-metropolis.

I examined two websites that have assembled future city art: One offers "45 incredible futuristic scifi 3D city illustrations" and the other "100 imaginative cities of the future artworks."[11] By my eyeball categorization, 106 of the images are vertical cities that rise to wild and giddy heights, compared to only 14 low-rise cities that stretch to distance horizons, 9 floating, hanging, or orbiting cities untethered from a planetary surface, and 16 images that combine the horizontal and vertical in ways that most resemble actual twenty-first-century cities with downtowns and suburbs. That is nearly a three-to-one margin for the vertical in the minds of artists of the fantastic—who also prefer the view from above or afar to depictions with a viewpoint in the midst of the urban action.

Future city drawing and paintings of the twenty-first century are strikingly similar to "King's Dream of New York," an image included in *King's Views of New York* (1908–9). Moses King was a prolific compiler of guidebooks and pictorial portraits of Boston and New York, combining text with hundreds of photographs. *New York, the American Cosmopolis: The Foremost City of the World* was a typically immodest title from his busy publishing enterprise. In his rendition, Broadway is a concrete canyon, the real Singer Building is dwarfed by higher towers connected by sky bridges, and blimps and dirigibles swarm the sky.[12]

INSIDE THE TOWERS

The artists highlight the point that is implicit in proposals for unbuilt super-duper skyscrapers: height itself is the techno feat. Whether created by Frank Lloyd Wright or a computer artist, what makes the building or city a speculative fiction is the assumption of building technologies that can scale up the typical individual Chicago skyscraper to something bigger than currently possible. From the building that depends on particular machines for circulating people, air, and water among multiple floors (the real skyscraper of 1890–1920), the science fiction imagination moves to high-rise cities that depend on the sets of machines assembled in currently impractical ways.

British writer Ian Whates invites readers to visit "the city of a hundred rows" in *City of Dreams and Nightmares* (2010).[13] The setting is Thaiburley, a high-rising city of a hundred levels or "rows." To a traveler from the rural hinterlands, "the towering city walls were just as magnificent and awe-inspiring as imagination had painted them. The closer the city grew, the more its sheer scale became apparent" (176). The elite live at the top in the City Above, and hardscrabble folks dwell at the bottom in the cavernous City Below. Communication is by stairs, by escalators that span segments of a dozen or fifteen levels, and elevators that are paired so one goes up while the other down. These lifts span a limited number of levels, and you have to get off and cross to another platform to get to the next stage (think about riding multiple cog railways and cable cars to reach the summit of the Schilthorn or the Jungfrau in Switzerland). Much of the space of the Rows is interior rooms and dwellings, but each level has terraces that open to the air . . . you can fall off!

Whates tries to imagine Thaiburley as a fully articulated city. There are food supply levels, Shopping Rows, and a ground-level Market Row that has spread beyond the base of the city. "From Streets Below to the Market Row / From taverns and stalls to the Shopping Halls" goes a nursery rhyme. Further down, beneath the Market Row, are subsurface levels for the poor in "the vast cavern which housed Thaiburley's lowest level" (56). Here are bazaars, aliens, street gangs, a river that provides power (and carries away waste), docks, factories, and "the Ruins" where there are taverns, whores, workers, bargemen, and beggars. Routes to the City Above are lucrative and claimed by groups and gangs who charge tolls. It is not clear how the basic large-scale supply of the City Above is organized, but there are scavengers called Swarbs (Sanitation Workers and Refuse Burners) who string nets to catch things and people that fall.

Even taller than Thaiburley is Spearpoint, the physical and conceptual pivot for Alastair Reynolds's *Terminal World* (2010). It is a towering city in the shape of a cone, with a relatively wide base, a curved taper to higher levels, and then finally a spire that goes beyond habitable levels. Its footprint at the base is fifteen leagues across, narrowing to one-third of a league across at fifty leagues above the ground, whence it keeps rising into the vacuum (86). At this scale, it is big enough to house thirty million people (101).

To complicate the impressive techno feat of enormous height, Reynolds throws in weird physics. In horizontal bands are zones in which different levels of technology are physically possible: from bottom upward are Horsetown, Steamville, Neon Heights, Circuit City, a cyborg zone, and the Celestial Levels (whose "angel" inhabitants have evolved the ability to fly). People live in complexes of buildings on the surface of the tower and partway into the interior. Connections are by mechanical funiculars and by a railroad that runs on a curving ramp that circles and recircles the tower like the Tower of Babel in the images of Pieter Bruegel the Elder and Gustave Doré. Horsetown encircles the base and spreads beyond it onto the surrounding planetary surface.

Despite their gargantuan height, Thaiburley and Spearpoint share a family resemblance with Burning Bright and Alphaville. Super-tall city buildings are cool, but height itself is not essential to the plot element of social hierarchy. Reynolds could just as well have imagined a horizontal city of concentric rings with different physical principles, with status declining from center to edge as in preindustrial cities. Whates has a lot more fun with the City Below than with the City Above, telling what is basically a story of cops, street gangs, and young people on the run through back alleys and abandoned buildings. Nor does the inevitable physical complexity of these tower-cities play an important role. Apart from describing the transportation systems, the authors do not take all that much effort to imagine how such cities might actually work as artificial ecologies. There are workshops and shops and apartments inside Spearpoint and Thaiburley, but they are ordinary spaces, and the exciting action takes place on the outsides of the structures as bodies are pitched or fall to their death and characters flee and are chased by air, stairways, and funicular railways that cling to the surface.

Although Spearpoint is an extravagant science implausibility, it was easy for writers in the later twentieth century to draw on the commonly accepted critique of massive public housing projects as alienating environments that nurtured social problems—whether U.S. examples like the infamous Pruitt-Igoe buildings in St. Louis or the sterile working-class apartment blocks of Paris or Moscow—and project social breakdown. Thomas Disch set his grittily detailed novel 334 (1972) in a subsidized twenty-one-story building at 334 East Eleventh Street, New York. In the 2020s its three thousand residents are supervised by a paternalistic bureaucracy, cope with malfunctioning elevators and deteriorating services, scam social workers to survive, and take refuge in drugs, television, and meaningless violence. As science fiction scholar Rob Latham has pointed out, Disch's near-future New York embodies much of the analysis of neo-Marxist geographers like David Harvey and Manuel Castells. Except for the elderly isolated in upper floors, residents are free to use the city around them, but only on the terms set by the structures of power and authority.[14]

Robert Silverberg and J. G. Ballard, in contrast, set novels entirely *within* high-rise buildings and use those settings to explore the impacts of concentrated and claustrophobic living on individuals trapped inside and unable to escape to freedom or adventure. Silverberg's *The World Inside* (1971) is pure science fiction, positing a world in which seventy-five billion humans live in megabuilding "urban monads"—urbmons—that could be characterized as cheerful dystopias. Ballard sets *High-Rise* (1975) in a skewed present in which an expensive condominium tower in the London Docklands erodes all social bonds and turns its residents into murderous sociopaths. In both books, however, the tall building is both a technological accomplishment and something more, a presence that conditions and drives individual behavior as much as the Alaska wilderness changes Buck from domestic pet to feral creature in *Call of the Wild*.

Silverberg wrote the linked stories that constitute *The World Inside* in 1970 and 1971, at a time when both the public and science fiction were obsessed with the threat of overpopulation. In good sf fashion, Silverberg decided to reverse the expectations and explore the possibilities of a society in which population growth was applauded—requiring vast buildings to house the multitudes and, in turn, elaborate systems of social regulation to maintain order. The social reversal draws directly on the sexual revolution of the baby boomer generation: urbmon society encourages sex for procreation from the early teens, has no nudity taboo, and promotes open promiscuity, with every woman theoretically available to any man. The structures that house the busy billions similarly extrapolate then-current urban thought. They are grouped in clusters with names like Chipitts, Sansan, and Wienbud (in Europe)—terms coined following publication in 1961 of Jean Gottmann's *Megalopolis: The Urbanized Northeastern Seaboard of the United States*, which described the Boston-Washington corridor as an emerging urban superregion. Silverberg began thinking about the structures themselves by projecting familiar New York skyscrapers, but he soon found Paolo Soleri's fantastic schemes for grotesquely gigantic self-contained arcologies that would concentrate human beings and free up the natural landscape (Soleri's *Arcology: The City in the Image of Man* is one of the most misnamed books ever).

Urban monads are indeed arcologies. An urbmon tapers upward from a relatively wide base to allow space for factories and supporting machinery on the lower levels. Each towers an identical one thousand floors high, divided into forty-floor cities that take their names arbitrarily from historic cities. In Urbmon 116 of the Chipitts cluster, where the stories take place, Reykjavik is on the bottom and Louisville is on the top. The original intent was fifty families per floor, but the population growth that the society so vigorously encourages means that most floors have more like 120 families, each crammed into an apartment that has been reduced to a single room. A relatively successful academic on a high floor has ninety square meters for six people, who use efficiently designed inflatable, wall-mounted, and built-in furnishings and appliances. The result is roughly eight hundred people per floor, thirty-two thousand per city, and eight hundred thousand per building. When Urbmon 116 reaches close to nine hundred thousand, it is time to hive off excess people to join with the extras from other towers to populate a brand-new urbmon.

Urbmonites never go outside, and many never stray beyond their own city except on school field trips. One character looks down at the manicured surroundings: "Below her are the tapered structures that hold the 40,000,000+ people of this urban cluster. She is awed by the neatness of the constellation, the geometric placement of the buildings to form a series of hexagons within the larger area. Green plazas separate the buildings. No one enters the plazas, ever, but their well-manicured lawns are a delight to behold from the windows of the urbmon" (49). Beyond the lawns, 90 percent of the continent is devoted to agriculture, with strangely primitive villagers operating vast industrial farms in exchange for manufactured goods from the cities—much like Soleri's scheme to free the landscape of nasty human beings.

This is a world of literal social climbing. The cities are stacked by status, from administrators on the top floors to maintenance workers at the bottom. Nightwalking is the socially sanctioned practice of males finding casual sex partners by prowling corridors and entering random apartments. To nightwalk in higher cities is to aspire; to nightwalk in lower cities is to go slumming. Sociocomputator Charles Mattern explains to a visitor from Venus that they try to encourage contact between cities. "Sports, exchange students, regular mixed evenings. Within reason, that is. We don't have people from the working-class levels mixing with those from the academic levels, much. It would make everyone unhappy, eh?" (29). Another character moves through Urbmon 116 as the liftshaft carries her upward in her imagination. "Up through Reykjavik where the maintenance people live, up through brawling Prague where everyone has ten babies, up through Rome, Boston, Edinburgh, Chicago, Shanghai, even Louisville where the administrators dwell in unimaginable luxury" (49).

Silverberg uses the massive physical presence of the urbmon as both the cause and the representation of inexorable social inertia. Several of the component stories deal with misfits whose vague dissatisfaction leads them to challenge the system. One commits suicide, and other "flippos" are summarily disposed of—arrested and immediately tossed down a recycling chute. Others find ways to reconcile themselves to their lives. Even the discontented understand and appreciate the vast interconnectedness of urbmon society. One misfit realizes, when describing Urbmon 116, that it is "a poem of human relationships, a miracle of civilized harmony" (207). A drug-tripping musician envisions the intricate connections: "For the first time he understands the nature of the delicate organism that is society; he sees the checks and balances, the quiet conspiracies of compromise that paste it together. And it is wondrously beautiful. Tuning this vast city of many cities is just like tuning the cosmos group [a musical combo]: everything must relate, everything must belong to everything else" (90).

The result, even as world population continues to rise from seventy-five billion toward ninety billion, is equilibrium. The final paragraph takes an irenic tone: "Now the morning sun is high enough to touch the uppermost fifty stories of Urban Monad 116. Soon the building's entire eastern face will glitter like the bosom of the sea at daybreak. Thousands of windows, activated by the dawn's early photons, deopaque. Sleepers stir. Life goes on. God bless! Here begins another happy day" (256). This ending repeats much of the book's opening paragraph, which starts: "Here begins a happy day in 2381" (15). We have come full circle to reaffirmation and stability.

If Silverberg's urbmons are vast machines for maintaining social equilibrium and keeping people happy, not so the building in J. G. Ballard's *High-Rise*, where stasis has no chance against chaos. Pity the ambitious and luckless Britons who have bought apartments in the brand-new tower within sight of the City of London. Set in the present of the 1970s, this is a book that has to work its way into the science fiction realm, and succeeds with devastating results. Things start a bit tense in the new building because of buried tensions between middle-class people on the lower floors and higher-status residents at the top. Upper levels have dogs, lower levels have children. Top-floor residents treat children as an intrusion and exclude them from an upper play area and pool to which they are supposed to have access. Everyone understands that there is a rough upper/middle/lower division (66–67).

The building itself is tiny compared with urbmons or Spearpoint, with two thousand residents in one thousand apartments in a forty-story high-rise. Nevertheless, it sucks people into its vortex. The building is largely self-contained; the entire tenth floor is a retail concourse with super-market, liquor store, hair salon, bank, school, pools and other recreation areas. In the beginning (the story starts after the building is occupied), residents commute to work, pick up their mail, and watch news on the telly. Quickly, however, the outside world loses its salience. Men cease to leave the building for their jobs. Moms keep kids home from school, hunkering in shuttered apartments. Even the strongest personalities find that they *can't* leave, even when they claim that is what they want. The police and other public authorities oddly ignore the building even as its parking lot fills with smashed and abandoned cars.

Tensions breed chaos over three short months. Trouble starts with a lot of noisy partying, as if all the residents are having simultaneous mid-life crises. Small incidents soon escalate into random violence. The water supply fails; electricity goes out floor by floor; garbage piles up. Man-agement ceases to respond to complaints. Residents of adjacent floors cluster into clans for self-defense and battle in the interior corridors with makeshift weapons. Each floor tries to block adjacent stairwells and guard elevator lobbies. Soon the clans fragment into small clusters of apartments. "The clan system, which had once given a measure of se-curity to the residents, had now largely broken down, individual groups drifting into apathy or paranoia. Everywhere people were retreating into their apartments, even into one room, and barricading themselves away." There are groups of wilding women, probably cannibalism, and finally everyone for him or herself. The last three survivors can look across the abandoned parking lot to see the same process starting in a newer tower.

High-Rise is barbed satire that skewers Britain on the verge of the Mar-garet Thatcher years, when the gospel of free markets impoverished the public sphere, and when the Docklands district would go through cycles of real estate boom and bust—although not as disastrously as the *High-Rise* high-rise. Ballard offers a dubious psychological explanation for the breakdown (the building is like a mother that allows residents to turn into uncontrolled two-year-olds). A better analogy is to see the building as a version of the generation starship (see chapter 4). Indeed, Ballard describes it both as a spaceship and as "a small vertical city, its two thousand inhabitants boxed up into the sky" (15). There are strong parallels to the generation ship in Brian Aldiss's *Non-Stop* (1958), where the command deck (building management) has ceased to function and society has devolved to tribal warfare within confined spaces. What is different is the external resolution and rescue that Aldiss provides. Ballard has no such hope, giving us, perhaps, *Non-Stop* meets *Lord of the Flies*.

Skyscrapers are particularly tempting techno feats that still fascinate after 120 years. Exciting visions of towering supercities from the early twentieth century influenced not only the golden age science fiction writers of the 1930s and 1940s but also the boomer generation who grew up with those stories as part of their SF universe. Some readers and writers have since repudiated it, but others have recapitulated or incorporated it into new work. The choices that designer Syd Mead made for *Blade Runner* very explicitly invert the techno-utopianism of Hugh Ferriss. William Gibson's early story "The Gernsback Continuum" from 1981 is both homage and critique of the visions of golden age science fiction. Its gentle satire posits an alternative history in which the world of the pulp covers breaks through into "reality," providing fleeting visions of cars like an "aluminum avocado with a central shark-fin rudder jutting up from its spine" and a city that mirrors that in *Metropolis*: "Spire after spire in gleaming ziggurat steps that climbed to a central golden temple tower ringed with the crazy radiator flanges of the Mongo gas stations. . . . Roads of crystal soared between the spires. . . . The air was thick with ships: giant wing-liners, little darting silver things . . . mile long blimps, hovering dragonfly things that were gyrocopters" (8–9). Gary Westfahl comments that the story "pays fond tribute to the now-quaint prophecies of science fiction writers and futurists of the 1920s and 1930s, and ponders how their visions still influence residents of the future they failed to predict."[15]

The exaggeration of these already larger-than-life buildings can authenticate otherness, as in thousands of drawings and paintings of future cities, but it can also call the whole idea of a bright urban future into question. In *The Futurological Congress* (1971; translated 1974) the brilliant Polish writer Stanisław Lem sends his recurring character Ijon Tichy to a scientific meeting held at the Costa Rica Hilton, which rears 164 stories into the sky and offers bomb-free rooms and the luxury of an "all-girl orchestra [that] played Bach while performing a cleverly choreographed striptease." At the meeting, convened to address seven world crises (urban, ecology, air pollution, energy, food, military, political), a Japanese delegate presents plans for the housing of the future: "eight hundred levels with maternity wards, nurseries, schools, shops, museums, zoos, theaters, skating rinks and crematoriums . . . intoxication chambers as well as sobering tanks, special gymnasiums for group sex (an indication of the progressive attitude of the architects), and catacombs for nonconformist subculture communities" (21). Seventeen cubic kilometers in volume, the completely self-contained building would reach from the ocean bed to the stratosphere. A scale model was already at work recycling all its waste products into food. The outcome of techno city may not be techno utopia, says Lem; it may be artificial bananas, ersatz wine, and synthetic cocktail sausages.

CHAPTER TWO

MACHINES FOR BREATHING

South Colony was arranged like a wheel. The administration building was the hub; tunnels ran out from it in all directions and buildings were placed over them. . . . Each was a hemispherical bubble of silicone plastic, processed from the soil of Mars and blown on the spot.—Robert Heinlein, *Red Planet* (1949)

"More money, more freedom, more air."—*Total Recall* (1990)

Deep Space Nine is a space station. Hovering over the planet Bajor, it monitors wormhole access to the Gamma Quadrant. It's a trade and diplomatic outpost with a permanent population of perhaps three hundred, augmented periodically by individual visitors and transients. Its population embraces multiple races—humans, Ferengi, Klingons, Bajorans—but the feel is small town. There is only one bar, after all, where everyone runs into everyone else.

Babylon 5 is another space station, floating in isolation at the intersection of translightspeed travel corridors. It is also a *city*—a place that is big, dense, and full of different sorts of people. Like Deep Space Nine, it has identifiable boundaries—it's a big metal container in the middle of nothingness—but Bab 5 is larger by three orders of magnitude. Its six levels teem with 100,000 humans and 150,000 members of other species. Interior spaces are specialized into residential neighborhoods and economic districts. A big bustling business district—the Zocalo—occupies part of Red Sector. Facilities range from baseball diamond to casino to courtrooms to factories and machine shops. There are officials, well-accounted citizens, a militant labor union, refugees, and an urban underclass in the partly finished Downbelow, where thieves and gang-

Silhouetted in the vastness of space, the space habitat city Babylon 5 sits astride inter-stellar trade routes that bring it residents and representatives from multiple species and worlds. Tensions between its human majority and its diverse communities model the conflicts of a cosmopolitan crossroads city like fifteenth-century Venice or twenty-first-century London. Courtesy Warner Bros. Television / Photofest © Warner Bros. Television.

sters run a thriving black market and illicit businesses. On Deep Space Nine, Constable Odo can pretty well keep tabs on every resident. On Babylon 5, security chief Michael Garibaldi is constantly surprised by new faces, new problems, new gangs, new conspiracies.

These imagined megastructures are the settings for two of the most popular—and simultaneously broadcast—science fiction television series of the late twentieth century. *Star Trek: Deep Space Nine*, which aired 174 episodes from 1993 to 1999, was a spinoff from *Star Trek: The Next Generation* with some secondary crossover characters. *Babylon 5* aired 115 episodes from 1994 to 1998. Both shows regularly make lists of the best examples of science fiction TV.

Analogies from the history of the American West help to point out why one of the space stations is a city and the other is not. A good match for Deep Space Nine is Fort Vancouver, the Hudson's Bay Company head-quarters on the Columbia River from 1825 to 1846. It was a trading node with multiple peoples—Scots, French Canadians, Métis, Iroquois, Crees, Hawaiians—but only a few hundred in total. Boss John McLoughlin could take in the single stockaded fort with a glance.

If Fort Vancouver was a tenuous extension of empire, San Francisco during the gold rush and after was another Babylon 5—big, brawling, barely able to hold on to middle-class respectability. It had its Zocalo along Market Street and Union Square, its Downbelow vice district in the Barbary Coast. San Francisco's population skyrocketed from a handful in 1847 to 57,000 by 1870 and 149,000 by 1880. It was a city of immigrants from Australia, South America, China, Europe, and the eastern United States—not so exotic a mix as at Babylon 5, but as disparate as you were likely to get in the nineteenth century.

Babylon 5 is a vast machine by definition. It is an enormously complex assemblage whose parts all have to work together, from power sources to airlocks, from ventilation systems to docking bays. But then, *every* city is a physical machine designed to sustain its residents. Into my house in Portland come water, natural gas, electricity, cable TV signals, Internet data to let me check on San Francisco's early population, bags of groceries, books, and a bunch of other stuff. Out goes water down drains and toilets; heat through my dryer vent and open windows (in summer) and poorly sealed cracks (in winter); solid unneeded objects to recycling containers and trash can; books back to my local library branch; and phone messages back to the world through nearby (and unpopular) cell towers. Multiply my house eight hundred thousand times for my midsize metro area, add millions of square feet of retail and office space, schools, fire stations, and museums, and then add some more—the roads, bridges, rail lines, conduits, pipes, wires, cables, drains, sewers, elevators, and broadcasting towers that hold it all together. Any city is a huge interlinked object, a three-dimensional artifact that reaches above and below the level ground. It is both a vast abstract sculpture and a machine for living.

Cities full of aircars and slidewalks are close cousins of mundane cities with current *pieces* of technology extrapolated to support story lines.

Superhigh cities of soaring towers extrapolate technologies like elevators and steel frame construction that have been available for 130 years. With space station cities, and domed habitats on airless worlds, and cities that float in air or water, and cities that pave over entire planets, something different is involved. Now the entire city with its overwhelming physical mass and form is the new technology that changes the ways that people can live. In short, the reimagined city itself is the new techno feat.

This chapter explores a particular type of city-machine whose fundamental imperative is to maintain and protect breathable atmosphere. A space station is, among other things, a sealed container of air maintained at pressure, humidity, and chemical composition appropriate for human beings. The science fiction future is filled, as well, with buried cities and domed cities that maintain usable air on moons and planets where a natural atmosphere is absent or deadly. "Dome breach!" is one of the most common and useful crises in the science fiction repertoire—after all, humans can live weeks without food and days without water, but only minutes without air.

Techno cities revolve around the promise of new products and technologies that will change everyday life. Bubble cities rely on the potential of engineering for their very existence, assuming the possibility of scaling up construction technologies by orders of magnitude; but they also raise the specter of fragility. First settlements in tunnels and domes are as vulnerable as isolated Massachusetts towns in King Philip's War or as tenuous as a mining town in avalanche country. Overgrown supercities depend on so many interacting systems that a single breakdown can trigger multiple failures and disaster.

BUBBLES IN THE SKY

"Pa had sent me out to get an extra pail of air." In 1951, Fritz Leiber opened the classic short story "A Pail of Air" with an irresistible hook that inverts the bucolic image of Jack and Jill. Leiber imagines Earth adrift from the sun and so cold that the atmosphere has frozen out into a layered snow of carbon dioxide, nitrogen, and oxygen. A solitary family huddles in an empty city inside a nest built from rugs and blankets, thawing buckets of frozen air to survive. The planet, in effect, has become a great space station with the conservation of breathable air as the purpose of rudimentary engineering. The fact that the family turns out not to be sole survivors doesn't undercut the impact of imagining air itself as a commodity that requires elaborate care.

Leiber's story directs our attention away from pipes and wires to the most fundamental technological imperative of spaceships and space stations—the value of breathable air. In a throwaway line, Linda Nagata in "Nahiku West" (2012) touches on the essence of orbiting cities as machines for breathing. She posits a space station city that orbits the sun just inside the orbit of Venus and notes that "most of the celestial cities restrict the height and weight of residents to minimize the consumption of volatiles" (544). The prime engineering directive for cities in empty space, on airless moons, and on planets with unbreathable atmosphere is to encapsulate living space in a way that absolutely delimits in-here from out-there. No terrestrial walled city—not Rome or Constantinople, Toledo or Tallinn—has been as completely separated from its surroundings as Babylon 5 or Nahiku West.

Pell Station in C. J. Cherryh's Hugo-winning novel *Downbelow Station* (1981) is a city comparable to Babylon 5. It is big, tightly packed, most definitely bounded, full of diverse races, social classes, and districts, and several generations old. Like other gigantic space stations, it is literally machine as city. It is also the major crossroads of the space lanes. It is the first station outward from Earth where major interstellar trading routes converge. Forty merchant ships are docked when the story opens. With access to in-system mines and to agriculture and mining on the planet that it orbits, Pell is also the key source of supply for a rogue fleet of warships that ostensibly are part of Earth forces but which operate as pirates. Here is Admiral Mazian speaking to his fleet captains: "Look at the map, old friends, look at it again. Here . . . here is a world. Pell. And does a power survive without it. What is Earth . . . but that? You have your choice here: follow what may be Company's orders, or we hold here, gather resources, take action" (242).

Pell is city-size. Cherryh does not specify its population, but two other stations recently destroyed in the ongoing Union-Company war had twenty-five thousand to thirty thousand each. When Pell has to absorb six thousand refugees, it needs to relocate only a small portion of its population. When the refugees come in, there are one thousand units available in guest housing and two thousand more available by emergency conversion of space. Another five hundred units will be available in 180 days through further space conversion. At three persons per unit, Pell could likely absorb more than ten thousand newcomers with social disruption but no serious stress on its basic systems; indeed, it absorbs nine thousand more refugees during the few weeks of the story. At that same time, Mazian's fleet is requiring new IDs for all the refugees. So far, says a fleet official, "we've identified and carded 14,947 individuals as of this morning" (423). The process will take two more weeks, implying that fifteen thousand is a minority. Seventy years later the population of Pell Station and its dependent planet has grown to roughly half a million, according to a follow-on novel, *Regenesis*, so we can assume a city-station population of one hundred thousand or more at the time of *Downbelow Station*.

As the population implies, Pell is physically extensive and complex enough that few residents know all its sections and corridors. They need street signs and color-coded corridors. Captain Signy Mallory, the fleet officer who has taken temporary control, orders all the signage removed. Station official Damon Konstantin complains,

> "The station is too confusing—even residents could get lost . . . without our color keys . . . "
>
> "So in my ship, Mr. Konstantin, we don't mark corridors for intruders."
>
> "We have children on this station. Without the colors."
>
> "They can learn," she said. "And the signs all come off." (255–57)

Pell station has the multiple economic functions of a city. All its sectors have retailing: There are "a score of bars and entertainment concessions along green dock and the niner access which had once thrived in the traffic of merchanters . . . a line of sleepovers and vid theaters and lounges and restaurants and one anomalous chapel completing the row" (433). When levels 5–9 on orange and yellow sectors are displaced, the result is "dockside shops, homes, four thousand people crowded elsewhere" (30). Two distinct working classes maintain Pell City. One of the characters gets assigned work on a salvage line, along with other human workers, taking apart worn equipment by hand and sorting parts for reuse. A social notch below, filling the role of the noncitizen proletariat, are nonhuman hisa from "downbelow" on Pell planet. They live in the maintenance tunnels and do the essential scut work that keeps the station alive.

Pell has persisted for at least two centuries with increasing independence. Seven generations of the Konstantin family have served—dominated—Pell administration as something like hereditary bureaucrats: "The Konstantins had built Pell; were scientists and miners, builders and holders" (50), and they are a powerful voice in the elected governing council. The station is theoretically subject to the control of the Company from distant Earth but effectively operates independently, a status that is confirmed at the end of the wartime crisis that drives the narrative. Pell had been evolving its own way, neither Union nor Company, with its own political values that its leaders try desperately to preserve. At the end of the book, Pell has ridden out a crisis that has nearly cracked it open to space when "a whole dock breached, air rushing out the umbilicals, pressure dropped . . . troopers who had been on the deck, dead and drifting. . . . The dock was void" (401–2). As the station-city avoids being ripped apart like earlier victims of the war, the newly formed Merchanters Alliance claims Pell as neutral territory, effectively making it an independent city state, and people begin to talk about "citizens of Pell."[1]

WILL WORK FOR AIR

New Klondike, as its name implies, is a boom town on the Martian prospecting frontier. The treasure this time is alien fossils, not gold, but New Klondike shares many of the traits of instant towns on the North American or Australian mining frontier. Featured in Robert Sawyer's *Red Planet Blues* (2013), New Klondike is jerry-built and already shabby: "The fused-regolith streets were cracked, buildings—and not just the ones in the old shantytown—were in disrepair, and the seedy bars and brothels were full of thugs and con artists, the destitute and the dejected" (9). Because the location is Mars rather than the Yukon, however, there is one major difference: it lies under a transparent dome that is four miles across and twenty meters high at its center. Public utilities include "air-processing facilities" as well as water and sewage treatment plants. And air is the most precious of the utilities. The private investigator who narrates the story offers a tongue-in-cheek take on noir fiction: "On the way to the place, I passed several panhandlers, one of whom had a sign that said, 'Will work for air.' The cops didn't kick those who were in arrears in their life-support tax payments out of the dome—Slapcoff Industries still had a reputation to maintain on Earth—but if you rented or had a mortgage, you'd be evicted onto the street" (32).

As New Klondike suggests, space station cities have planet-based cousins. Science fiction could scarcely survive without its hundreds or thousands of air-protecting cities built under domes, under transparent tents, buried under the surface of moons and planets. The most basic job of these cities as physical constructions is to encapsulate breathable air at breathable pressure. Residents must always be on guard for breaks and blowouts that vent the usable air, void the pressure, or perhaps let in the poisonous atmosphere that has been swirling outside. These are cities protected from the vertical dimension—from meteors, from poisonous gases, or from vacuum that stretches upward to infinity.

Air is the one unregulated and unmetered input into our ordinary urban ecology. It is just there. It is not piped and monitored like water, nor packaged and vended like food and fuel. It is just there as we go about our lives—sometimes dry and sometimes rainy, sometimes smoggy, sometimes crisp and clear after a weather front has swept through. It can do violence when stirred into tornadoes and hurricanes, but usually we notice only its attributes—it's too hot, too cold, too wet. To imagine air requiring technological intervention is a disquieting novum. Science fiction readers may be so accustomed to domed and buried cities that they scarcely notice, but the idea is actually startling, just as Fritz Leiber points out with the very title of his story.

Consider the dual role of air in the film *Total Recall* (1990). Mars is a mining colony controlled by a corporation directed by the creepy Vilos Colhaagen, who squeezes his workers by charging for the very air they breathe. When Douglas Quaid, played by Arnold Schwarzenegger, arrives on the planet, workers are being driven to revolt as the price of air keeps rising: "More Freedom! More Air!" At the same time, the half-buried, half-domed city is terribly fragile. Quaid's arrival on Mars triggers a shoot-up in the arrivals hall that shatters a window and creates a blowout that sweeps people outside—very exciting and very dangerous, although we wonder who would design such a brittle dome, not to mention being stupid enough to arm guards with projectile weapons.

Writers have converged on consensus architecture for the stages of settlement on airless worlds. Allen Steele in *Lunar Descent* (1991) describes the moon early in the colonization process. Moon miners live in a single company town constructed from a bunch of "low, square and rectangular monocreete buildings clustered together under bulldozed soil, interconnected by subterranean tunnels and above ground crosswalks" (53). The mess hall / meeting hall has a couple of deeply recessed windows onto the drab moonscape, but the workers live inside under a layer of regolith or outside in pressure suits. Larry Niven set his SF detective novel *The Patchwork Girl* (1980) on the moon at a later stage of development, but the city is still buried under "rock and moondust piled high atop it for meteor protection" (15). The top level has windows, however, enabling an assassin to attempt murder by targeting a victim in his room with a powerful laser aimed from outside, setting up a reverse locked-room mystery. As lunar settlement continues to mature, we may find the characters living on the surface under a dome, as in the opening of *Anniversary Day* (2001), a recent entry in Kristine Kathryn Rusch's "Retrieval Artist" series about a science fiction detective in Armstrong City: "Bartholomew Nyquist parked his aircar in one of the hoverlots at the end of the neighborhood. The Dome was dark this morning, even though someone should have started the Dome Daylight program. Maybe they had, deciding that Armstrong was in for a 'cloudy' day—terminology he never entirely understood, given that the Moon had no clouds and most people who lived here had been born on the Moon and had never seen a cloud in their entire lives" (15).

The consensus sequence is similar for Mars. South Colony in Robert Heinlein's classic *Red Planet* (1949) has a population of a few hundred pioneers, living in double-layered plastic domes connected by tunnels. Arthur C. Clarke's first published novel, *The Sands of Mars* (1951), is set sometime in the 1990s in Port Lowell, the largest city on Mars, with two thousand people. Lowellites live inside six nearly invisible plastic domes (the largest half a kilometer across) held up by internal air pressure and intertied by tunnels. Under the domes are "uniform metal houses and a few public buildings" giving the appearance "more of a military camp than a city." Oxygen is extracted from the oxidized red Martian soil. Residents practice blow-out drills with the goal of getting to cover inside a sealable building within ten seconds.

Heinlein's and Clarke's colonists are in the first decade of settlement, but Greg Bear's *Moving Mars* (1993) is set on a substantially developed planet in the year 2171. Residents still live underground, but with large domes over the central spaces. Off to the edges of the university, for example, is a maze of old tunnels: "Forty orbits ago—over seventy-five terrestrial years—these tunnels had connected several small pioneer stations. We filed past warrens once used by the earliest families, dark and bitterly cold, kept pressurized in reserve only for dire emergencies" (8). Now Martians live in domed trench complexes, well protected but still vulnerable to pressure-loss accidents and power failures leading to oxygen deprivation and recycler failures. When political crisis explodes, "the white walls and pressure arches [of the new Mars capital] stood out against the ochre and red all around, a beacon for assault" (367)— although it will prove to survive.

Descriptions of cities are secondary in Bear's narrative, but they are central to Kim Stanley Robinson's intentions in his trilogy about the terraforming of Mars. He opens the first volume, *Red Mars* (1993), with a civic festival celebrating Nicosia, the planet's first fully surface city, coming seventy-five years after initial settlement. "The first town of any size to be built freestanding on the Martian surface; all the buildings were set inside what was in effect an immense clear tent, supported by a nearly invisible frame." The town is a large triangle on a slope (great views!) with seven radiating avenues and low buildings in Fauvist hues. Its five thousand residents have already divided into ethnic neighborhoods. The air has enough oxygen and weight that the city does not have to be fully sealed, but the atmosphere is still so thin and cold that one cannot survive for long outside without protective suits. "After all those years in Underhill it was hard to grasp. . . . We're out of our holes, Maya, we're on the surface at last" (4–6, 19).

Decades earlier in Robinson's planetary epic, Martian settlement had started with an expedition camp of modules scattered on the surface, such as might be found in Antarctica or Greenland. Soon Underhill is built as a permanent underground habitat. A double glass dome holds the pressure and keeps out ultraviolet radiation, roofing over a central atrium, with underground rooms branching off. "The sky was a ruby color through the glass panels, and the magnesium struts gleamed like tarnished silver" (163). Settlers built other habitats also largely underground, but with gradually increasing exposure, such as a set of rooms dug into the side of a thirty-meter trench, with three levels of stacked rooms faced with glass, and reflective material on the other side of the trench to direct sunlight. Then the increasingly confident Martians scaled up that model. Japanese immigrants built Senzeni Na, an industrial community at the bottom of Thaumasia Fossae's deepest canyon. Production facilities on the canyon floor are connected by walktubes because pressure suits were still needed outside. "The town's actual living quarters were built into the southeast wall of the canyon. A big rectangular section of the cliff had been replaced by glass; behind it was a tall open concourse, backed by five stories of terraced apartments." The biggest and most beautiful new city is Burroughs, the de facto capital as the base of the United Nations Office of Mars Affairs. It is another cliff city, carved into a set of mesas: "Big sections of the mesas' vertical sides had been filled by rectangles of mirrored glass, as if postmodern skyscrapers had been turned on the sides and shoved into the hills" (271).

The Martians revolt against Earth domination, UNOMA being the tool of big Earth corporations, but their cities are vulnerable to tent breach. They "lay helpless under the lasers of orbiting UNOMA police ships" (514). Refugees have crowded into Cairo, which is surrounded by UN police. "At 4:30 alarms went off all over the city. The tent had been broached, apparently catastrophically, because a sudden wind whipped west through the streets, and pressure sirens went off in every building. The electricity went off, and just that quick it went from a town to a broken shell, of running figures in walkers and helmets, all of them rushing about, crowding toward the gates, knocked down by gusts of wind and each other. Windows popped out everywhere, the air was full of clear plastic shrapnel" (529).

Heinlein, Clarke, Bear, and Robinson are all authors who respect engineering. Their Martian cities converge in appearance and structure because the logic of pressure gradients, oxygen pressure, and materials mandate a common form. Moreover, it is a form that readers with basic physics can understand, agree with, or critique. Engineering challenges and solutions are not another decorative gizmo like a bounce tube or dilating door, but rather essential background. In *The Sands of Mars*, for example, Clarke devoted several paragraphs to the completion of a seventh dome.

Hello, Earth. This is Martin Gibson speaking to you from Port Lowell, Mars. It's a great day for us here. This morning the new dome was inflated and now the city's increased its size by almost a half. . . .

You know that it's impossible to breathe the Martian atmosphere—it's far too thin and contains practically no oxygen. Port Lowell, our biggest city, is built under six domes of transparent plastic held up by the pressure of the air inside—air which we can breathe comfortably though it's still much less dense than yours.

For the last year a seventh dome has been under construction, a dome twice as big as any of the others. . . .

Imagine a great circular space half a kilometre across, surrounded by a thick wall of glass bricks twice as high as a man. Through this wall lead the passages to the other domes, and the exits direct on to the brilliant green Martian landscape all around us. . . .

When I entered Dome Seven yesterday, all this great circular space was covered with a thin transparent sheet fastened to the surrounding wall, and lying limp on the ground in huge folds beneath which we had to force our way. . . . The envelope of the dome is very strong plastic, almost perfectly transparent and quite flexible—a kind of thick cellophane. (422)

Several ensuing paragraphs describe the process of pumping in air and inflating the dome. The scene is perhaps not all that high on the sense-of-wonder scale, but Clarke knew that his own technical bent matched that of his readers.

CITIES UNDER THE SEAS

Underwater cities are the mirror image of lunar and Martian bubble cities. The basic challenge is to maintain a bubble of usable atmosphere within an environment at a different pressure. Dome breach is just as much a fear, but the problem is reversed—keeping massive overpressure at bay and preventing implosion rather than holding in air against explosive escape.

Underwater cities have seldom made for good fiction because of the storytelling problem of setting action in dark ocean depths where neither characters (nor readers/viewers) can see or move freely outside. Consider that submerged movies tend to be submarine warfare thrillers, mysterious shipwreck thrillers, or adventures revolving around alien objects that just happen to have fallen to the ocean floor. In *The Abyss* (1989), the best of the genre, ambience and action are dark and claustrophobic. A cinematic alternative like the cheesy *Captain Nemo and the Underwater City* (1969) offers implausibly cheerful interiors and no gestures to technical verisimilitude.

A pulp writer's favorite option was to ignore science in favor of a mythical Venus with warm seas and networks of underwater cities. Henry Kuttner and C. L. Moore in *Fury*, originally serialized in *Astounding* in 1947, posited a set of undersea Venusburgs: "The Earth is long dead, blasted apart, and the human survivors who settled on Venus live in huge citadels beneath the Venusian seas in an atrophying, class-ridden society ruled by the Immortals—genetic mutations who live a thousand years or more." The domes themselves, both beneath the waters and covering newer colonies on land, are made from "impervium." What a handy material that is, excusing the authors from actually thinking through the engineering problems so they can focus the plot on tensions and conflicts within the ruling class. Nevertheless, impervium makes the machines for breathing possible: "Now he stood on the land of Venus, with a transparent impervium dome catching rainbows wherever the fugitive sun broke through the cloud blanket. . . . The free air of Venus was short on oxygen and long on carbon dioxide; it was breathable, but not vintage atmosphere. . . . Here, under the dome, the atmospheric ingredients were carefully balanced. Necessary, of course—just as the impervium shell itself seemed necessary against the fecund insanity that teemed the Venusian lands" (93).

Isaac Asimov left only part of his science at the door when he wrote for the juvenile market as Paul French, describing an entire network of fifty undersea cities in *Lucky Starr and the Oceans of Venus* (1954). Because the atmosphere contains no oxygen, Venusians make the planet livable by using electrolysis to oxygenate their bubble cities. Rather than Kuttner's implausible mile-deep citadels, these lie just below the ocean surface so their tops nearly break into the sky at low tide. The dome is two-layered, with carbon dioxide sandwiched in between to absorb shocks. Honeycomb structures between the layers minimize danger, and internal barriers can shut off different sections of the city in case of breach (the first half of the book centers on threatened sabotage). This said, however, the domes themselves are made from a handy super-duper plastic called transite, which is completely insoluble, doesn't etch, won't change chemically in reaction with the ocean, and never gets encrusted with slime or Venusian barnacle equivalents. Moreover, the domes are actually supported by power beams that are, explains a city official, "dia-magnetic force fields in steel housings. It looks as though steel beams are supporting the dome, but that's not so. Steel just isn't strong enough. It's the force fields that do it" (58).

Maureen McHugh in *Half the Day Is Night* (1994) made a much more serious stab at imagining underwater cities, in this case a set of cities two hundred meters under the Caribbean that constitute the nation of Caribe. The plot itself—a story of two innocent individuals who slowly realize that they have been caught up in political and corporate ma-neuvers and scheme to escape—does not require the undersea setting. Much of the action occurs in the boardrooms, cheap hotels, and mean streets that are the familiar settings of noir and thriller fiction. Subma-rines rather than ferries connect the cities, buses operate on city streets, including the Caribe equivalent of Kenyan matatu and similar vehicles of the third-world poor. The ethnicity of the French Vietnamese and Chinese American protagonists contrasts with the darker-skinned Hai-tians of Caribe, paralleling the plot tension of individuals from the global North caught up in problems of the global South that drives many stories of intrigue, from Graham Greene novels to the 1982 film *The Year of Living Dangerously*.

Nevertheless, McHugh refrains from introducing impervium or transite or diamagnetic force fields and pays particular attention to the problems of temperature and air. She never describes the domes or con-tainment systems themselves, but the ambient cold of the deep ocean overburdens heating systems and renders the cities always chill. Only a handful of construction workers and fish jockeys work in the sea outside, taking drugs to speed their metabolism and eating vast piles of carbo-hydrates to survive the cold. Inside, pressure variations between upper and lower levels affect the composition and quality of the atmosphere. The rich get clean, dry air. The poor on the lower levels breathe damp, oxygen-poor air laden with odors and pollutants because recirculation systems are ill-maintained. Open fires are illegal, a stricture violated in poor districts, but richer residents still drive cars with internal combus-tion engines. Air is not yet metered like water and power, notes one resident, but the implication hovers that Caribe is not that far removed from New Klondike.

SUPERSIZE US

In 1974, author and editor Frederik Pohl had a brief conversation with New York mayor John Lindsay about whether the city was governable (Lindsay thought that the basic problem was not enough tax revenue). The next year Pohl published *The Years of the City*, five chronologically sequential novellas about the future of New York. The unifying concern is the problem of governance as the changing cast of characters deal with labor union power and racketeering, political corruption, and changing legal systems.

In the third novella, "The Blister," Manhattan is being enclosed under one large dome up from the Battery to Canal Street and another over the middle of the island, with a smaller dome to connect them, making a sort of lopsided dumbbell shape like "two humps on a camel, the tall igloo one down around lower Manhattan, the lower connecting bridge from Canal Street to the twenties, the big elongated one covering midtown and Central Park" (177). Pohl might have been drawing on Buckminster Fuller's 1969 proposal for a dome covering Twenty-Second Street to Sixty-Fourth Street, river to river.[2] In line with New York's tradition of work in high steel, the domes are a network of girders and cables holding plastic panels. The engineers use peripheral skyscrapers as anchors, some of which have to be sheared off to fit the slope. It will not be a Martian-style bubble tent but rather a gigantic cousin of a geodesic dome, although with hexagonal instead of triangular panels.

Pohl never explains why it is necessary or desirable for the Big Apple to become the Big Blister. He refers briefly to creating an enclosed, relatively self-sustaining system—garbage will be recycled rather than barged and dumped at sea, gas-powered cars will be replaced, there will be more recycling of materials—but in the next story the barges are still at work. The dome is periodically vented to get rid of radon, but readers otherwise do not know how air circulates. The dome does allow climate control within the range of 15–28 Celsius, perhaps the reason that a city like Tucson followed with its own smaller "thermal dome." In the fourth and fifth sections, the existence of the dome is background (it allows for exciting but illegal hang gliding, for example).

A few years after Pohl imagined the evolution of New York, C. J. Cherryh took on the same task in "Highliner," one of six stories about the distant future of earthbound cities collected and published as *Sunfall* (1981). Her New York is a superhigh, ever-growing pyramid whose "single spire aimed at the clouds, concave-curved from sprawling base to needle heights" (106). The city is constantly expanding, building and rebuilding its burdened foundations, pushing higher, adding space to intermediate levels. Smaller suburban towers cluster around it, metropolis and mountain range at the same time.

Both authors are careful to undercut the impressions of grandeur that their megastructures might evoke. Pohl's city is socially messy, with a touch of political repression. His protagonist in "Blister" is an ordinary worker who helps to assemble the great dome. Cherryh's city is an ultimately futile effort on a dying planet with a fading sun. Like Pohl, she centers her story on the city's "highliners," the skilled specialists who risk their lives to inspect and repair the exterior of the tower while dangling from flimsy ropes and harnesses. Her basic plot is routine—workers unite to resist corrupt corporations—but the name of the central character, John Tallfeather, recalls the Mohawk Indians who worked skyscraper construction in twentieth-century New York. With both stories, readers get indirect answers to the questions in Bertolt Brecht's poem "A Worker Reads History," which asks "Who built the seven gates of Thebes? . . . In the evening when the Chinese wall was finished, where did the masons go?"

Cherryh's future New York is a mighty and monstrous artifact, but it has nothing on Isaac Asimov's definitive supersized city. Eager readers who bought the first volume of Asimov's *Foundation* for its cover art when it appeared in book form in 1951 might have expected, from the lines of rocket ships swirling toward the center of a vast galaxy, to plunge immediately into a space battle or an expedition to alien worlds. Instead they found themselves on the very strange planet Trantor . . . and in the world-encompassing imperial city of Trantor.

Asimov's readers were visitors in the ultimate covered city. It's *big*, with a population of forty-five billion, many of them administrators who manage the affairs of the twelve-thousand-year Galactic Reich. The city covers all seventy-five million square miles of the planet's land surface and creeps out onto the continental shelves. Only occasional parks and the imperial palace offer touches of green to relieve Trantor's metallic gray. Nearly everyone lives underground. Asimov introduces the city by tracing newcomer Gaal Dornick's breakneck trip from spaceport to hotel in an air taxi that plunges into a high wall "riddled with holes that were the mouths of tunnels" and flies on through blackness "with nothing but the past-flashing of a colored signal light to relieve the gloom" (8). When he wakes the next day, he cannot tell day from night, for "all the planet seemed to live beneath metal" (9). Trantoropolis extends only a few hundred feet above the surface but reaches a mile belowground. From an infrequently used viewing tower Gaal "could see no horizon other than that of metal against sky, stretching out to almost uniform grayness . . . all the busy traffic of billions of men were going on, he knew, beneath the metal skin of the world" (11). In follow-on books, as the atmosphere deteriorates, Trantorians erect domes to cover their surface buildings in addition to carrying on their lives in the climate-controlled underground.[3]

Trantor is a long way in time and space from New York, but Pohl and Asimov shared the same impulse to imagine a city as a stupendous engineering project. There is no apparent reason to dome over New York —the ambient atmosphere is quite breathable—but it is definitely an intriguingly futuristic idea that assumes the ability to consume impressive volumes of resources. To imagine Trantor is to take this sort of fascination with the sheer physicality of future cities to its extreme, and also to put their operating systems front and center in the same way as in air-bubble cities, although again there is really no practical reason offered for the gee-whiz gigantism. A world-encompassing city makes extreme demands on the urban metabolism—the importation of the food, fuel, and materials that keep it functioning and the elimination of waste products ranging from excess heat to garbage. Trantor gets its power from the temperature difference between the surface and the deep planetary interior. It depends on the agricultural production of twenty-four planets in the same way that Rome depended on grain from North Africa, wine from Greece, and olive oil from Spain—one of the many parallels to the history of Rome on which Asimov built his galactic history.

Trantor is an ultimate entry in the reimagination of cities along the horizontal plane that began in the later nineteenth century, when the spread of railroads and streetcars broke the physical limits of cities based on walking. Not long after Arturo Soria y Mata imagined a single linear city stretching between opposite corners of Europe, Patrick Geddes, in 1915, coined "conurbation" to describe the growing together of previously distinct cities in industrial regions like the Ruhr and the English Midlands. The U.S. Census tried to give bureaucratic precision to the idea by defining "metropolitan districts" in 1920 and "metropolitan areas" in 1940 to encompass cities and increasingly sprawling suburbs in a single unit. Jean Gottmann simply took the effort another step in arguing that the entire northeastern United States from Boston to Washington functioned as a single "megalopolis"—a concept quickly adapted in Japan as *megaroporisu* for the Taiheiyo Belt along the southeast-facing coast of Honshu. It got new life in the twenty-first century as "megaregion" in the United States and "mega-urban region" in China.[4]

Megalopolis is an easy transfer to science fiction, offering writers a quick way give a sense of verisimilitude to their near-future settings. Much of the action in William Gibson's *Neuromancer* (1984) takes place in "BAMA, the Sprawl, the Boston-Atlanta Metropolitan Axis" (57). The Judge Dredd comics, published since 1977, take place in the twenty-second century in Mega-City One, which extends roughly from Florida to Ontario (or is it Georgia to Montreal—consistency not being a strong point over decades of comic books) with somewhere between one hundred million and eight hundred million residents (ditto). However, fiction has struggled to out-extrapolate mundane planning discourse, especially the work of the enthusiastic Greek planner Constantinos Doxiadis, who envisioned Ecumenopolis—a single supercity that might extend its tendrils across entire continents. Assuming a planetary population of forty or fifty billion, he projected from metropolis to megalopolis to world city in an essay on "Ecumenopolis: Tomorrow's City":

> All cities will be interconnected in major urban complexes where no distinction between large and small will be possible; they will all have become one. . . . Such cities, growing dynamically over the next two or three generations, will finally be interconnected, in one continuous network, into one universal city which we can call the ecumenic city, the city of the whole inhabited earth, or Ecumenopolis. If we speak, therefore, of the cities of the future one century from now, we can state that they will have become one city, the unique city of mankind.[5]

At this final Trantorian scale, of course, the idea loses any attachment to the economies, transportation systems, and people of actual places. Even Megalopolis is too big to be useful on a daily basis; people will tell new acquaintances that they hail from South Philly or White Plains or Providence, but it is unlikely that anyone normally claims to be from BosWash, and presumably the same might be true of BAMA. A city-machine that covers an entire planet is even more abstract. It can be imagined as a whole but never fully described because we see it either from great distances or in close-up. Doxiadis wanted ecumenopolitan neighborhoods to maintain human scale, but what we remember decades after his manifesto are his maps in which the single supercity looks like the subterranean connections of a giant fungus. Descriptions of Trantor kept morphing through the initial and follow-on books because it was an idea rather than a place.

A half century after Trantor made its appearance, Coruscant, the globe-girdling city at the political heart of the Star Wars universe, works —and doesn't work—in the same ways. Referenced generically as the Imperial Center in the early movies, it got its name in Timothy Zahn's *Heir to the Empire* (1991), the first of scores of spin-off Star Wars novels. "Since a largely urbanized world would probably sparkle wonderfully in the sunlight (as well as glittering with its own lights on its dark side)," he comments in the foreword to a reprint edition, "I gave the planet the name *Coruscant*, which means 'glittering.'" Beyond the name, Zahn briefly describes the city as a vast busy surface: "Even in the middle of the night the Imperial City was a bustle of activity, with the lights of vehicles and streets intertwining to form a sort of flowing work of art. Overhead, lit by both the city lights and those of occasional airspeeders flitting through them, the low-lying clouds were a dim sculptured ceiling stretching in all directions, with the same apparent endlessness as the city itself" (17).

Coruscant has since featured prominently in the three Star Wars movie prequels. *The Phantom Menace* (1999) brings Queen Amidala to plead the case of the planet Naboo before the Galactic Senate, which deliberates in an appropriately galactic-sized auditorium, and then pleads again to the Jedi Council. In this latter scene the city stretches endlessly below the windows of a high tower where the Jedi meet. *Attack of the Clones* (2002) serves up the airspeeder chase through the city's high-rise canyons. *Revenge of the Sith* (2005) opens with a space battle far above the city-planet surface. When viewers aren't positioned in flying machines, however, they see the city from windows and balconies in shots that are conceptually identical to views from Manhattan skyscrapers.

When actual actors enter the frame, the city-as-a-whole fades into a backdrop, as in Amidala's visit to the Jedi. Instead we see meeting rooms, apartments, and other bits and pieces at human scale. Similarly, the army of writers who have produced scores of Star Wars novelizations and spin-offs are limited by their inability to draw on the visual powers of artists and model builders. Like every other suspense and adventure writer, they zoom in to specific buildings, like the elite apartment tower 500 Republica in the Ambassadorial Sector, where nabobs and politicos live, and neighborhoods like the derelict manufacturing district The Works. Dex's Diner in Coco Town ("collective commerce") is especially popular as a greasy spoon restaurant where dockworkers mingle with nonhumans and important figures like Obi-Wan Kenobi.

These choices reflect the reality that nobody lives in an entire "Chicago" or "Los Angeles" or "Coruscant." Environmental psychologists and social geographers have long known that we spend the bulk of our lives in very limited parts of our cities. We know our neighborhood, favorite shopping districts, and perhaps downtown. We know routes to school, work, movie theaters, and friends across town, but much of the rest of the metropolis is mental white space that we see in passing from freeways —a sort of urban flyover country. We tend to look for new housing within a few miles of our current residence because we trust our judgment about familiar areas. Before the takeoff of Internet dating sites, we even found girlfriends, boyfriends, and spouses within limited subareas. If Portland at 2.5 million people is too big for a curious urban studies professor like me to know completely, Coruscant with its supposed population six orders of magnitude greater is too big even for Yoda—who does manage to make an appearance at Dex's Diner.

Trantor and Coruscant are more than physical constructs. They also function as galactic capitals. Earthly empires have needed metropolitan capitals like Byzantium and Baghdad. Vast networks of economic activity have needed global cities like New York and Tokyo to pull the strings of power. So too does a galactic empire need a capital of appropriately large scale. Trantor, wrote Asimov in *Foundation and Empire*, "was more than a planet; it was the living pulse of an Empire of twenty million stellar systems. It had only one function, administration; one purpose, government; and one manufactured product, law" (67).

In the literature of urban criticism, such world cities have a bad reputation. Saskia Sassen sees places like London and Tokyo, the head cities of finance capitalism, as breeders of inequality. Even more pessimistic was Oswald Spengler, who in the aftermath of German defeat in World War I wrote *Der Untergang des Abendlandes*, translated as *The Decline of the West*. His "world city" was the center of high but decadent civilization that had turned vibrant cultures into stone and inevitably led to collapse and barbarism: "And then begins the giant megalopolis, the city-as-world, which suffers nothing beside itself and sets about annihilating the country picture. . . . There arises the monstrous symbol and vessel of the completely emancipated intellect, the world city, the center in which the course of a world history winds up by winding itself up. . . .

[This] stone Colossus, 'Cosmopolis,' stands at the end of the life-course of every great Culture."[6]

A cyclical understanding of history also underlies the *Foundation* narrative, written explicitly to the model of the expansion and collapse of the Roman Empire. What that meant for Trantor, of course, was nothing good. By *Second Foundation*, set three hundred years after the first volume, the mighty city of forty-five billion has fallen in the Great Sack that accompanied the implosion of empire: "Its drooping powers had been bent back upon themselves and broken forever. In the lasting ruin of death, the metal shell that circled the planet wrinkled and crumpled into an aching mock of its own grandeur. The survivors tore up the metal plating and sold it to other planets for seed and cattle. The soil was uncovered once more and the planet returned to its beginnings" (181). Will Coruscant suffer the same fate by Episode IX of the Star Wars saga?

Science fiction world cities may be metaphors for the accumulation and dissipation of power, but *as cities* they don't actually do much work in terms of narrative or development of ideas. They are awesome scene-setters. Once the protagonists land and start to interact, however, we are in specific buildings and neighborhoods, and the vastness of scale recedes and loses relevance. Contrast our scanty knowledge of Trantor with the way that the scale, variety, and character of Chicago are creative constituent elements in James T. Farrell's Studs Lonigan novels or Saul Bellow's *The Adventures of Augie March*. Think about the role of Paris as an active force that has shaped innumerable films.

Although the Galactic Senate Chamber is indeed impressive, a far more plausible take on the science fiction world city simultaneously undercuts its pretentions and refocuses attention on its simple physical improbability. *Bill, the Galactic Hero* (1965) is Harry Harrison's mash-up of *Candide*, *The Good Soldier Schweik*, and *Catch-22* as a space opera satire. Bill, a naïve recruit to the space troopers, finds himself in one absurd situation after another. By mid-book, he is stranded on Helior, the Imperial Planet and "first city of the galaxy," whose population of 150 billion triples that of Trantor. The supercity turns out to be incredibly confusing, especially after Bill loses his map book: "A city as large as a planet! The concept was almost too big to grasp! In fact, when he thought about it, the concept was too big to grasp" (ibook edition, 2001, 83). Without a guidebook, poor Bill wanders lost and befuddled among "the endless miles of metal corridors, the constantly rushing crowds, the slipways, slideways, gravdrops, hellavators, suctionlifts, and all the rest" (95).

AWOL and a nonperson, Bill flees lower and lower into the city, where he encounters the systems that make it work. He hacks into a food delivery pipe that spews out endless links of green chlora-filly sausages that he roasts over a wastebasket fire. Stumbling ever deeper through spider-webbed corridors, he comes at last to the heart of the imperial city—the Department of Sanitation with its divisions for Refuse, Waste, Rubbish, Plumbing, and Sewage Disposal. The department deals in cycles. Food comes in from agricultural planets, sewage flows to the lower levels, Sanitation processes it into "the finest bricks of condensed fertilizer in the civilized galaxy," which are shipped to the agricultural planets. Rainwater is pumped from basement levels to the surface. But solid trash is a problem: "Did you ever think how many newspapers 150 billion people throw away every day?" a sanitation inspector asks Bill. "Or how many dispos-a-steins? Or dinner plates?" The stopgap is to create fake flea infestations that require the evacuation of cubic-mile dormitory blocks, which can then be stuffed full of discarded plastic dinner trays. A longer-range effort to boost the rubbish off planet toward a neighboring sun proves too dangerous because the volume of material nearly destabilizes the sun's energy cycle and pushes it to go nova.

By the time Bill moves on to other misadventures, Harrison has reminded readers that it is easier to dream up a city that sounds impressive than to figure out how it might work. The problem is endemic to every scale of design—architects design nifty-looking buildings where nobody wants to work, utopian planners sketch out enticing schemes while leaving someone else to figure out the details. World-city science fiction operates at the same scale, and here in marked contrast to the work discussed earlier in this chapter. Writers who choose a space-station city or a Mars-bubble city as their setting have to pay some attention to the practicalities of air and energy to maintain credibility in a way that the Star Wars franchise does not. When imagining future cities it's not necessary to write engineer-as-hero science fiction in the mode of *Astounding*, but it helps to remember that it takes bus operators, transportation planners, utility managers, water engineers, pipeline monitors, produce vendors, pizza delivery kids, and, yes, garbage truck drivers to keep big cities going. For the future, we'll need to add atmosphere chemists and air pressure technicians to the list. Without them even the most impressive supercity is on the verge of cascading collapse.

CHAPTER THREE

MIGRATORY CITIES

Fleeing from the Cylon tyranny, the last Battlestar *Galactica* leads a ragtag fugitive fleet on a long quest . . . a shining planet known as Earth.
—*Battlestar Galactica* (1978)

Puerto Angeles adrift on the blue Pacific and Arkangel skating on iron runners across the frozen northern seas . . . —Philip Reeve, *Mortal Engines* (2001)

Manhattan is on the move . . . throughout the galaxy. The invention of the "spindizzy," a real doozy of an antigravity device named for tricks with electron rotation, has allowed entire cities to cut themselves loose from planetary surfaces and zip through space at super-light speeds. First one, then another, then every Earth city has gathered up its bedrock and buildings and atmosphere in a force field bubble to go flying off in search of work and adventures. James Blish introduced his upwardly mobile New York in stories for *Astounding Science Fiction* in 1950 and combined several related stories into the book *Earthman Come Home* in 1955. He wrote two prequel novels and one sequel over the next few years and published them together as *Cities in Flight* in 1970.

New York and other migratory metropolises are Okie cities—eighteen thousand of them at the time of *Earthman Come Home* about fifteen hundred years into the future. Like refugees from the Dust Bowl of the 1930s, they roam the stars looking for worlds where they can trade scientific or industrial expertise for resources like petroleum, germanium, and food. Business is regulated by contracts enforced by a bureaucratic galactic police force that hassles the cities just as cops in the early twentieth century harassed itinerant laborers. Migrant cities like New York that are on the up and up think of themselves as hobos or migratory workers. Cities that have gone rogue are bindlestiffs, a synonym for tramp that Blish uses as a pejorative. New York encounters a hobo jungle where three hundred cities have huddled without work because of economic collapse, before eventually flying off to ever more distant adventures.

Half a century later, Stephen Baxter in *Flood* (2009) imagined a migrating city as far removed and different as could be from high-flying New York. The year is 2031, and global climate change and massive tectonic disruptions are causing water to pour into the oceans at an astounding rate. Mean sea level rise has already passed two hundred meters over the base datum for the twentieth century, on its way to an eight-hundred-meter rise by 2035. What had been an organized settlement of sea-rise refugees in the Texas panhandle only a few years earlier is now Walker City. Its tens of thousands of residents are on the move. They stretch in miles-long columns, flanked by the community's armed guards. "This was Walker City, a city on the move. To walk was the world. To walk was life" (290).

The community wanders the still unflooded parts of the Great Plains—Kansas, Iowa, Nebraska. It stops for days or weeks to offer labor in exchange for food and supplies; because gasoline is available only to the remnants of the military, organized muscle power is invaluable. One of the characters who has ended up in the city describes it to a visitor:

> We're organized. You can see that. We're a city on the move. We have a mayor, who we elect, although it has to be a show of hands. We have cops and medical facilities, and we barter with other communities. When we stop, we get organized, we dig latrines, we post guards. We have chaplains in every denomination, and imams and rabbis. We help each other; we bury our dead; we care for our children. And we stay out of trouble. . . . We work in return for lodging or food. It's not ideal, but it's not meant to last forever. We're looking for a place to put down some kind of roots. Until we find that, we're on the move. An Okie city, but a city nevertheless. (300–301)

Tell a science fiction fan that you're writing about mobile cities, and *Cities in Flight* is likely to pop up first in the conversation. James Blish was one of the more popular science fiction writers of the 1950s and 1960s and well connected with the Futurians, the New York club that included Isaac Asimov, Frederik Pohl, Cyril Kornbluth, Donald Wollheim, Damon Knight, Judith Merril, and many other writers who shaped the field from the 1940s to the 1970s. Blish wrote big-picture science fiction of grand sweep over many millennia, framed by Oswald Spengler's ideas about the rise of cultures and the decline of civilizations from *The Decline of the West* (1919). It's future history of the sort that Isaac Asimov and Robert Heinlein were toying with in the same era.

But Blish doesn't actually do much with the *city* part of his story line. Mayor John Amalfi makes his appearance standing on the top level of New York City Hall (is it the "belfry" of a building or the "bridge" of a spaceship? he wonders). Blish scatters occasional references to New York streets and landmarks, but the city as city doesn't drive the action. Neither the scale nor variety of urban life really figures. The narrative is a series of exciting episodes at different planets and star systems where a few key characters get to show their cleverness and courage. For all that we learn about the dynamics of neighborhoods, the interplay of cultural groups, or the maintenance of urban services, we could just as well be on a traditional starship having space opera adventures with Mayor Amalfi and City Manager Mark Hazleton as captain and first mate.

Baxter's wandering community is a more limited and more plausible projection that just meets the criteria for cityhood. Roughly the size of the Union and Confederate armies that marched back and forth across Tennessee to clash at Shiloh and Chickamauga, it is large enough to be a city. Its population is a heterogeneous hodgepodge of races and ages and backgrounds. It has government and services. It is certainly not tied to one location, but the ability of Walker City to survive for a decade in a context of cataclysmic geophysical change that has destroyed cities with millennia of history means that it substitutes persistence for permanence.

Blish and Baxter have set a challenge. Normal cities are stationary — they spread from a center and don't move (with the occasional exception of small towns that governments relocate because of dam projects or similar public works). London is still where the Romans built Londinium nearly two thousand years ago. Names may change with politics and migration—from Byzantium to Constantinople to Istanbul for a world-class example, from New Archangel to Sitka for a U.S. case—but the cities are in the same place. Plenty of cities have disappeared into history, but they died on the ground where they were born. We have seen that one of the common tropes of science fiction is the city that could not possibly move because it already covers an entire planetary surface.

But what if a city *could* move? That is the premise for startling, even shocking, reversals. Unlike staid social scientists and historians, science fiction writers can imagine cities that fly, walk, crawl, roll, creep, and float. Cities can move by hard inches and slow miles, they can barrel along tracks and strike out across oceans. How could they do this, we wonder, hoping for more technologically satisfying suggestions than spindizzies. Why should they move at all? What is gained and what is lost when a city pulls up stakes?

HUNTER-GATHERERS

In 1964, British architect Ron Herron published drawings of Walking City—a huge self-contained mini-city that looked like a combination of giant building cranes, 1950s robots, and praying mantis. He envisioned urbanoids with vast extensible legs that could stalk through future New York or London like benevolent monsters. Walking cities could assemble into an ad hoc metropolis, or their residents could decide to pack up and move their entire city if their environment grew too polluted or local politics too repressive. Walking City citizens wouldn't have to leave their apartments as the superstructure trundled across the landscape, the entire city turning into a giant caravan (or RV, for U.S. readers).

Herron was a part of Archigram, a group of young British architects who came together in the early 1960s to stage a conceptual revolt against stuffy academic modernism. They published their ideas in an ephemeral magazine beginning in 1961, staged exhibitions, and even snagged a handful of commissions. They were part of the transformation of British intellectual life as a new generation of artists and professionals pushed to supplant their elders who had been shaped by depression, war, and post-war austerity. Results ranged from the explosion of British rock music to the New Wave science fiction that would soon appear in the magazine *New Worlds*.

Archigram drawings are thought experiments and visual jokes in what people a few years later might consider the Monty Python mode. The Archigram watchwords were flexibility and motion, in contrast to Le Corbusier's proposals for massive building complexes fixed in place and Paolo Soleri's emerging drawings of vast permanently sited arcologies. Herron proposed the Walking City. Peter Cook proposed Instant City, a set of airships freighted with performance spaces and culture to enliven drab towns like a flying circus. Given their celebration of movement and what critic Michael Sorkin called their "nomadic fantasies," we can read the Archigram vision as a direct send-up of Lúcio Costa's and Oscar Niemeyer's Brasília, designed to resemble a great *grounded* bird and already four years into construction when Herron published.[1]

Much more recently, Spanish architect Manuel Domínguez has published drawings for a Very Large Structure half a kilometer in span that could crawl across the landscape on huge caterpillar tracks. Lower levels would house the mechanical systems and infrastructure, and the top deck would be the living area. More like a land-based cruise ship than a city, it is another quasi-utopian thought experiment, not all that different in basic goals from the ideal cities that Renaissance thinkers sketched out in two dimensions—just more mechanically complex and mobile.[2]

Greg Bear's mobile cities in *Strength of Stones*, published in 1988 and including stories from 1978 and 1981, read like supersized projections of Herron's vision. On the planet God-Does-Battle, thousand-year-old sentient cities "walk" by partly disassembling themselves and then reassembling along a chosen route like a disarticulated slinky. "The city that had occupied Mesa Canaan was now marching across the plain. . . . It had disassembled just before dawn, walking on elephantine legs, tractor treads and wheels, with living bulkheads upright, dismantled buttresses given new instruction to crawl instead of support, floors and ceilings, transports and smaller city parts, factories and resource centers, all unrecognizable now, like a slime mold soon to gather itself in its new country. The city carried its plan deep within the living plasm of its fragmented body" (1).

More than a millennium before the story starts, the planet had boasted 153 mobile cities, each rising hundreds or thousands of feet and able to house half a million people. They were intended as homes and refuge for the galaxy's surviving Jews, Muslims, and Christians, but something went terribly wrong. The city operating systems decided that their humans were sinners, threw out them out, and kept them out. Without a purpose, however, the cities slowly decay. Some have gone mad. Others are unable to create spare parts or repair themselves. Those that survive move sometimes aimlessly, other times deliberately to place themselves where they can gather new supplies of water and resources. As the three linked novellas proceed, covering a span of 111 years, the central theme is the potential variety of artificial intelligence: master urban AIs, mobile city fragments with rudimentary robotic capacity, avatars, simulacra, and the original city architect reconstituted from stored memories. Nevertheless, the image of vast cities that lumber over the landscape like gigantic Transformer toys in their hunt for survival is hard to shake.

Armada is another "nomadic city" on the hunt. Front and center in China Miéville's *The Scar* (2002), Armada is a great composite raft constructed on the hulls of hundreds of ships that have been lashed and chained together, some voluntarily and some as prizes from war and piracy. It spreads across a square mile of sea like an unmoored Venice, linked by bridges and walkways, served by "flat-bottomed canal runners" in the watery cracks between ships.

> Each vessel was a pontoon in a web of rope bridges. Boats coiled toward each other in seawalls of embedded ships, surrounding free-floating vessels. Basilio Harbor, where Armada's navy and visitors could tie up, repair or unload, sheltered from storms. The largest ships meandered instead around the edges of the city, beyond the tugs and steamers tethered to Armada's

sides. Out in the open water were fleets of fishing boats, the city's warships, the chariot ships and whim trawlers and others. These were Armada's pirate navy, heading out across the world, coming in to dock with cargoes plundered from enemies or the sea. (81)

Armada is a city by all criteria. It is ancient, and it is big. The first ships began tying together a thousand years earlier. Rebuilt from the inside and topped with new superstructures that represent the aesthetics of a hundred cultures, it supports a population in the hundreds of thousands. The city is both a hunter and a gatherer—raider, trader, deep-sea miner. Armadans engage in far-flung trade with nations of the mainland and inhabited islands. But the Armada navy also hunts down salvage and stray cargo ships, bringing back loot to feed the city's economy. "This was a pirate city, ruled by cruel mercantilism, existing in the pores of the world, snatching new citizens from their ships, a floating freetown for buying and selling stolen goods, where might made right" (82).

And the city itself moves, sometimes making a great circle around the ocean at the whim of winds and currents, sometimes at its own intent, pulled by hundreds of tugboats that latch on with thick chains. Progress under tow is painfully slow: one mile per hour by tugs and maybe twice that if wind and current assist. It may get under way to avoid foreign vessels, to contact trading partners, or to find and tap sources of petroleum. Here the ponderous city makes steam: "The steamers, the tugs, the squat industrial vessels were moving back toward the city, like iron filings toward a magnet. . . . When all the servant ships had attached themselves to the city, they bore off to the southwest, venting black smoke, their gears grinding, devouring huge quantities of stolen coal and anything else that might burn. With appalling slowness, Armada began to move" (397–98).

Things go awry when the city falls under fanatical leaders fixated on reaching a geophysical anomaly at the far end of the ocean, a rift or "scar" where probability works in unusual ways and possibilities for wealth and power may be multiplied. The action involves capturing a huge sea monster and tethering it to Armada with gigantic chains, so that it pulls the city like a huge draft animal. As the city draws closer to the literal edge of the ocean, inhabitants rise in revolt, and after many dire events, the city turns away: "Raucous gangs, reeling at what they did, turned the winches that tugged at the avanc's reins. And slowly, over miles, the avanc turned its nose in dumb obedience, and the city's massive wake began to arc, and Armada turned. It was a long, very shallow curve that took the rest of the day's light to complete" (619).

Armada is piratical out of necessity and some choice, but the Traction Cities that roam a postapocalypse world in Philip Reeve's "thrilling predator cities quartet" exist in a world of pure municipal Darwinism. Crashing across the landscape on treads, London and its rivals pursue, capture, and dismantle smaller cities—and each other when they can. In *Mortal Engines* (2001), London has to flee from the huge and deadly Panzerstadt-Bayreuth, "a conurbation formed by the coupling together of four huge Traktionstadts" (140). Smaller cities attract swarms of predators and carrion-eater cities. The city of Motoropolis, for example, runs out of fuel and finds itself stranded, to be picked apart by scavenger towns: "Tom realized that its tracks and gut were gone, and that its deck plates were being stripped out by a swarm of small towns that seethed in the shadows of its lower levels, tearing off huge rusting sections in their jaws and landing salvage parties whose blowtorches glittered and sparked in the shadows between the tiers." In turn, "a pack of tiny predator-suburbs were harrying the scavenger towns on the northwestern side, singling out the weakest and slowest and charging after it" (81–82).

London towers two thousand feet with six tiers (roughly enough height for a 150-story skyscraper). The elite live in the open air on the top level. The lowest factory level is the city's gut, where captured cities are dismantled. The clanking machinery of traction occupies the bottommost tier—the city runs on steam. We get no horizontal dimensions or population figures, but a small mining city that London captures has nine hundred people. The finest place on earth to Londoners, the city suffers when seen from the air: "It was bigger than he remembered, and much uglier. Strange, how when he lived there he had believed everything the Goggle-screens told him about the city's elegant lives, its perfect beauty.

Now he saw that it was ugly; no better than any other town, just bigger: a storm front of smoke and belching chimneys, a wave of darkness rolling toward the mountains with the white villas of High London surfing on its crest like some delicate ship" (267).

The books are written for the middle-school market, so the chief characters are a plucky teen boy who sees through adult deceit and a plucky teen girl from outside the cities who offers her own cynical views. *Mortal Engines*, the first volume, offers confrontations with bad adults, a narrow escape from a pirate city, a thrilling airship ride, and other fascinating adventures. By the second volume, *Predator's Gold* (2003), Tom and Hester have made their way to a different city, London having perished in fire. Their new home is pursued by the greedy urbivore Arkangel, which claws its way across the northern ice: "eight tiers of factories and slave-barracks and soot-spewing chimneys, a sky train riding the slipstream, parasite airships sifting the exhaust plume for waste minerals, and down below, ghostly through veils of snow and powdered rock, the big wheels turning" (11). Accompanying Arkangel like escort ships around an aircraft carrier are hunter-killer suburbs like Wolverinehampton (a pun for British readers, as is the mobile suburb Tunbridge Wheels). If the hero, the heroine, and their adopted city fail to escape, their fate is visible: "The city flexed its jaws, giving the watchers on Anchorage's stern an unforgettable glimpse of the vast furnaces and dismantling-engines that awaited them" (299).

Real cities have enormously intricate energy systems. They use electricity generated by distant dams, steam plants, and atomic reactors; they burn coal from distant mines and natural gas piped in from hundreds of miles away and perhaps even delivered in liquid form by ship; they depend on petroleum sourced in a world market but delivered to gas stations and home heating systems by tanker trucks; and a few buildings may directly tap solar radiation from ninety-three million miles away. This complexity makes a mobile city an imaginative stretch, since it would need power not only for internal needs but also to move its immense tonnage. Miéville has the advantage of wind and current for Armada, while Reeve takes refuge in the steampunk aesthetic for his post-electronic cities, with giant red-hot boilers powering gears and drive trains. It's fun, ramping up nineteenth-century steamboat races and loco-motive chases, but it also puts him firmly on the fantasy side of science fiction that doesn't care about pesky physics formulas on the relation-ships between energy and work.

RIDING THE RAILS

Powering across the Mars-scape of the future, the Catherine of Tharsis is a barreling supertrain that crisscrosses the surface of the Red Planet in Ian McDonald's *Ares Express* (2002). Looming like an ocean liner, it hauls hundreds of freight cars to keep the Martian economy humming. It is also a small traveling town, the permanent residence of a big interlock-ing clan. Clans and guilds from dozens of independent trains exchange information, compete for business, and intermarry to cement alliances.

There is something about trains that helps to marry past to future for science fiction and fantasy. Clanking, hissing, tooting, rumbling loco-motives are steampunk SF standbys. Few American kids ride intercity trains, but millions know about the magic train platform and the steam locomotive that carries Harry, Ron, and Hermione to Hogwarts School. At the same time, the streamlined locomotive was one of the principal signifiers of the technologically superior future when science fiction was entering its golden age in the 1930s and 1940s, a role assumed more re-cently by the bullet trains that connect European and Asian cities at two hundred miles per hour, such as Japan's Shinkansen, the Alta Velocidad Española, France's TGV, and South Korea's KTX.

Both the French and Korean trains may have been inspirations for the French comic *Le Transperceneige*, source for the Korean-made English-language film *Snowpiercer* (2013). After ecological disaster has frozen the Earth, a tiny remnant of humans have found shelter on a train that end-lessly circles the globe. The train is divided rear to front by class divisions enforced by armed police. An unemployed lumpen proletariat living on the dole crowd the rear cars, petty officials fill the middle cars, and the indulgent elite live in exotic comfort close to the engine. The action involves a revolt of the underclass, who slowly fight their way forward until the hero confronts the mad genius who designed and runs the train. At the climax, an avalanche shatters the train and leaves only two young survivors to step out into the wintery wasteland, their fate ambiguously left to the imagination of the audience.

The train is a moving world—it contains all surviving humans— but it is questionably a city because it has no hinterland, no trade, no interactions with a larger world. Its population is unspecified but probably in the range of five hundred to two thousand, and its size apparently somewhere from thirty to fifty cars.[3] The closest analogy to the train is the science fiction standby of a generation ship, a large spaceship that takes several generations from departure to destination at sublight speeds. The train moves along an endless loop, as a generation ship moves through space. As in Robert Heinlein's classic story "Universe," the goal of the protagonist is to explore the far reaches of the container and reach its control center. As the story progresses, the people from the rear cars learn more and more about the miniature world in which they are confined. In the end, however, gaining control does not help— there is no forgotten purpose toward which the train/ship can be redirected and no new world waiting.

Kim Stanley Robinson's Terminator inflates the streamlined train by orders of magnitude. Terminator is an entire city that rolls around Mercury at forty-five degrees south latitude, carried on "twenty gigantic elevated tracks," pacing the planet's rotation and keeping just inside the shadow zone and ahead of Mercury's searing dawn. The city, as Robinson describes it in 2312 (2012), is bigger than Venice, whose historic island districts were home to about sixty thousand people in the early twenty-first century. The city is domed, of course, for temperature control and breathable air. Its power supply is a marvel of creative engineering: "The sleeves on the underside of the city are fitted over the track with a tolerance so fine that the thermal expansion of the tracks' austenite stainless steel is always pushing the city west, onto the narrower tracks still in the shade. A little bit of resistance to this movement creates a great deal of the city's electricity" (28). Around and around the planet it glides, circumnavigating the barren globe in 177 days, powered by the sun and thus solving the problem of a city finding and carrying enough concentrated energy to be able to move.

Terminator made an earlier appearance in Robinson's "Memory of Whiteness" (1986), and Geoffrey Landis echoed or paralleled it in "Proposal for a Sun-Following Moonbase" in the *Journal of the British Interplanetary Society* in 1991. The narrative imagination and the engineering imagination combine to reach toward the technological sublime, the sense of wonder and exhilaration that comes from contemplating newly made objects that push the limits of human accomplishment, like Boulder Dam, perhaps, or the space station that we approach with a sense of awe in the film *2001*. Robinson enjoys thinking up new and unusual cities like the Martian cliff-wall cities we have already encountered or the city in *2312* that rings the Saturnian satellite Iapetus, built along a continuous High Street that follows the moon's odd equatorial ridge. Its engineers have used seashell genes to engineer calcium into scallop shapes that make the city resemble a giant coral reef. Terminator is equally awesome. Seen from outside by sunwalkers who enjoy the splendor of the Mercurial surface, the city is sublime. Sometimes it rolls through darkness, sometimes it is struck by sunlight reflected off cliffsides ahead. "During these cliffblinks, nothing has a shadow; space turns strange. . . . Changes in light, slight tilts in pitch, these make it seem as if the town were a ship, sailing over a black ocean with waves so large that when in their troughs, the ship drops into the night, then on the high points crests back into day" (28–29).

Inside the city, ambience and scale change. Terminatorians enjoy neighborhood cafés, parks, human-scale apartments, and similar benefits of traditional urban life. Robinson's future cities are consistently walkable, reflecting the best of current theory about the fabric of successful urbanism. He assumes that no matter how exotic the urban shell and location on Mars or Mercury, people will prefer everyday environments that recall Paris or Brooklyn. It would be hard to think of a future city as comfortable as Odessa in *Green Mars* (1994), for example, where Maya Toitovna and Michel Duval work interesting jobs during the day and take evenings at tables along the seawall facing the yet-to-be filled Hellas Sea, with dark copper clouds in the purpling sky and music from the café behind them.

Advanced technology is vulnerable, especially when it is a single non-redundant system, but social inertia is a powerful counterforce. Terrorists destroy Terminator by diverting and crashing a chunk of solar system debris onto the tracks ahead of the city. Although there is time to evacuate, the city dies when it reaches the break in the tracks and stalls for the sun to catch it. Like New Orleans after Katrina or Tokyo after its earthquakes and fire bombings, Mercury has the capacity and the emotional will to rebuild. The central character Swan Er Hong is caught outside when the disaster strikes and immediately cries in anguish: "Oh, my town, my town, *ohhhh*. . . . We'll come back! We'll rebuild! *Ohhhhh* . . ." At the book's end Swan is back in the rebuilding city: "It's good to be home," she tells another citizen. "Thank God we rebuilt." "We had to," a friend replies (341).

The ramshackle rail-riding city that Christopher Priest imagined in *Inverted World* (1974) certainly should be rebuilt, or at least renovated, but the chances are unfortunately minimal. The city, whose inhabitants call it "Earth," is in constant motion like Terminator, but it grinds rather than glides. It travels on four tracks that are gathered up after it passes and hauled around to the front to be laid down again so the city can continue to move. Huge winches haul it along a stretch of track and then have to be repositioned when the track is relaid from behind the city to front. This numbingly repetitive process has been going on for 192 years at the rate of one-tenth mile per day. In seventy thousand days the city has moved seven thousand miles. Residents number their age in miles, not years, setting up the striking opening sentence: "I had reached the age of six hundred and fifty miles"—17.8 Earth years.

The city is on the move because it is compelled to chase a constantly retreating "optimum" that recedes at a constant pace. The city can sometimes make up ground when the going is easy, only to falter in pursuit when it reaches rough terrain and has to detour around obstacles or delay for its engineers to throw up bridges. We learn at the end that the optimum is an energy source that travels slowly across the Earth (a bit like a shifting magnetic pole). The optimum interacts with a machine in the city to supply its power, thus the necessity to keep up. The seven thousand miles started in China and end on the coast of Portugal.

To residents it is a city, and it functions like a city. The population appears to have been drawn from China, Russia, Italy, France, Germany, and England, for instructions and maps can be found in all those relevant languages. Labor is divided and differentiated into roles ranging from teacher to synthetic food factory worker. Government is by guilds of Future Surveyors (scouts and explorers), Traction, Track-Laying, Bridge Builders, Barter, Militia, and Navigators (the senior council). The roles of the Traction, Track, and Bridge specialists are obvious, but the Barter guild is the key to survival, for the city trades with its constantly changing hinterland. Barter specialists negotiate labor contracts with local villagers, who help with the track-laying process. "By and large, the city could fulfill [the needs of the settlements]. With its high degree of organization, and the technology available to it, the city had over the miles accumulated a large stockpile of foodstuffs, medicines, and chemicals, and it had also learned by experience which of these were most required. So with offers of antibiotics, seeds, fertilizer, water-purifiers—even, in some cases, offers of assistance to repair existing implements—the Barter guildsmen could lay the groundwork for their own demands" (115).

"Earth" is a satirical stand-in for the British Empire. It passes through impoverished landscapes across the span of Eurasia and uses technical superiority to impose its will on the backward natives. In particular, it leases young women as breeders, because women born of city families overwhelmingly produce male children. Female children remain in the city, but boys can return to the village with mothers. This sexual exploitation is not necessary to the basic plot, but it highlights the unequal relationship between the city and its surroundings. There is much dissatisfaction in the villages, expressed at one point by a destructive but ultimately unsuccessful attack by angry natives. Why do the locals resent us, the central character Helward Mann asks his track guild mentor: "Surely we pay for their services." "Yes, but at our price. This is a poor region. The soil's bad, and there's not much food. We pass by in our city, offer them what they need . . . and they take it. But they get no long-term benefit, and I suppose we take more than we give" (86). The people of India and Uganda would agree.

If the city is Western imperialism, it's in just as bad shape as all the real empires were in the postwar era. The winches are slowly wearing down, parts are failing, cables are fraying with sometimes deadly results, rails are warping out of true. It is slow moving, ungainly, its most vital parts exposed to attack. When Helward Mann first sees it from outside, as a new guild member, he is surprised how small and grubby it looks. An outsider with wider experience agrees that it doesn't appear very city-like: "She had heard the men refer to it as a city . . . but to her eyes it was not much more than a large and misshapen office block. It did not look too safe, constructed mainly of timber. It had the ugliness of functionalism . . . this strange structure was nowhere more than seven storeys high" (276). Priest gives its dimensions as 1,500 feet long, 150 feet wide, and 200 feet high with seven levels. He never specifies a population total, but an allocation of three thousand cubic feet of space per resident would allow a population of fifteen thousand. Alternatively, the floor space on the seven levels could house five thousand people at three hundred square feet each, or maybe double that if there are mezzanines and secondary levels.

The city—"Earth"—also exists in its own perceptual bubble, with a self-satisfied insularity and distorted worldview. The optimum creates an "inverted world" by warping local space-time into a hyperbola that stretches to infinite height in front and infinite flatness behind. Things get flatter behind and taller ahead. Because of relativity effects, people age more slowly relative to the city/optimum if they travel backward from the city and age faster if they travel forward into the future. Given that people from outside the city can come and go without apparently feeling the same effects, we are left uncertain as to whether the city people suffer a mass delusion in their perceptions of the world, or whether they are truly physically influenced.

The city dwellers are ignorant of the larger world outside, where it is two hundred years after the crash caused by exhaustion of fossil fuels. Civilization is being rebuilt in places like England. The key outside character/observer Elizabeth Khan is a nurse from England who has come to Iberia to work with villagers (an example of the nongovernmental organization work that can be considered, by critics, as neo-imperial) and visits the city. At the end, however, the city grinds to a halt, stopped by the Atlantic Ocean and by a revolt among younger residents who want to stop the city and get off. "We've been cheating and stealing our way across this land, it's that which has created this danger," says one. "It's time for it to stop" (234). And it does. The moving city comes to rest, and "Earthers" leave it to take up life according to normal Earth physics.

The city's mobility, it turns out, has been a source of ignorance. Blinkered by their real/perceptual space warp, the city folks haven't a clue and think they are on another planet. Encapsulated in the city and compelled, they think, to follow the optimum, residents structure their entire society around keeping the city moving. Promising young people like Helward Mann are educated and trained for the single purpose of keeping the tracks advancing and the city with them. There is never time to learn anything about the regions and people through which they pass, save for their ability to furnish food and labor. The situation is like a column of nineteenth-century explorers passing through the African jungle, intent on a distant goal and interested in their surroundings only to the degree that they can supply porters.

DISTRIBUTED CITIES

The Swarm is a fleet of at least 150 dirigibles that ceaselessly crisscross their planet in the recent action-packed novel *Terminal World* by Alastair Reynolds. Once they were the defense force for the vast city of Spearpoint, but they along ago declared independence and have become a complete society. Reynolds does not supply full details, but it is clear that different airships serve different functions, much like the neighborhoods or districts of a city. An oversize super-aerostat serves as the city's "downtown" and government center. There are military airships, and presumably industrial and agricultural airships to serve the different needs of the Swarmers, who live their lives in the air. In effect, they constitute the physically disconnected pieces of a single city.

Like a real city, the Swarm governs itself (through an airship oligarchy), trades with communities outside itself, accepts immigrants who meet its standards, and has persisted over generations. Reynolds is explicit: this is an "aerial city" where the protagonist Quillon, on arrival, hears "four thousand subtly different engine notes, not one tuned to exactly the same tone as any other, but combining, merging, threading, echoing off the crater walls to form one endless, throbbing, harmonically rich chorus that was utterly, shockingly familiar. The hum of the city" (195).

The Swarm is a "distributed city," a concept that is emerging simultaneously in urban planning theory and science fiction. The term can be derived by analogy from distributed computing, where a single task is parceled out among multiple networked but physically separate machines. A distributed city is one whose neighborhoods and districts are widely parceled out over space and form a unit by interacting over distance. It retains the spatial specialization of a normal city, but the pieces are scattered rather than adjacent. A distributed city is not simply suburban sprawl, which is a phenomenon that we can map as a single contiguous geographic entity. Geographers and planners can debate where exactly to draw boundaries around metropolitan Toronto or Phoenix, but they agree that it can be done. A distributed city is something different. It can be mapped only as a discontinuous scattering of nodes or pieces, each of which plays a distinct role as part of a larger whole.

There is really no distributed city yet to be found on our planetary surface. Mega-regions like the BosWash megalopolis of the northeastern United States or Japan's Taiheiyō Belt (Pacific Belt) from Tokyo to Osaka and beyond might look at first glance like they fit the model—they consist of several nodes located along a corridor like beads on a string— but each component is fundamentally independent of the others. Baltimore could exist without Philadelphia, Nagoya without Kobe, Portland without Seattle. The closest we have come in North America is the relationship between Los Angeles and Las Vegas, the latter of which boomed in the later twentieth century as, in essence, a specialized recreational annex of LA separated by a hefty chunk of desert.

Another comparison is the "global cities" described by sociologist Saskia Sassen. She argues that the global economy has produced an interchangeable elite of corporate managers and financiers who inhabit the most expensive apartments and prestigious office buildings in New York, London, Tokyo, Paris, Hong Kong, Singapore, and Dubai and move with complete ease from one place to the next. Their "upper city" (think *Metropolis* here) is effectively a single place that happens to be distributed among several continents, given that the highest-level .001 percent are at home anyplace their expensive wants and tastes can be satisfied. An example in contemporary fiction is the twenty-eight-year-old protagonist in Don DeLillo's aptly titled *Cosmopolis* (2003), an asset manager who spends the novel in a limousine between his Manhattan apartment and a haircutting salon while running a bet against the yen.

In urban theory circles, interest in distributed cities comes in part from concerns about urban survivability in the face of disasters like Hurricane Katrina and anticipation of the long-term crisis of climate change. In response, a few planners have begun to explore the creation of resilient cities through massive decentralization that goes many steps beyond classic suburbanization. This is not nostalgic, antiurban, back-to-the-land thinking of the sort that permeates much of American culture and some of its science fiction. It is about using the power of long-distance communication to create new urban forms.[4]

The government of Scotland offers an example. A report by Design Innovation Scotland recently offered up the idea of a distributed city as a new way to think about regional economic development. The report calls it an "imagined city" in which enterprises and communities across a large region (it suggests the Highlands and Islands) are linked laterally into a functioning whole that is greater than the sum of its parts. Thinking in these terms, the Scottish planners see a distributed city as a way in which "apparently disparate resources—intellectual, physical, social and material—can be usefully related to one another to create motivational, distributed enterprises within a regional ecology of cultural and economic activities." The economic development jargon from Edinburgh bureaucrats is a bit painful to read, but the idea is there.

We can understand the radical implications of distributed cities by revisiting *Terminal World*, where Reynolds contrasts the Swarm with Spearpoint, a vast towering city in the shape of a tapering cone that is home to thirty million people. Fifteen leagues across at its base, it narrows to one-third league across at fifty leagues above the ground and keeps rising into the vacuum. As discussed in chapter 1, Spearpoint represents the much more common science fiction type of the city as megastructure, imagined as the ultimate coalescence of high-rise Manhattan or Chicago into a single accreted superstructure. Distributed cities offer a sharp contrast, with some innovative ways to think about urban futures in science fiction as well as urban planning. They also do the science fiction work of upsetting the image and reality of cities as vast, fixed agglomerations that grow higher and wider as time passes. They embody the ability of science fiction to challenge basic economic and social assumptions.

The antecedent of the radically distributed city is a brief theoretical speculation by the early Soviet sociologist and planner Mikhail Okhitovich, who wrote in opposition to high modernist theorists of the high-rise city like Le Corbusier. Associated with the radical Soviet architects of the Constructivism movement, Okhitovich in 1929 published a short article, "The Problem of the City," that proclaimed the idea of "disurbanism." With modern technology, he said, the new socialist society would not have to crowd together in the centralized capitalist city. His alternative was the Red City of the Planet of Communism—perhaps envisioned for Earth or perhaps as a socialist utopia for Mars in the tradition of Alexander Bogdanov's *Red Star* (1908). The new city would be structured by social relations rather than territory, he argued, and the different functions of a city no longer needed to exist in one physical place. Instead, he wrote, "the whole world is at our service." He envisioned activity waves of greater and lesser intensity that would span the planet, sometimes overlapping and reinforcing to create a network of urban nodes that together constituted urban society. Okhitovich himself ran afoul of Joseph Stalin and was executed in a gulag in 1937, plunging his ideas into official disrepute. Architectural historians in the 1980s resurrected his work along with that of other advocates of radical Soviet architecture. His ideas now make it into blogs on architecture and utopias.[5]

The distributed cities that are now appearing in science fiction, with their indirect debt to Okhitovich, have yet to settle into a standard pattern. In a simple example, Iain M. Banks in *Surface Detail* (2010) uses the term "distributed city" for a set of supersize high-rise structures scattered over a planetary surface. It is as if the suburban "edge city" nodes described by journalist Joel Garreau were uprooted from their locations outside Washington and Houston and plopped randomly across a much wider landscape. Jay Lake takes an opposite tack in imagining a distributed "Cascadiopolis" in the near-future Pacific Northwest. His story "Forests of the Night" appears in the original anthology *Metatropolis*. The stories from other contributors such as Tobias Buckell and editor John Scalzi take place in recognizable extrapolations of regular cities like Detroit and St. Louis, and their plots revolve around the classic tension between privilege and powerlessness in urban centers and peripheries. Lake, in contrast, imagines an alternative city that weaves its way through the forests and mountains of the Cascade Range in the Pacific Northwest. His city consists of a networked set of isolated enclaves that look individually like forest compounds but together amount to something much more. As he said in an e-mail, "It's not like I had a map or anything. Just visualizing a distributed, zero-footprint city environment spread out through lava tubes, tree platforms and low-impact temporary surface structures."[6]

The refugee fleet that comes together in the reimagined television series *Battlestar Galactica* (2004–9) is also a distributed city. It consists of several dozen physically distinct and sometimes quite distant units. Because series continuity was not always great, the number of ships at different times and in different episodes ranged variously around several dozen. There are big "neighborhoods" like *Galactica* with more than twenty-five hundred people and smaller ships with populations in the mid-hundreds. The total population of this discontinuous settlement amounts to just about fifty thousand, the size of a small city like Binghamton, New York, or Grand Junction, Colorado.

Like cities with neighborhoods and districts, the fleet's individual ships specialize in particular activities that together make up a functioning city. There are cargo ships, mining ships (*Monarch*), industrial ships like the tylium refinery ship *Daru Mozu*, a hospital ship (*Rising Star*), a prison ship (*Astral Queen*), residential ships like *Cloud Nine*, a government center on *Colonial One*, and, of course, military ships like *Galactica*.

They function together, exchanging personnel and residents, sometimes shifting functions, and battling over politics. The fleet lacks the permanence of a real city, but for a few brief years it amounts to a city parceled out among vast reaches of space.

These are innovative ways to think about cities, which have always been grounded in very specific locales, but there is a precedent from 2,450 years ago, as recounted from the Greek-Persian wars. *Battlestar Galactica*'s William Adama had an ancestor in Themistocles, also the captain of a distributed city-fleet standing against the overwhelming might of an implacable enemy. Here is what Herodotus reported about debates among the Greek leaders after Athens had fallen to the invaders:

> When Themistocles thus spoke, the Corinthian Adeimantos inveighed against him for the second time, bidding him to be silent because he had no native land, and urging Eurybiades not to put to the vote the proposal of one who was a citizen of no city; for he said that Themistocles might bring opinions before the council if he could show a city belonging to him, but otherwise not. This objection he made against him because Athens had been taken and was held by the enemy. Then Themistocles said many evil things of him and of the Corinthians both, and declared also that he himself and his countrymen had in truth a city and a land larger than that of the Corinthians, so long as they had two hundred ships fully manned.[7]

A distributed city highlights interrelations among the different parts of a great city—their simultaneous specialization and interaction. It also requires flexibility that is the opposite of a vast, stable arcology. A distributed city can grow by accretion and shrink by secession, like the Galactica fleet. It adds flexibility to the mobility of flying Manhattan or Terminator. Half a century ago, urban planner Melvin Webber proposed that the increasing power of communication technologies would allow "communities without propinquity." Webber was thinking of the loosened constraints of geography within metropolitan areas, but his idea of a "non-place urban realm" is excellent shorthand for distributed cities envisioned on much vaster scales. Planners and theorists are still coming to grips with the possibilities, and imaginative writers have an open invitation to step in and help.

CHAPTER FOUR

UTOPIA WITH WALLS
THE CARCERAL CITY

"Earthmen are all so coddled, so enwombed in their imprisoning caves of steel, that they are caught forever."—Isaac Asimov, *Caves of Steel* (1954)

To everyone in Diaspar, "outside" was a nightmare that they could not face. They would never talk about it if it could be avoided; it was something unclean and evil.—Arthur C. Clarke, *The City and the Stars* (1956)

Here's a story: A young boy or girl grows up in a closed society that is tightly structured in the best interests of the whole. But all is not well. Individual possibilities are limited, and creativity withers. Even worse for the immediate future, things that used to work are breaking down, and the social fabric is fraying and unraveling. The frustrated teenager or young adult chafes at restrictions, rebels, and escapes to a place and a future with more possibilities.

Over the centuries, this plotline has accreted innumerable variations —both Huckleberry Finn and Benjamin Braddock light out for the territories, after all. It is also the structure for a very specific type of science fiction story in which people, for their own good, live in isolated and enclosed cities whose physical form embodies social rigidity. More often than not, these future cities are hidden underground (although walls and domes also come into play). Something awful has happened that made the world dangerous or uninhabitable, driving survivors to a refuge where the authorities regulate the details of everyday life to keep the artificial ecology and the planned economy humming. Young people seldom like adult rules, and they really don't like them when the machinery of the city is growing unreliable or the social rules limit their choices, so the protagonists declare their independence by finding ways to flee the city for what they hope are wider possibilities.

These underground cities and walled-in cities are urban machines of a special type. They are cousins of the buried and bubbled cities designed for environmental protection, but they are places in which the initial goal of physical protection has come first to expect and then to require social stability rather than exploration—they are exercises in social engineering layered on top of physical engineering. In this plot parabola, society withdraws into the city for protection and survival but sinks slowly into stasis. The protective city, as an end-state utopia, has frozen its possibilities, and its physical limitations represent and enforce those societal limits. The city may have been constructed originally for a material purpose such as safety from nuclear fallout, but it survives as an institutional machine to implement social and political purposes. If you are underground—or behind high walls—the range of your senses and thus your range of knowledge are limited. People are supposed to be happy because they are secure, but a few people see through the superficial harmony, aren't satisfied, and find ways to rediscover a wider world. A buried city, after all, is a metaphor for a society with its head in the sands . . . and also for a society that is dead and buried.

These are carceral cities—cities that imprison their residents even with the best of intentions. The term comes from Michel Foucault's chilling idea of the "carceral archipelago" of physical and social institutions that constrain individual freedoms in the modern era of intrusive government, prying corporations, and ubiquitous surveillance. Foucault started with Jeremy Bentham's idea of a panopticon prison, a physical space where prisoners would be under constant observation and control, and extended it to the wide variety of modern institutions that regulate and direct individual actions.

Bentham aimed for the moral reform of individual inmates, but anthropologist James C. Scott has expanded the idea to the scale of national policy. He argues that nation states have a tendency to set ambitious goals that take on a momentum of their own—Five-Year Plans, Great Leaps Forward, high modernist cities like Brasília, and high dams across the Yangtze gorges. The slope from beneficial projects and protective regulations to coercive requirements is paved with banana peels. And in the twenty-first century, of course, panoptic society can function without bars and walls, by tracing calls, monitoring key clicks, and tracking GPS locations.[1]

In the carceral cities of science fiction, social goals and standards of right behavior grow so rigid that isolation becomes absolute and the city becomes a fortress-prison that effectively imprisons its inhabitants for their own good. The goal of safety takes on life of its own. As the buried or walled city strives to survive in isolation, everyone must do his or her part by taking assigned jobs, obeying authorities, turning aside doubts. These places are all walls and no gates, unlike space station cities that are open to commerce or domed cities whose raison d'être is planetary settlement. The structures of confinement that were pragmatically necessary in the initial years have become codified and culturally ingrained. The purpose of the city is no longer to be a safe base for survival or exploration, like a buried city on the moon or a tented city on Mars, but rather simple self-perpetuation, with a population educated, enculturated, and regulated to accept the limits of the city. Residents embrace the city's limits as well-ordered participants in hegemonic systems like the "good subjects" described by Marxist critic Louis Althusser, people who accept and maintain the practices of the dominant ideology that is embedded in social institutions and the practices of government. They have so internalized the values of their restrictive society that they obey social and cultural norms without needing explicit external controls. In Althusser's well-known phrase, they work all right all by themselves.

SPUNKY KIDS

In 1962, Place Ville Marie opened in downtown Montreal. This mixed-use development included a soaring office tower over an underground shopping mall that connected to the train station and the Queen Elizabeth Hotel. Over the next four decades, *La Ville Souterraine* expanded to include twenty miles of interconnecting tunnels, shopping arcades, department stores, hotel lobbies, and subway stations. The Underground City has been a selling point for real estate developers and a boon to Montrealers in cold and blustery Canadian winters, and was imitated on a smaller scale in Toronto. A year after the builders of Place Ville Marie began to put portions of central Montreal underground, French Canadian author Suzanne Martel published *Surréal 3000* (1963), soon translated as *The City under Ground* (1964). Writing for upper elementary children, Martel described a future in which Montreal has been replaced by a subterranean city built under Mount Royal, the seven-hundred-foot-high hill that looms over the central city. The city of Surréal was a response to the Great Destruction that had ravaged the entire planet and supposedly killed off all life, leaving an atmosphere of poisonous gases. "Only those who had taken refuge in the caverns under Mount Royal had been saved. A few people, foreseeing the disaster, had prepared a shelter many years before. These fortunate ones, only a few hundred, had sealed the leaden gates behind them and built a city. Above them, the civilized world had perished, destroyed by the stupidity of man" (19).

A thousand years later, Surréal displays the future-will-be-smooth-white-surfaces aesthetic that dominated the postwar imagination. Inhabitants no longer have hair (too messy in a closed environment), endure disinfecting showers every time they enter their white-walled apartments, take meals in the form of nutritionally balanced food pills, and go by names like Luke 15 P 9 and Eric 6 B 12, the book's twelve-year-old heroes. All adults have productive jobs, and residents are forbidden to leave. Only four people had ever tried, all of them quickly caught, judged insane, and institutionalized—the municipality protects its own.

It is not a bad city to live in, as long as you are a mildly unimaginative adult, but it's really boring for active teenagers, and it's worrisome when the main power source begins mysteriously to fail after an earthquake. Eric's brother Bernard 6 B 12 bravely finds the source of the problem by slithering along power conduits too narrow for grown-ups. Meanwhile, adventuresome Eric has used a rift opened by the quake to reach and explore the world above, where the air is breathable after all and where a peaceful tribe of Lauranians (from "Laurentian," presumably) live close to nature. Luke and his brother Paul 15 P 9 save the Lauranians from a plague with Surréal medicines and skillfully use a television broadcast to open the eyes of their fellow citizens to the reality of the outer world, showing flowers, birds, blue sky, and green grass. "We now know that, no matter what happens, we need never be imprisoned underground without air or light," says Paul. The Grand Council agrees, and the gates of Surréal open to the world of "the sun and moon, and the forests and rivers of prehistory" (153).

Surréal is a benign prison-city with happy families and a leadership that is not too set in its ways. Not so the city in Jeanne DuPrau's popular *City of Ember* (2003), another book for avid readers in grades four to eight. DuPrau recycles Martel's plot in literally darker tones, for Ember is built in a deep cavern and lit by electric floodlights. Beyond the streets of the city are trash heaps, and then outer darkness that can drive you insane with fear. The ambience is Victorian gaslight, given the preciousness of light and the fact that there is a nightly curfew when all illumination switches off, an ambience carried into the 2008 film version. The map at the front of the book is drawn with an old-time look. The streets are "lined with old two-story stone buildings, the wood of their window frames and doors long unpainted. On the streets level were shops; above the shops were apartments where people lived. Every building, at the place where the wall met the roof, was equipped with a row of floodlights— big cone-shaped lamps that cast a strong yellow glare" (17).

The city originated after an unspecified disaster caused authorities to construct an underground refuge to ensure that humans survive; originally it contained one hundred people over age sixty and one hundred babies for them to rear. The city was supposed to remain hidden and protected for two hundred years, at which time a sealed box would open and reveal the instructions on how to leave. The box is entrusted to the mayor, who is to pass it down the line to successors in office. However, it is lost, and the city keeps going to year 241, well beyond design specifications of its infrastructure and the capacity of its supply rooms. Now

Doon Harrow and Lina Mayfleet, played in the movie version of *City of Ember* by Harry Treadaway and Saoirse Ronan, epitomize the spunky teens who manage to break free from self-isolated cities in stories about carceral cities. Courtesy Walden Media & Twentieth Century Fox / Photofest © Walden Media & Twentieth Century Fox.

everything from canned goods to lightbulbs is running out; the generator that provides electricity from an underground river is aging and failing, and blackouts are starting. Everyone is getting increasingly edgy, afraid, and desperate. Some of them join in a cult that expects salvation from the return of the Builders. Others find secret stashes of goods and hoard them or create black markets: "At the supply depot, crowds of shopkeepers stood in long, disorderly lines that stretched out the door. They pushed and jostled and snapped impatiently at each other. Lina [the plucky heroine] joined them but they seemed so frantic that they frightened her a little. They must be very sure now that the supplies were running out, she thought, and they're determined to get what they can before it's too late" (100). Ember was set up for people's own good, but it has become rigid and outlived its usefulness, and it takes young people who have not locked into the routine to break out.

Governance is strict but also corrupt—the mayor is the beneficiary of a secret hoard of food and liquor. Children go to school until age twelve, at which time they pick jobs out of a hat. It is therefore a regimented society, with a place for everyone . . . and you must work, although it is possible to trade your job assignments, as long as they're covered, as do twelve-year-olds Lina Mayfleet and Doon Harrow. DuPrau, not being an urban studies sort, does not specify the size of Ember at the time of the story. However, there are twenty-four students in Doon and Lina's class; if there are the same numbers in each cohort from ages one to eighty, the population would be about two thousand.

Lina and Doon discover and decipher the secret instructions and notify the authorities, only to find themselves wanted as criminals for spreading nasty rumors. Taking flight, they find the passageway that takes them on a long, harrowing journey that finally leads them to the surface of an earth that welcomes them with a rising sun. The story ends as they find a fissure that gives them a view of the lights of Ember far, far below; they tie a message of escape around a rock and toss it down in the hope that the other Emberites will also rescue themselves.

These novels for fifth graders have straightforward plots and simple resolutions—their cities are confining and in trouble, but not malevolent, and escape is possible. In *Wild Jack* (1974), John Christopher colored the imprisoning city more darkly. He posits a future London city-state whose bosses are much more effective authoritarians than the bumbling leaders of Ember. Oligarchic families enjoy a bucolic post-petroleum city that has arisen after the Breakdown on the foundations of twentieth-century London. Like the other new city-states scattered around the globe, it offers a comfortable life to the elite and a strict regimen for a hereditary servant caste. Walls and guards keep out the supposedly antisocial and dangerous inhabitants of the wild Outlands, "the name for everything outside the boundaries of the cities and the holiday islands. There were roads running through them linking the civilized places, and the ground was kept clear for fifty yards or so on either side of the roads" (6). Electronic monitors and airships fend off threats from Outland barbarians.

The plot is elementary. Clive Anderson, the high-school-age hero, runs afoul of the government because his family is politically out of favor. He

Doon and Lina make their perilous escape from their subterranean city in *City of Ember*. The looming darkness of the cavern that surrounds the city is both a physical barrier and metaphor for the shrunken horizons of its inhabitants. Courtesy Fox-Walden / Photofest © Fox-Walden.

endures a nasty reeducation camp on the Channel Islands but steals a boat and escapes to the English countryside, where he discovers a rough-and-ready egalitarian society with Robin Hood (whoops, Wild Jack), a band of merry men (who dress in green!), and Jack's attractive and woods-wise teenage daughter Joan. The hero overcomes tenderfoot trials and proves his mettle. After more adventures that demonstrate that soft and corrupt plutocrats behind their walls are no match for stouthearted Englishmen, the hero casts his lot with the "savages" of the Outlands, where life will be physically harder but a lot more fun. Clive has escaped the social limitations and metaphorical prison of the city, but thousands of the servants remain trapped in place, perhaps waiting for Clive and Joan to lead a revolution in a sequel that normally trilogy-prone John Christopher never wrote.

The Hunger Games trilogy, aimed at eighth graders and read happily by adults, depicts a more conflicted and morally ambiguous world than the ones Clive or Lina have to deal with. As tens of millions of readers and moviegoers know, sixteen-year-old Katniss Everdeen never has the opportunity to enjoy innocence. Her father dead from an industrial accident, she grows up poor and hungry in an impoverished coal-mining community, one of twelve districts of a future North America that are dominated by an oppressive central government arisen out of postapocalyptic war. Like everyone else in the districts, she knows that the authorities in the Capitol may compel anyone from ages twelve to eighteen to participate in an elaborate annual gladiatorial event that has only a single survivor. In *The Hunger Games* (2008), she survives the game with a combination of physical skill and wit. *Catching Fire* (2009) shows several of the suppressed districts on the edge of revolt and subjects Katniss to an unprecedented second round of the game. She sees friends killed, and she herself kills to live.

At the start of *Mockingjay* (2010), District 13 looks like an answer to readers' prayers. Katniss has been spirited away from the Hunger Games arena and brought to a buried city complex that she thought had been destroyed long before. In fact, District 13 has retained nuclear weapons and exists in a standoff with the totalitarian regime of the Capitol. Dug dozens of levels deep to withstand attack, it is a tightly controlled society on a war footing, where everyone has a job to serve the rebellion that is being fomented in the other districts. It has survived only "due to strict sharing of resources, strenuous discipline, and constant vigilance" (17). Residents wear identical gray clothes and are expected to call each other Soldier Everdeen and Soldier Hawthorne. Each morning a special machine writes their day's schedule on their arms in ink that disappears only after 22:00. Mealtimes are fixed, seating is assigned, and food is rationed, with portions programmed for individual needs.

District 13 on one level may be a sort of nightmare high school instantly recognizable by preteen and teen readers with its equivalents of assigned seating and class schedules, but it is also a fascist state that strictly limits freedom of movement and access to the admittedly dangerous outside. Katniss slowly realizes that its leaders have been corrupted by their own sense of righteousness and the stress of perpetual struggle against the Capitol. As the other districts rebel in a violent civil war, District 13 offers support but also takes on many of the values of its enemy. Success with the revolution will simply replace an evil regime with a marginally more benevolent tyranny.

Because of her status as a heroine and symbol of rebellion, Katniss does not have to engineer a physical escape from the controlled—carceral—city of District 13. Out of its direct control, however, she makes what we can call a mental escape. As the trilogy moves to its climax, she participates in a mission to infiltrate the Capitol and take down its president—a hollow victory. When the hypocritically ambitious leader of District 13 seeks to restart the Hunger Games with the children of the Capitol as the new victims, Katniss kills her to prevent a new dictatorship. Katniss survives to raise a family, but at the cost of losing her sister and her closest friend. In the moral universe of the Hunger Games, as in other young adult stories, cities require control, and control corrupts the powerful and stifles the young.

VOLUNTARY COMMITMENT

In the year 2805, the starliner *Axiom* has been carrying hundreds of thousands of passengers on a centuries-long voyage among the stars while Earth slowly recovers from being turned into a vast garbage dump. The passengers have grown grossly fat, confined to mobile chairs that allow them to suck nutriment from tubes and entertainment from giant screens. They are stuck inside the confines of a very large metal container, stuck in their chairs, stuck with the endless recycling of canned experiences. They are comfortable in body and mind, and they know no better, condemned to an endless voyage on a hypertrophied Carnival Cruise ship.

Axiom is literally the cartoon version of a particular kind of carceral city. The starliner figures prominently in the enormously successful animated film WALL-E (2008), in which active, conscientious, and heroic robots help to save humankind by cleaning up their planet and bringing new life into the closed, encapsulated system of the space liner. In so doing, they save the Axiomites from self-imposed imprisonment. Humans have, after all, withdrawn from a contaminated Earth and then settled in for seven hundred years of aimless cruising and contented isolation. The ship, given its size, amounts to a very large, plush, and self-created prison city whose mental chains only the very cute and robotic WALL-E (Waste Allocation Life Loader–Earth Class) and EVE (Extra-Terrestrial Vegetation Evaluator) can break.

WALL-E has interesting ancestors. Ninety-nine years before the film hit the cineplex, E. M. Forster published "The Machine Stops" in the *Oxford and Cambridge Review*. Humankind in the future has withdrawn from the surface of the Earth, living in underground cities scattered across the globe. Airships allow travel from one city to another, but the overwhelming majority of inhabitants prefer to stay put in small hexagonal cells where the only furnishings are a reading desk and a powered armchair.[2] These lumps of flesh with faces "white as a fungus" communicate by hand-held screens (seemingly like Skyping on iPads) and attend lectures by remote broadcast, never stirring from their rooms. The underground urbanites internalize an aversion to the surface as they recycle old ideas and follow the admonition "Beware of first-hand ideas!" Vashti, an older woman who passes her time putting together lectures on "Music during the Australian Period," is "seized with the terrors of direct experience" when she ventures to try an airship voyage: "She shrank back into the room, and the wall closed up again." She is more than willing to let the all-encompassing Machine keep her safe and connected to others whom she need never meet in person (253).

The challenge comes from her son Kuno, the rebellious youth and "bad subject" who has the courage actually to visit the surface. There is no good reason to walk the surface, Vashti tries to explain: "The surface of the earth is only dust and mud, no advantage . . . no life remains on it, and you would need a respirator, or the cold of the outer air would kill you" (250). Kuno sees that his society is dying from inertia, "that down here the only thing that really lives is the Machine. . . . We created the Machine, to do our will, but we cannot make it do our will now. It has robbed us of the sense of space and the sense of touch . . . it has paralyzed our bodies and our wills" (266). Kuno's minuscule rebellion, leaving the underground without an Eggression-permit, earns him the threat of Homelessness—exile from the cities and certain death. Time passes after Kuno's "escapade," and the cities grow even more confined. Respirators and airships are abolished, for leaving the underground is determined to be impossibly vulgar and unproductive. And then the Machine slowly and inexorably fails: "There came a day when, without the slightest warning . . . the entire communication-system broke down, all over the world, and the world, as they understood it, ended" (276).

Isaac Asimov depicted similar—though far less totalizing—cities in *Caves of Steel* (1954), a science fiction detective story whose plot puzzle requires that the twenty million inhabitants of future underground New York be psychologically incapable of leaving their city for the open air. Each of Earth's eight hundred cities has become "a semiautonomous unit, economically all but self-sufficient. It could roof itself in, gird itself about, burrow itself under. It became a steel cave, a tremendous, self-contained cave of steel and concrete. . . . Practically none of Earth's population lived outside the Cities. Outside was the wilderness, the open sky that few men could face with anything like equanimity" (21). Although the city once had hundreds of exits to the surface, most have been blocked (like those of Surréal). Asimov's New Yorkers can, if absolutely necessary, venture into the open air, but they really, really prefer that automatic systems harvest their food and raw materials. It is inconceivable that any potential murderer leave the city to approach the isolated Spacer quarter from outside: "Impossible!" says police detective Lije Baley. "There isn't a man in the City who would do it. Leave the City? Alone?" (66). And yes, indeed, it turns out that the murderer used a robot to fetch the murder weapon, carry it to him through open country, and then return it across the open fields where no human wished to go.

Asimov has a clever solution for a murder mystery in an agoraphobic society, but he also wants to critique the temporary stability achieved through what we might call voluntary commitment to a sort of urban asylum. He posits a three-way tension between the city people who like the comfortable reliability and protection of their caves of steel, a very small minority of Medievalist agitators who want to return mankind to the surface of the Earth, and an even lesser number who are willing to envision breaking beyond Earth itself and sending new generations of people to join the fifty inhabited worlds of the Spacers—the offshoot of humanity who didn't hunker down and turn their backs on the stars. We end optimistically, in classic science fiction style, with the expectation that Earth's dirt-bound city dwellers will throw off their mental chains and rejoin their fellows who have been exploring the galaxy.

Forster offered no such optimism as he aimed his "counterblast" at multiple targets, including the supposed technological optimism of H. G. Wells.[3] More substantive was the fear of racial degeneration and devolution that Forster's contemporaries saw as the dark side of evolution and that figures in Wells's The Time Machine (1895) and Jules Verne's late story "The Eternal Adam" (1910). To stretch a bit, Forster's implicit endorsement of the superiority of actual exercise on the planetary surface to chair-bound subterraneality came a year after Robert Baden-Powell published Scouting for Boys, which took Britain a bit by storm. That is one facet of the larger point that self-sequestration is a downward spiral. Like the passengers on *Axiom*, the Machine-dependent city dwellers have been seduced by convenience to become their own jailers, applauding and even worshiping the system that keeps them confined. Forster illustrates the effects of this voluntary incarceration with a wicked parody of the academic belief that scholarship consists of commenting on other scholars: "First-hand ideas do not really exist. . . . Let your ideas be second-hand, and if possible tenth-hand, for then they will be far removed from that disturbing element—direct observation. . . . And in time there will come a generation that had got beyond facts, beyond impressions, a generation absolutely colourless, a generation seraphically free from the taint of personality" (276).

Where Forster envisioned stasis over centuries or millennia (he is not very specific about the date, but people still remember the French Revolution), Arthur C. Clarke extended the time frame to plus/minus one billion years. *The City and the Stars*, published in 1956 after nearly two decades of sporadic writing and an earlier, shorter version as *Against the Fall of Night* (1948), is the ultimate novel of the self-incarcerating city. This is a canonical work of science fiction by one of the field's superstars, read by multiple generations and eliciting a small mountain of criticism and commentary. It is a philosophical parable in which a sweeping vision of the far future is presented as a plea for humankind to think big—to think about reaching for the stars beyond the city.

If the stars are freedom and possibility, the city, of course, is the opposite. Diaspar, the last and only city on Earth, has existed in truly splendid isolation for unknowable aeons. Clarke introduces it in the language of high fantasy of the Lord Dunsany ilk:

> Like a glowing jewel, the city lay upon the breast of the desert. Once it had known change and alteration, but now Time passed it by. . . . It had no contact with the outer world; it was a universe itself.
>
> Men had built cities before, but never a city such as this. Some had lasted for centuries, some for millenniums, before Time had swept away even their names. Diaspar alone had challenged eternity, defending itself and all it

sheltered against the slow attrition of the ages, the ravages of decay, and the corruption of rust.

> [The people of Diaspar] were as perfectly fitted to their environment as it was to them—for both had been designed together. What was beyond the walls of the city was no concern of theirs; it had been shut out of their minds. Diaspar was all that existed, all that they needed, all that they could imagine. It mattered nothing to them that Man had once possessed the stars. (7)

Imagining a city that survives over millions of years, Clarke is not interested in the social and political processes that might have created it—just that it is the result of a colossal failure of nerve. He does offer a solution for the intellectual stagnation that bothered Forster, however. The minds of residents are stored in a huge data base and periodically reincarnated from memory banks. They live a thousand years or so, get rested, get revived. This combination of immortality and population control leaves the city with a steady state but recycling population. Only 1 percent of all Diasparites walk the streets at one time. The intervals for revivals are staggered and random, so that there is an ever-changing mix: "So we have continuity, yet change—immortality, but not stagnation" (17). Nevertheless, there is the fundamental weakness that nearly infinite permutations of the same people and same memories still add up to change without new inputs. Diaspar is an effort to build a perpetual intellectual motion machine, and we therefore know that ultimate failure is inevitable.

Only one individual has the capacity to challenge the bounds of the city. Alvin is a "unique," the fourteenth individual in the span of the city who has been newly constituted rather than reconstituted from the memory bank. As a new rather than recycled person, he is first able to understand the limitations of the city and then to take the initiative actually to leave through a subway system unused for aeons. He finds first a bucolic society that looks initially like a real alternative to Diaspar but that proves to be equally committed to the status quo (each society tries to block access to the other in order to fend off change). Eschewing a simple antithesis of bad city / good countryside, Clarke suggests that breaching the walls of the carceral city is not enough.[4] Over the course of the second half of the book, Alvin learns that only casting loose the bonds of Earth itself and reaching again for the stars will rescue humanity from its billion-year funk.[5]

Forster's story and Clarke's novel are science fiction milestones, and they are prime exhibits for Gary Wolfe's carefully developed argument that science fiction tends to depict cities as dead ends. In *The Known and the Unknown: The Iconography of Science Fiction*, he lists several urban traits that are "antithetical to the traditional attitudes of the genre." As centralized places, cities contradict the SF value of expansion in space. As dense environments, they require enforced conformity and authoritarian rule that sets the stage for "the widespread theme of escaping from the city." As stable communities, cities are more often stagnant than utopian. As bounded or even walled systems, they limit exploration of a larger world and trap the imagination. As closed systems, cities will eventually run down, perhaps from the gradual failure to support themselves through parasitic control of the countryside or, more important, from the failure to generate new ideas. As Wolfe sums up: "The city is indeed one of the most important iconic images in science fiction, but the ways in which this image is used in the genre suggest that it is less a realization of human plentitude than a barrier to it. . . . The walls of the cities become images of barriers that must be broken, of a past that must be transcended."[6]

What Wolfe presents as *the* science fiction "icon of the city" (in parallel to the icons of the spaceship, the robot, and the monster) is more specifically a description of the carceral city. In some of his examples, hypertrophied cities are unhealthy, planet-bound alternatives to expansion through space—*Caves of Steel*, for example. In others, such as *The City and the Stars*, cities are the antithesis of change, locked-in and locked-down dystopias where only a lonely hero understands the need to challenge the balance. As we shall see in the last section of this book, social theory, from nineteenth-century writers George Tucker and John Stuart Mill to twenty-first-century economist Edward Glaeser, also offers an alternative view in which the variety and sometimes chaos of cities are the true generators of new ideas.

ESCAPE FROM . . .

The most interesting adult fiction by writers from Forster to Clarke explores the internal dimension of confinement, imagining carceral cities where the residents are their own jailers, bound to the city by its physical comfort and by the security that buffers them from the stress of the outside. In two key science fiction films from the 1970s, in contrast, confinement is more blatant, actively enforced by explicitly totalitarian regimes. The extreme logic of the carceral city is front and center in *THX 1138* (1971) and *Logan's Run* (1976). Both present physically closed cities whose residents are under tight control in the interest of population management—a hot-button issue of the 1950s and 1960s. Each city is organized around the prime goal of maintaining a steady-state population—meaning that the basic desire to reproduce and/or survive becomes the source of rebellion and motivation for breakout.

THX 1138 was the first feature from George Lucas, expanded and developed from a film-school project. It flopped initially but became a cult favorite when Lucas followed with *American Graffiti* and *Star Wars*. Lucas drops viewers into a version of the underworld from Fritz Lang's *Metropolis*, redone in the stripped-down postwar aesthetic of bare white spaces. Workers have alphanumeric codes for names, just like in Surréal. The authorities dose them with drugs to suppress emotions and sex drive and enforce rules with robot police. Slotted into their jobs, the citizens ritualistically invoke the "blessings of the state" in the manner of *1984*. Trouble comes when LUH 3417 (she's female) alters the drug mix fed to THX 1138 (he's male). Actual sex happens, and the authorities imprison THX 1138, leading to his escape and flight to the edge of the city along underground roads (the film used unfinished BART tunnels). At the end he reaches the surface to view a sunset for the first time in his life.

Logan's Run was based on a 1967 book by William Nolan and George

Clayton Johnson. Writing when the hippie-radical slogan "don't trust anyone over thirty" was in the air, they projected a society in which people lived only to age twenty-one before being euthanized. A box office success, the film spawned a short-lived TV series in 1977–78. The film extends the terminal age to thirty, again the reason being a supposed need to enforce equilibrium between population and resources. In the year 2274, residents live in a domed city, multigenerational descendants of refugees from a presumably devastated outside. Logan 5 is an enforcer or Sandman who makes sure that people don't escape their termination date (echoing the Firemen who burn books in Ray Bradbury's *Fahrenheit 451* and anticipating Deckard's function of tracking down replicants in *Blade Runner*). At the command of the central computer, he leaves the city in the company of the lovely Jessica 6. What they discover is not the fully functioning alternative society the computer sent them to find, but a wilderness that has the possibilities of social rebirth. Logan returns to the city, where his answers to interrogation by the computer overload its systems, blowing the external seals and allowing everyone to flee the ruined city.

Both films are ultimately unsatisfying as either prison city movie or prison escape movie because they are set in social vacuums. We don't know why the city where THX 1138 lives is so repressive—it just is—nor do we know how Logan 5's city came up with such a curious solution for population control. We can contrast both films with the well-loved *Escape from New York* (1981), which projected a near future 1997 in which urban crime had become so intense that Manhattan has been evacuated, walled in, and turned into a prison colony. Viewers in 1981, already fed a diet of New York–in–crisis stories in news media and movies, could easily imagine a city gone from bad to very worse in a decade and a half. Carceral Manhattan embodied the paranoid fears of both the libertarian right and the radical left that the government was preparing concentration camps for rioters and dissidents, as indeed the FBI and Justice Department considered in the early 1950s. The government eventually decided not to establish "commie camps" (to be used only in an emergency, of course), because of fears that they would offer the Soviet Union a propaganda opportunity comparable to the germ warfare stories that came out of the Korean War. Academics like political science professor Norton Long were simultaneously suggesting that national policy was to turn black ghettos into something analogous to Indian reservations where residents would be confined and fed dribbles of help—only one step short of Manhattan as prison.

On the other side of the narrative arc, viewers or readers of "real" prison break stories know something of what awaits outside Alcatraz or a German POW camp or Devil's Island, and they are able to anticipate the set of problems and opportunities that may follow the escape. In some instances (*The Count of Monte Cristo, The Defiant Ones*) what happens after is more important than what happens before. In contrast, we bid farewell to THX 1138 silhouetted against the totally unknown and Logan, Jessica, and other city dwellers fleeing into a wilderness.[7] We observe well-justified rebellion, but to what outcome we do not know.

Far more challenging than THX 1138 or *Logan's Run* is "Escape from Topeka," known in actuality as "A Boy and His Dog," a novella published by Harlan Ellison in 1969 and made into a low-budget movie in 1975. Whereas things turn out very promising for Doon and Lina, and Katniss is able at least to settle into the semblance of a normal life, even if haunted by her past, not so for Quilla June Holmes in "A Boy and His Dog," where the story line twists and inverts the spunky kid plot. Spunky, plucky, doughty, or spirited . . . these adjectives might work for Paul 15 P 9, Lina, Clive, or even Katniss, but we are not likely to use them for either of the leads in Ellison's dark story of the year 2034. After two world wars, the surface of North America is the province of roverpaks, gangs of violent young men who live and loot among the ruins. Below the surface are "downunders," entire underground cities that have reproduced a nostalgic image of the early twentieth-century town as understood by "Southern Baptists, Fundamentalists, lawanorder goofs, real middle-class squares."[8] This was not a compliment coming from Ellison, notorious for self-defining as one of the coolest people in science fiction and maybe in all of Southern California.

Vic is a solo survivor who roams the surface with his sentient and telepathic dog, Blood. Quilla June Holmes is a luscious young woman from deep Topeka who has been sent to the surface to entice a potent male below to improve the gene pool. Unlike the cities of THX 1138 or *Logan's Run*, Topeka wants more sex, not less, seeking survival through intercourse with the surface world. Quilla pulls it off, leading Vic to her city of 22,680 dull, middle-class Americans (that's roughly the size of Galesburg, Illinois, at the time that Carl Sandburg had just left home and Ronald Reagan was entering school). Topeka is one of two hundred downunder towns that middle-class refugees have carved out of mine shafts and caverns. It covers the floor of a buried tube twenty miles across and 660 feet high, but it looks just like a small town with "neat little houses, and curvy little streets, and trimmed lawns, and a business section and everything else a Topeka would have. Except a sun, except birds, except clouds, except rain, except snow . . . except freedom."[9] In quick sequence, Vic recognizes the iron hand of social regimentation, realizes his mistake, and escapes the stifling city with Quilla June. Unfortunately, they find an injured and starving Blood waiting for them at the top of the entrance shaft. When Quilla demands that Vic choose between caring for a woman and caring for Blood, he decides that what is needed is fresh meat: after all, "a boy loves his dog."

In its cult-favorite movie version from 1975, Topeka is cartoonish. Vic first sees Topeka to the sounds of John Philip Sousa played by a fully outfitted marching band that is entertaining picnickers in the park— we are in a parody of *Music Man* country where Professor Harold Hill might appear at any moment. The town council wear clownish white makeup, and citizens stand quietly to be condemned to death for "lack of respect, wrong attitude, and failure to obey authority." The original makes the same point without the caricature by simply listing the behaviors that mark the place as quintessentially stagnant and uncool, such as raking lawns, playing hopscotch, sitting on park benches, throwing sticks for dogs, or rocking on front porches (one might contrast Ellison's take on front porches with James Agee's eloquent evocation of summer evening in 1915 in Knoxville, Tennessee, at the opening of *A Death in the Family*).

The combination of well-justified feminist criticism, Ellison's exploration of the contradictions of the 1960s sexual revolution as understood in its midst, and the extra grotesqueries of the cult movie—plus the ending—have made Vic's responses to Quilla the center of critical analysis. Most tellingly, critic Joanna Russ raked the film as a boy/dog buddy movie in which the female character exists only to point up the bonds of deep but innocent homosocial affection.[10] The movie makes Quilla simultaneously helpless and manipulative. She entices Vic into Topeka and then eggs him to attack the oppressive Topeka administration in the hope of taking over. Thinking she has succeeded in making Vic into her tool, the manipulative bitch who threatens the buddy relationship finds the tables turned at the end when she becomes the means that Vic uses to save Blood.

Revisit the story, however, to think how it might look if Ellison had written Quilla June as the central figure. The writer, and especially the screenwriter, may have made her a cipher and pawn, but a little reflection shows that she would have to be remarkably confident and gutsy to undertake her mission to the surface. Russ acknowledges that the plot requires her to have physical courage and brains to put her life on the line for the betterment of her community by venturing out among the wild boys. She holds her own as she helps Vic and Blood fight off a roverpak and then has the smarts to knock sex-besotted Vic on the head so she can get away and lure him below. Taking this line further, Quilla deserves credit for recognizing the oppression of the city—one of the few residents who can make that mental leap. In their escape she handles a firearm like a pro and shows plenty of Katniss-like gumption in fleeing familiar comfort for dangerous freedom with Vic. What is nasty is the plot reversal: the spunky girl breaks free of her carceral city only to die in a world that is far more dangerous than the one she left. Given that "the War had killed off most of the girls" and that roverpaks tend to greet strange women with rape and murder, Quilla's death is one more example of how men think only in the short run.

ESCAPE FROM THE GENERATION SHIP

It is a long leap from Harlan Ellison's world to that of Molly Gloss in *The Dazzle of Day* (1997), a novel about self-imposed confinement in which it is not a heroic individual but an entire society that challenges and breaks the limits. Gloss is a writer of historical novels and science fiction who is seldom considered in tandem with Harlan Ellison—it's hard to imagine them in the same room—but *The Dazzle of Day* takes place in a generation starship that is a physical counterpart of Topeka. Driven through space by vast light sails, the *Dusty Miller* is a wheel with a central hub and a habitable ring that maintains gravity and supports dense rural settlement on its floor and sloping sides. For several generations its three thousand or so residents have farmed, gardened, maintained mechanical systems, and waited for the voyage to end at what they hope will be a habitable planet. Now 175 years out, the ship has arrived at a solar system with a disappointingly marginal planet. It is cold, rocky, inhospitable, greatly unlike the subtropical interior of the ship with its gardens and vineyards, but it is a place where Millerites could survive if they are willing to adapt and trade what is essentially a Caribbean existence for Iceland or the Hebrides.[11]

The physical containers may be similar, but the social systems are—of course!—vastly different. Where Ellison deliberately caricatures his Topekans, Gloss draws Millerites as deeply realized individuals. The book is organized around a series of individuals from overlapping families, each of whom is commendable and flawed at the same time. Gloss understands the intense physicality of people's existence as they work the soil, eat, sleep, and have sex. She describes in detail one character's experience of a stroke and the effects of a flulike plague on housing clusters. When people live close together in apartment complexes with shared spaces, they hear what's going on next door and know each other's business.

Generation ships occupy the overlap zone of spaceships, space stations, and cities. A generation ship is a large habitat that is dispatched, usually from Earth, to carry colonists to a new planet through real space-time. Without benefit of wormholes and hyperdrive, the trip will take multiple generations, with those in the middle decades or centuries knowing only the ship. It is an enclosed, self-sustaining environment like a space station. It moves like a starship. It has some of the social complexity of a town or small city—although not, of course, contact and commerce. If residents of the carceral city are waiting through time for a new world (that is, for the Earth's surface to again become habitable), the people inside a generation ship are voyaging to new worlds through time and space. Generation ships are thus protective mini-cities whose purpose is directly or indirectly to preserve the human race.

The problem with a generation ship is social entropy—falling into chaos or congealing into stasis. Since the 1940s, the plots in these stories have used the premise that people after several generations have forgotten that they are in a ship and have come to see it as the whole world. It requires a brave young misfit, if not a spunky kid, to test the boundaries, challenge the old ideas, and find the truth—that there is a control center that has been forgotten (Robert Heinlein, "Universe," 1941); that the ship is actually in orbit around a planet but no passengers know it (Brian Aldiss, *Non-Stop*, 1958); or that it has already landed on a hospitable planet and all but a few passengers have been too scared to come out (Chad Oliver, "The Wind Blows Free," 1957). They are, in short, ironic breakout stories about confinement that has been self-imposed through the loss of knowledge and nerve. As science fiction scholar Simone Caroti points out in *The Generation Starship in Science Fiction: A Critical History, 1934–2001*, these are also generational stories, about knowledge and passion that is or is not passed down over time and thus, in essence, family stories, with the inhabitants of the generation ship as a large family.[12]

In *The Dazzle of Day* the crew/inhabitants of the *Dusty Miller* (on Earth a foliage plant with soft silvery leaves) are Quakers who value simplicity in life and make decisions through group discernment that looks like consensus to outsiders but is an explicitly spiritual practice. The novel starts with a chapter set in Central America before the ship departs and ends with a chapter showing a younger generation responding to the challenge of their new planet. In between the Millerites have to decide what to do. Should they choose this planet, unpleasant as it seems, or should they keep going for another fifty years to the next solar system? It means that in between there is a lot of talk. There are conversations among individuals and in the context of Quaker "meeting for business" in which there are no motions or votes, but rather the expression of views and opinions by anyone present until a sense of the meeting emerges, or sometimes fails to emerge.

The *Dusty Miller* has become a mental prison through its familiarity. The ship encapsulates and protects its inhabitants, but at the expense of a quietly mounting sense of unease and dissatisfaction. In meeting for business, we hear speakers voice practical concerns about the new planet and, simultaneously, their comfort with the familiar. If they are seriously thinking about dismantling their ship to reuse its elements on the new planet, why not stay in the ship and save the trouble? "What is the point of taking the *Miller* apart and rebuilding it down there? It think it's crazy, this scheme. . . . If we're going to go on living under a roof, we ought to just stay where we are . . . [where] people with arthritis can go on without the weight getting into their bones" (209). That comment triggers more: "I don't see why we need to come out into the sunlight. We're doing pretty well, after all. . . . This place is an Eden, it's the body of God. . . . We ought to just stay right here" (210).

As the meeting continues, other voices arise. Millerites may fear the new, but they also fear for the future of their ship. Social pressure can be intense in a community with no physical escape valve—no hills to head to, no rivers to cross. Many suffer *šimanas*, feelings of loneliness and powerlessness that lead to depression and sometimes suicide. Systems may function smoothly from day to day, but as one says, "We're living in a mechanical thing, eh? And we've got to work hard to keep it from going to ruin. People can't be expected to carry such a burden, can they?—knowing it's our human intervention prevents the whole world from collapsing" (216). Having started with ideas about reproducing a protected environment on the planet, then veering into arguments for avoiding the surface entirely, the group finally acknowledges that the *Miller* is frightening as well as comforting. They begin to hold up the value and excitement of taking the planet on its own terms and re-entering the natural world: "We ought to be listening to this New World instead of asking it so many questions." "We ought to be asking ourselves whether there's a place for us there, and what it is" (216).

The meeting ends without obvious resolution or summarizing speeches, but with a growing sense that the ship is a prison that has locked people's minds and spirits into narrow tracks. In this carefully structured book, Gloss does not follow this understated climax with dramatic action. Instead she rounds out part of the shipboard story by resolving a deep tension between an estranged married couple who are two of the main characters. She doesn't care to show any details of the follow-up decisions or the initial colonization. Instead, the epilogue skips ahead by decades to show the planet-born now adapted to a new life, having found through much trouble what kind of place the new world had for them.

The Dazzle of Day challenges the standard formula of the generation ship story in specific and the carceral city story more generally. Comments on sites like Amazon show strongly polarized reactions, with complaint after complaint about the lack of action. Science fiction writer Jo Walton has commented that "I'd have hated *The Dazzle of Day* when I was eleven, it's all about grown-ups . . . and while being on the generation starship is essential to everything, everything that's important is internal. . . . If there's an opposite of a YA book, this is it."[13] So Molly Gloss does several things to stretch the limits of the carceral city. As Walton notes, Gloss shows that middle-age people as well as rebellious youth can understand the need to break away from imprisoning places and ideas. By depicting a society that can think its way out of a trap by community process she challenges the science fiction model of hero/heroine adventure stories (there doesn't have to be an escape scene to get out of this imprisoning environment!). She quietly critiques utopia, imagining a well-designed and democratically managed community that doesn't fail spectacularly, just begins to run down with lack of new energy. And she offers the possibility that societies have the capacity to reinvent and reimagine their futures—making this, after all, mainstream science fiction and grounding the high-flying message of *The City and the Stars* in the lives of believable human beings.

CHAPTER FIVE

CRABGRASS CHAOS

The view from the bench was slightly depressing, fronting as it did on street
after street of vacant, deserted houses and weed-grown, unkempt yards.
—Clifford Simak, "City" (1944)

In his grandparents' time, even the commute between an old Expansion suburb and a city center was impossible. His grandparents used to tell stories of
exploring abandoned suburbs, scavenging for the scrap and leavings of whole
sprawling neighborhoods that were destroyed in the petroleum Contraction.
To travel ten miles had been a great journey for them.
—Paolo Bacigalupi, *The Windup Girl* (2009)

The picture window in the modest suburban house in Belle Reve,
New Jersey, is marred by a long crack from top to bottom. Built in
the late 1940s for World War II veterans who are about to launch
the baby boom, the house isn't aging well. The foundation is settling and cracking after ten or fifteen years, the plumbing is permanently
out of sorts, and there is no spare money to fix the fifteen-foot window
that was supposed to be the symbol of upward mobility.

Forward another eighty years and the once hopeful community of
Belle Reve has turned into the dangerous slum of Belly Rave, the key
setting for Frederik Pohl and Cyril Kornbluth's 1955 novel *Gladiator-at-
Law*, a story of corporate malfeasance and intrigue in the socially divided
society of the twenty-first-century United States. Some of the houses are
abandoned, some are burned-out shells, and some have been turned into
dens of vice. The house in which Norvell, Virginia, and Alexandra Bligh

find themselves after a precipitous ejection from corporate comfort may be the same that we have seen generations earlier. The roof leaks, the stairs are rotten, and the cracked window is now boarded over, with just a chink left for scoping out dangers in the front yard.

The year after Pohl and Kornbluth's book, journalist John Keats titled his best-selling diatribe against the new suburbia *The Crack in the Picture Window*. A signature feature of atomic age residential design, picture windows opened up the wall between dwelling and neighborhood and blurred distinctions between private and public. The cracked window was a multiple metaphor, calling out the suburbs for failing as physical places, falling short of hopes for shiny technologies, and betraying expectations for building more harmonious communities.

Pohl and Kornbluth's depiction of Belly Rave is a classic extrapolation of the disdain with which intellectuals in the 1950s treated the massive growth of middle-class suburbs. It is also an early example of a recurring science fiction vision of feral suburbia. In tacit dialog with critics of American urban planning, SF writers have offered a series of variations on the theme of crabgrass chaos. In the future, they say, affluent society may survive in comfort with the help of private security forces that protect downtown cores and gated enclaves. Inverting J. G. Ballard's narrative of high-rise hell, these stories project aging suburbs as the new ghettos and slums, free-fire zones of danger and depopulation where it's everybody for him or herself and wilding gangs take the hindmost.

This is also science fiction written in close dialogue with contemporary criticism and analysis of suburban trends. Extrapolating near-future suburbia, writers from Pohl and Kornbluth to Octavia Butler to John Scalzi have paid attention to the current consensus from journalists and scholars who have tried to understand suburbs and suburban living. If science fiction suburbs are usually troubled and dangerous places, it's in part because popular discourse about suburbia has been equally negative—from aesthetic and moral censure in the 1950s to critiques of suburban isolation in the 1980s to the trope of "slumburbia" in the present century.

SLAMMING THE SLURBS

Gladiator-at-Law appeared in the midst of a national debate over the implications of postwar suburbanization in which fierce indictments took center stage.[1] Sociologist David Riesman, professor at the University of Chicago and then at Harvard and author of the best-seller *The Lonely Crowd* (1950), penned an essay titled "The Suburban Sadness," writing, he said, as someone who loved both the city and the country, but *not* the suburbs. Riesman was one of many American intellectuals after World War II who began to lambaste suburbia for a litany of physical and social deficiencies at the same time that Americans were moving there in the tens of millions. Suburbs were and still are attacked as tacky, inauthentic, stifling, inefficient, boring. They were the very opposite of Morningside Heights or Cambridge, Massachusetts (which is a former suburb, of course, but don't tell anyone).

Anti-suburbanites wrote variations on the long-established themes of American antiurbanism: that corrupt cities were inimical to a successful democratic nation and sinful cities pernicious to the morals of individuals. To many intellectuals—even those safely ensconced in very urban universities and editorial offices—rural life held out the promise of authenticity and, especially during the Great Depression, the allure of self-sufficiency. Agrarian theorist Ralph Borsodi called for the middle class to return to the land in *Flight from the City* (1933). The federal Resettlement Administration promoted mini-farms with a Subsistence Homesteads program that planted several dozen semirural communities across the country. Frank Lloyd Wright floated his scheme for Broadacre City in which families would live on one-acre lots where they could tend gardens, fruit trees, chicken coops, and rabbit hutches.

Clifford Simak turned these ruralist ideas into fiction in the ironically named story "City" in 1944. For Simak, the values of his rural Wisconsin upbringing (the background as well for Frank Lloyd Wright, not to mention Frederick Jackson Turner) trumped those of the Twin Cities where he made his living as an editor with the *Minneapolis Star and Tribune*.

Telephones and personal airplanes have allowed people to abandon cities for their own "broad acres" in the country, enjoying easy access to one of those thousands and thousands of Minnesota and Wisconsin lakes. In the story, the only people left in the city are a few squatters in an abandoned neighborhood and a few old codgers sticking it out in their old suburban houses. By the end, the corrupt city government has been dissolved (it didn't have much to do in a shrunken city anyway), and one small neighborhood has been preserved as a memorial to a vanished way of life: "In another hundred years men will walk through those houses down there with the same feeling of respect and awe that they have when they go into a museum today. It will be to them something out of what amounts to a primeval age, a stepping stone on the way to the better, fuller life."

For Simak, cities and suburbs were an unfortunate transition between the rural nineteenth century and what he hoped might be a broad-acre society for the twenty-first century—in effect, the less said, the better. Social scientists like Riesman, however, elaborated a set of common criticisms: Suburbs were alienating environments where the bonds of community were unavailable. They lacked the intense interpersonal interactions of city neighborhoods and the overlapping social networks of small towns. Real connections to others were replaced by frantic neighboring that was both artificial and superficial. At best, they bred mindless conformity among well-adjusted children, while their hapless parents led equally empty lives as "John and Mary Drone" (names that Keats invented for his diatribe). Even a supposed rise in suburban churchgoing was not so great, said University of Chicago religion professor Gibson Winter in *The Suburban Captivity of the Churches* (1961), because too many people went for superficial socializing rather than profound religious experience.

The outcomes could not be good. Critics claimed that the suburbs were really "disturbia," where rates of treatment for mental illness were skyrocketing, even though the tiniest bit of research would have shown that rates were going up in every American community because of the declining stigma on seeking psychiatric help. Suburban alienation was said to turn teenagers into juvenile delinquents, or at least the teenagers who weren't well adjusted. James Dean's troubled teenager in *Rebel without a Cause* (1955) put the problem persuasively on screen.

Meanwhile, the new suburbanites may have been transient, conformist, and materialistic, but their materialism was betrayed by what one writer called the split-level trap. Critics translated the initial monotony of mass-produced suburbs like Levittown, New York, into expectations of physical shoddiness. Composing her lyrics from the intellectual safety of Berkeley in 1962, Malvina Reynolds summed up fifteen years of criticism in her song "Little Boxes": Shoddy and monotonous suburbs like Daly City, California, which triggered the Reynolds muse, create shallow and monotonous people destined for boxed-up lives in ticky-tacky houses.

That catchy two-minute song is a good entry point for a closer look at Belly Rave, a community whose first houses sold for $350 cash down and $40.25 monthly payments, with washing machine, freezer, and that fifteen-foot picture window. With the severe housing shortage of the late 1940s a recent memory, Pohl and Kornbluth describe buyers lining up to view model homes and opening their checkbooks before real work has begun on the larger development. The scene could have been taken from the real community of Lakewood, California, designed for veterans and workers at a nearby Douglas aircraft plant where a selling point was a garbage disposal in every house.

Things turn sour fast. To set the scene for their twenty-first-century action, the authors take four pages (27–30) to trace the community's downward spiral in its first generation. The tiny houses are only partly finished inside. Unexpected fees and taxes for schools, fire protection, sewers, and other services eat up money that might have gone to upkeep. The market for the houses dries up as newer neighborhoods are built, and bad elements move in, including moonshiners with a still in their living room (it would now be a meth house). The father is caught in a dead-end job, the son turns into a layabout and petty hoodlum. The house itself begins to collapse because it sits on poor land that is impossible for lawns or gardens: "You start digging out there and first you go through two feet of garbage and trash, then maybe six inches of cinder and fill. Then you hit the real pay-dirt. Sand" (76).

By 2050, more or less, Belly Rave has turned nasty and brutish. People huddle in their houses with guns at the ready to prevent shakedowns. The economy runs on barter, stoked by the government food allowances that every resident receives from central handout stations (73–75). Alcohol and narcotics circulate freely. Brave thrill-seekers arrive at night for illicit sex, but the city police only come in armored cars (58), leaving gangs of preteens and teens to roam the streets, some armed with broken bottles, some with knives, some nine-year-olds with carbines. The Wabbits are the "nicest" and play a part in the action as messengers and finders, having avoided being sold as pickpockets and child prostitutes.

Belly Ravers are society's outcasts. Apart from the captains of finance who still can maintain Westchester estates, the majority of other Americans are corporate workers who enjoy steady paychecks but who are locked into nearly unbreakable long-term contracts (like major league baseball players before free agency). Their greatest perk is the opportunity to live in a super-high-tech bubble house with smart closets, self-minding appliances, and walls that turn transparent or opaque as needed. Bubble cities sit protected behind wide beltways—but once you leave the safety zone on the way to Belly Rave, you are on the disintegrating remnants of the old six-lane expressway, passing toll booths "crumbled into rock piles and rust" (58).

In describing Belly Rave, Pohl and Kornbluth drew directly on the older literature about the underside of industrial-era cities. "Wabbits" for a juvenile gang echoes the Dead Rabbits of antebellum Manhattan as immortalized in Herbert Asbury's *Gangs of New York* (1928). The street kids and gangs draw more generally on descriptions of Victorian London by Henry Mayhew in *London Labour and the London Poor* (1851–61) and Charles Booth in *Life and Labour of the People of London* (1891–1901)—not to mention *Oliver Twist*. The cookie-cutter money pits recapitulate everything that was wrong with the flimsy house that traps Jurgis Rudkus and his family in Upton Sinclair's muckraking classic *The Jungle* (1905).

Charles Platt in *The Twilight of the City* (1974) offered an equally dangerous future for suburban New Jersey. New Vista is a vast new town built by the government as a safety valve for New York. It is "kind of a showplace. The government did it to inspire confidence," says a character. "Surrounded by man-made hills of brown earth churned by the wheels of giant excavators, the city stood like a vast, grandiose piece of modern sculpture. Hundreds of towers of shining white concrete, soaring ramps and pedestrian walkways, walls of glass, shopping precincts, rows and rows of apartment blocks" (55). But it is neither finished nor occupied before American society collapses from resource scarcities. The novel's protagonists are able to find temporary refuge among the instant ruins, huddling in unheated apartments and scrounging from the malls that were stocked but never opened for business. "People in the zone wandered freely; sometimes one little group would encounter another and would pause to trade what news there was, but most of the time was spent within one's own nomadic party, in isolation. Little was said, nothing was planned" (126–27). Things can quickly get anarchic and violent among the few folks wandering New Vista: "There is no center. There's a dozen little independent groups of people wandering around and a handful of crazy old folks. . . . That's all" (156).

The reality of 1950s New Jersey and its counterparts, of course, was not half so bad. The suburban myth, as analyst Scott Donaldson called it, or even the suburban slander, was a moral and aesthetic judgment. Critics who threw out terms like "slurb" and "sloburb" were not interested in objective analysis of social data. Urban planning intellectuals like Lewis Mumford disliked mass-produced suburbs because they seemed to betray the ideals of carefully sequenced decentralization through green Garden Cities. Leftists feared that relocated and shuffled populations would be harder to organize than the urban working class of the 1930s. Conservatives worried that new communities lacked the established institutions that helped to maintain social stability (echoing the fears of nineteenth-century Tories about industrial Manchester and Birmingham). Columbia University architecture professor Peter Blake, in *God's Own Junkyard* (1964), used a photographic sequence of the construction of Lakewood to epitomize the contribution of the new suburbs to the devastation of the American landscape, in an early salvo in a swelling critique of the impact of suburban sprawl on the natural landscape.[2]

The reality of new suburbs was not social disorder à la Belly Rave, but rather the reconstitution of community in new settings. When University of Pennsylvania sociologist Herbert Gans decided to study Levittown (now Willingboro Township), New Jersey, as a participant observer by moving there rather than critiquing it from afar, he found that 85 percent of his new neighbors preferred the new suburb to their old city neighborhood for the down-to-earth reason that it offered the biggest and best house for the money. Few Levittowners were changed by their new environment, and even fewer saw any reason to be embarrassed by their suburban home. For many, after all, the alternative was a walk-up apartment or a South Philly row house shared with in-laws. Bennett Berger found that autoworkers at the new Ford assembly plant in suburban Milpitas, California, acted a lot like autoworkers in Detroit. In a sense, all that the new suburbs lacked was sufficient age, so that suburban children could grow up and look back nostalgically at the neighborhoods of their school days—as D. J. Waldie would observe in Lakewood, California, in *Holy Land: A Suburban Memoir* (1995). As the acerbic urban planner and commentator Charles Abrams once put it in *The Language of Cities* (1971), community "is that mythical state of social wholeness in which each member has his place and in which life is regulated by cooperation rather than by competition and conflict. It has had brief and intermittent flowerings through history but always seems to be in decline at any given historical present. This community is that which each generation feels it must rediscover and re-create" (60).[3]

CALIFORNIA BEHIND WALLS

Far up Topanga Canyon on the west side of Los Angeles sits Arroyo Blanco Estates, an affluent community inhabited by writers, real estate brokers, corporate executives, and entertainment industry functionaries. At the beginning of T. C. Boyle's biting novel *The Tortilla Curtain*

(1995), Arroyo Blanco Estates is a normal, albeit pricey, suburb with open street access. Residents have already claimed the literal and metaphorical high ground of ridgetops and view lots. As real estate whiz Kyra Mossbacher knows, hilltops are refuge against invaders, for many of her clients "wanted something out of the way, something rustic, rural, safe—something removed from people of whatever class or color, but particularly from the hordes of immigrants" (106). As the story proceeds, the increasingly nervous Arroyo Blancans gate and wall themselves in as protection against the threats of "coyotes," their shorthand for intrusive poor people—but they hire undocumented Mexican immigrants to do the work, of course.[4]

Arroyo Blanco Estates, despite its wall, is an entry point into a particular science fiction vision for suburban California that exploded onto pages in the 1990s. The anti-suburban indictment had moved beyond the moral and aesthetic posture of the 1950s to an explicitly political argument about the way that increasing economic polarization plays out on the metroscape. Coming soon to Southern California, or already arrived, said novelists and social scientists alike, was the deeply divided metropolis of global capitalism. Urban sociologists such as Saskia Sassen in *The Global City* (1991) and Manuel Castells in *The Information City* (1997) and *End of Millennium* (1998) saw the global market sorting the world into winners and losers—among nations, within nations, within cities. The metropolitan command centers of the international economy, they have argued, are increasingly bifurcated societies in which a growing servant class tends the needs and wants of the bankers, advertising executives, consultants, and corporate executives who run the world. What is disappearing is an urban middle class. Local businesses fall to global franchises, routine white-collar jobs evaporate, and neighborhoods become either derelict slums or protected enclaves of privilege.

The feisty historian and critic Mike Davis popularized the vision of the dual city in *City of Quartz: Excavating the Future in Los Angeles* (1990) and *The Ecology of Fear: Los Angeles and the Imagination of Disaster* (1998), both bitter attacks on the ways in which the large landowners and their hangers-on have shaped the metropolis to their own benefit and to the detriment of everyone else. The founding dynasties of greater Los Angeles, associated with the *Los Angeles Times*, banks, oil companies, and land speculators, presided over "one of the most centralized—indeed, militarized—municipal power structures in the United States. They erected the open shop on the bones of labor, expelled pioneer Jews from the social register, and looted the region through one great real-estate syndication after another." In the last half century, horizontal growth and the rise of the entertainment, aerospace, and electronics industries have fragmented the single power elite, but the result is more of the same: "Darwinian place wars as new centers and their elites, from Century City to Orange County's Golden Triangle, have challenged the squirearchy of Downtown L.A."[5]

The physical result of unequal power, says Davis, is the creation of Fortress LA. In the San Fernando Valley, the middle class tries to defend its status by protecting home values and neighborhood exclusivity with every political tool available. On the south side of the city, police department helicopters hover over the poor neighborhoods of South Central and play their searchlights along its mean streets, while police ground forces mount search-and-destroy operations against gangs and drug houses. Meanwhile richer neighborhoods in the canyons and hillsides isolate themselves with walls, security patrols, and closed-circuit television surveillance. A biting diagram in the *Ecology of Fear* puts the pieces together in a parody of standard sociological models of urban form: In place of a downtown, working-class zones, and middle-class suburbs are "natural" districts with labels like Neighborhood Watch, Armed Response, Narcotics Enforcement Zone, Prostitution Abatement Zone, and Toxic Rim. Combine Neighborhood Watch and Armed Response and the result is the imagined future of Southern California as a mosaic of gated and protected communities—Arroyo Blanco taken to logical extremes as Fortress LA.

The polarized and decrepit Los Angeles in Cynthia Kadohata's *In the Heart of the Valley of Love* (1992) is a case in point. Francie, the protagonist, is nineteen years old in 2052, but she lives in an aging city. With her parents dead of a wasting disease that is a metaphor for cultural malaise and economic decline, she is living with her aunt in a rundown Los Angeles bungalow and working for the family's financially marginal delivery service. As the aunt's life falls apart, Francie strikes out on her own to live in tacky apartments, work odd jobs, and attend community college. She endures an auto accident, gets fired as a waitress, investigates stories for the college newspaper, goes to unsuccessful parties, finds a boyfriend, gets a tattoo. Francie and her friends are constantly driving across town, but they usually find that one nondescript location doesn't offer much more than another.

Francie's Los Angeles is leading the downward spiral of the American economy, an exhausted reflection of the more exuberant twentieth century. A new highway system—intended originally to relieve the old freeways—looms unfinished over the landscape, started "before everything ran out of money, back at the beginning of the century." American banks are bailing out of the city, and "hardly anybody was as rich as they'd once been." While Francie lives off her dead-end service jobs, her acquaintances make do with petty crime and an off-books barter economy. The family house, bought by her great-great-grandmother, is now "in a section of town largely abandoned by anyone who mattered to the country's economy." Riots are spreading across the nation, and Francie sometimes wakes to the smell of burning buildings not too many blocks away. Meanwhile, upscale cemeteries maintain armed security guards, and the people of "richtown" (her term for places like Brentwood) are increasingly moving to "camps," communities "enclosed by high metal fences and guarded by uniformed, armed men and women" (2, 8, 33, 124). We can assume that Kadohata, of Japanese American ancestry, picked the term "camp" to recall the internment experience of 1942–45 and relishes the inversion of the image as the elite pull barbed wire around themselves rather than stringing it around others. The city, and presumably its nation, are now incapable of reforming themselves, with the leadership elite having voluntarily interned themselves for safety.

Neal Stephenson takes Kadohata's "camps" and runs with them. *Snow Crash* (1992) anticipates a city of franchised Burbclave city-states, or FOQNES—Franchised-Organized Quasi-National Entities. All of them post guards and customs agents at gates and require visas for entry— although couriers and pizza delivery vans have electronic chips to open gates automatically. Some of the FOQNES such as New South Africa and Mr. Lee's Greater Hong Kong handle their own security, and Narcolombia depends on its reputation. Access to the microplantations of White Columns is race restricted: "WHITE PEOPLE ONLY. NON-CAUCASIANS MUST BE PROCESSED." Jails are private franchises, Stephenson's take on the recent phenomenon of private prisons that had begun to take off in the later 1980s.

Lesser Burbclaves hire WorldBeat Security or Metacops Unlimited, which also patrol private highway systems run by Cruiseways (World-Beat) and Fairlanes Inc. (Metacops). "You are hereby warned that any movement on your part not explicitly endorsed by verbal authorization on my part may pose a direct physical risk to you," says a deputy of Metacops Unlimited who has just snared a skateboarder trying to get through a gate. "Or, as we used to say," the other Metacop says, "Freeze, sucker!" With their claims of effective sovereignty, Burbclaves and FOQNES can enter into security treaties with neighboring burbs. "Under the provisions of The Mews at Windsor Heights Code," says Metacop no. 1, "we are authorized to enforce law, national security concerns, and societal harmony" on the territory of White Columns. "A treaty between The Mews at Windsor Heights and White Columns authorizes us to place you in temporary custody until your status as an Investigatory Focus has been resolved." The second Metacop again translates: "Your ass is busted" (44).

The facts of gated communities are more complex than Kadohata or Stephenson might seem to suggest. The spread of gated suburbs has been a very real trend, especially in Sunbelt cities like Miami, Houston, Dallas, and Phoenix. Census data showed that seven million American households lived behind walls and fences by 2001. By estimate of urban planner Ed Blakely, 40 percent of new housing in California was in walled or access-controlled developments at the start of the twenty-first century. Residents of "Fortress America" or "Privatopia," to borrow two book titles, are seeking freedom from crime and freedom from strangers. Bringing the upper-class compounds of Latin American cities to the United States, they are the suburban equivalent of expensive New York apartments with doormen.[6]

But not all gated communities are "richtowns." Census data show that millions of lower-income Americans live in communities with walls or access control—for example, in modest apartment complexes or mobile home parks with single entrances. Residents of distressed neighborhoods, including some in Los Angeles, sometimes ask that through streets be closed off to block passage of drug dealers. Dayton, Ohio, consulted with Oscar Newman, the architect responsible for promoting the concept of defensible space, about how best to close streets, erect gates, and install traffic barriers to limit through traffic in several modest older neighborhoods experiencing increasing crime. Five Oaks, where I used to study piano with Miss Elizabeth Stuart as a junior high and high school kid, became, for a time, "Fort Five Oaks."

In perhaps the most wrenchingly realized of the gated suburb fictions, fortress LA is literal, and the extinction of the middle plays out in fire and blood. Octavia Butler in *Parable of the Sower* (1993) imagined defensible space not as a policy experiment but as a basic survival strategy for a community at the same socioeconomic level as Five Oaks. The story centers on Lauren Olamina, who grows up in a collapsing Los Angeles. Her parents and the other homeowners have created the ultimate cul-de-sac, having surrounded their street of eleven houses with a locked gate and wall that is "three meters high and topped off with pieces of broken glass as well as the usual barbed wire and the all but invisible Lazor wire" (74).

By 2024, the internal combustion era is over, with rusting vehicles cannibalized for metal and plastic, and three-car garages turned into rabbit hutches. In this quiet apocalypse, potable water costs more than gasoline. To be clean is to make a target of yourself, so "fashion helps. You're supposed to be dirty now." A money economy survives, but barter is taking its place. The shrinking middle class holds on and hopes for better times. Foreign corporations are buying up the United States and turning Americans into agricultural slaves or white-collar debt peons in defended enclaves, such as Olivar on the California coast. Like their counterparts in *Gladiator-at-Law*'s bubble cities, Butler's characters are enticed by the possibility of enlisting for life with one of the multi-national corporations that are buying up the United States, in order to live in a defended company town.[7] It is the economically bifurcated society of the early twenty-first century made manifest, and Lauren muses about the new economy: "Maybe Olivar is the future—one face of it. Cities controlled by big companies are old hat in science fiction. My grandmother left a whole bookcase of old science-fiction novels. The company-town subgenre always seemed to star a hero who outsmarted, overthrew, or escaped 'the company.' I've never seen one where the hero fought like hell to get taken in and underpaid by the company. In real life, that's the way it will be. That's the way it is" (114).

Middle-class families live in constant fear inside their walls that enclose one block, two blocks, even five blocks. "We hear so much gunfire, day and night," muses Lauren, "single shots and odd bursts of automatic weapons fire, even occasionally blasts from heavy artillery or explosions from grenades or bigger bombs" (50). There is really no safety outside, even in supposedly safe neighborhoods like this one not far from Elliott's house in the film *E.T.* "Last week Mrs. Sim's son, his five kids, his wife, her bother, and her brother's three kids all died in a house fire—an arson fire. The son's house had been in an unwalled area north and east of us, closer to the foothills. It wasn't a bad area, but it was poor. Maybe it was a vengeance fire set by some enemy of a family member or maybe some crazy set it just for fun" (23).

Churches become forts, and the only truly secure place is a huge indoor mall that protects vendors with a massive security force. Adults venture outside on jobs or errands, but only in daylight and always on watch: "That's the rule. Go out in a bunch, and always go armed" (8). Lauren's walled street is on the northern side of the San Fernando Valley near the 118 Expressway, a sad survivor of the Valley isolationism described by Mike Davis. The whole community learns to handle guns; the only safe respite from the tiny community is a group excursion for target practice in the surrounding ravines, where they are likely to encounter feral dogs and human corpses.

As far as possible, Lauren's neighbors keep to themselves. Fathers still work in guarded offices, schools, and clinics, but they sometimes don't come home—killed for their bicycle, perhaps, or caught in drug-war crossfire. Residents grow as much food as they can, valuing every fruit tree and turning yards into gardens. They home-school their own children or cooperate in a rudimentary living-room school—young children who manage to wander out of the tight compound are not likely to survive. There is still a real fire department, but it is always late, leaving bucket brigades as the only practical way to fight accidental blazes. Increasingly aggressive thieves force residents to establish an armed nightly security patrol (the police, too, are always late, and charge a fee for service).

Lauren's neighborhood is squeezed between the privileged and the desperate. Outside the walled neighborhoods are drug dealers and the street poor who envy the modest security and wealth of people behind the gates. The rich live in protected communities or mansions protected by multiple walls, while the poor squat in burned-out houses. On a group expedition out of the neighborhood, Lauren sees the contrast: "Up toward the hills there were walled estates—one big house and a lot of shacky little dependencies where the servants lived. . . . We passed a couple neighborhoods so poor that their walls were made up of unmortared rocks, chunks of concrete, and trash. Then there were the pitiful, unwalled residential areas . . . squatted in by homeless families with their filthy, gaunt, half-naked children." And it gets worse, farther up into the brown California hills: "There are always a few groups of homeless people and packs of feral dogs living out beyond the last hillside shacks. People and dogs hunt rabbits, possums, squirrels, and each other. Both scavenge whatever dies" (9, 38).

As Lauren comes to realize, her community is staring into the abyss. The older generation hopes that things will get better, back to normal, but she knows better—that someday "a big gang of those hungry, desperate, crazy people" will come over the wall (55). Her brother runs away to a short life of robbery, drug dealing, murder, and then his own death. Her father never returns from one of his weekly trips outside the wall. As the story unfolds, thieves grow bolder, scaling the wall and cutting the wire, first to strip the gardens, then to ransack houses for anything they can sell. Invaders set one house on fire to distract neighbors while they pillage the others, exercising one of the few ways that they can exert any power—by making others as miserable as they are. Three years after the story opens—it's now 2027 and Lauren is eighteen—the community dies in a night of riot and fire, murder and rape. She escapes by luck and returns in the morning to a neighborhood of ash-covered bodies, a host of tattered strangers plundering the ruins and stripping the dead. With the two other survivors out of dozens of neighbors, she salvages what she can and starts a long trek north on what will be the road to a new, hard-won, tentative, and very rural utopia.

THE EVERTED METROPOLIS

In the nearly six decades since *Gladiator-at-Law* hit the shelves, Americans have continued to vote with their Chevrolets and Volkswagens (they could scarcely vote with their feet when many suburbs have no sidewalks). By the 1970 census, a plurality of Americans lived in suburban areas around major cities (76 million people, more than the number either in central cities or in rural areas and small towns). In 2000 the nation was officially suburban—146 million people, or 52 percent of all Americans.

But the suburban triumph can also be read as a suburban crisis. As early as the 1980s, social scientists realized that the aging of the baby boom generation was bringing problems to inner-tier suburbs. Moving beyond the cultural critique of Columbia and Harvard professors, they looked at reams of data to see that demand for housing was stagnant or falling and that declining numbers of students were rattling around in schools built for 1950s families. By the turn of the twenty-first century, it was clear that older suburbs often shared "central city problems" of declining tax base and crumbling infrastructure.

These declining environments make cameo appearances in Douglas Coupland's novels about the suburban West Coast. On the outskirts of Palm Springs, where the cast of *Generation X* (1991) idle away their lives, sits West Palm Springs Village, "a bleached and defoliated Flintstones color cartoon of a failed housing development from the 1950s. . . . In an era when nearly all real estate is coveted and developed, West Palm Springs Village is a true rarity: a modern ruin and almost deserted save for a few hearty souls in Airstream trailers and mobile homes, who give us a cautious eye upon our arrival through the town's welcoming sentry —an abandoned Texaco gasoline station surrounded by a chain link fence" (14–15). There is a failing shopping mall in Lancaster [Richland], Washington, in *Shampoo Planet* (1992), half its stores plywooded up or burned out. Even booming Palo Alto in *Microserfs* (1995) has an empty corporate research campus, unused after only two decades—"a 1970s utopian, *Andromeda Strain*ishly empty tech complex" (211).

This very devaluation has made older suburbs the destinations of choice for new waves of international immigrants, turning the older suburbs of Boston, Atlanta, Portland, Los Angeles, and most other large cities into new melting pots. By the 2010 census, 51 percent of immigrants to the United States lived in the suburbs of the hundred largest metropolitan areas. In metropolitan areas as different as Hartford, Washington, and Orlando, more that 80 percent of foreign-born residents were suburbanites. The suburbs also pick up more and more folks on the economic margins; the number of poor people in suburban rings rose by a whopping 67 percent from 2000 to 2011. The political impacts of these trends have been well documented by urban scholar and activist Myron Orfield in *American Metropolitics: The New Suburban Reality* (2002).

In a larger framework, geographers Rob Kitchin and James Kneale have suggested that the everted metropolis is the natural product of information-age capitalism. Reversing the suburban flight of the first post–World War II generation, those with resources follow information and economic power toward the metropolitan center. In positive terms, this concentration of energy and real estate demand involves the heralded renewal of the city by the middle class, but that trend supports increasing bifurcation: "The edges of these concentrations and the sprawl are predominantly home to the disenfranchised [and] those on the outside of the information economy."[8]

The devalued and recycled suburb makes brief appearances in David Brin's *Existence* (2012). In the mid-twenty-first century, the United States has recovered from Awfulday, which has left behind nuclear contamination from radiation plumes. The upper middle class has fled the Washington suburbs of Fairfax and Alexandria, but "those briefly empty ghost towns quickly refilled with immigrants—the latest mass of *teemers*, yearning to be free and willing to endure a little radiation in exchange for a pleasant five-bedroom that could be subdivided into nearly as many apartments" (163). Newcomers from Congo and Celebes have turned garages into stores, swimming pools into trash dumps, and old quiet suburbs into new lively (if dangerous) communities.

The result is the everted—or perhaps reverted—metropolis that has begun to reverse 150 years of suburbanization. As in preindustrial cities, the center is again the favored location, attracting the upwardly mobile young, the successful middle-aged, and the comfortable retirees who have triggered an outpouring of celebratory writing about the "return to the city." The flip side of celebration, however, has been a counter-explosion of newspaper opinion and blogging about the rise of "slumburbia," stoked by an *Atlantic* article by Christopher Leinberger that appeared at the height of the housing crash of 2008.[9] Older suburbs in the Rustbelt and brand-new suburbs in the Sunbelt are both described as losing the middle class; falling into abandonment and disrepair; attracting vandals; becoming homes to drug gangs. The urban crisis rhetoric of the 1960s and 1970s has thus been transferred part and parcel to the suburbs of the new century, with *Escape from New York* being reimagined as "Escape from Nassau County." Here is Timothy Egan in the *New York Times*, describing the very recent suburb of Lathrop, near Stockton, California: "Drive along foreclosure alley, through new planned communities that look like tile-roofed versions of a 21st century ghost town, and you see what happens when people gamble with houses instead of casino chips. Dirty flags advertise rock-bottom discounts on empty starter mansions. On the ground, foreclosure signs are tagged with gang graffiti. Empty lots are untended, cratered with mud puddles from the winter storms that have hammered California's San Joaquin Valley. Nobody is home in the cities of the future."[10]

This trend is background for John Scalzi's vision of future St. Louis in "Utere Nihil Non Extra Quiritationem Suis" (roughly, "use everything but the squeal"), his contribution to the original anthology *Metatropolis* (2009). The story combines a satirical take on the carceral city with a painfully realistic vision of feral suburbia. New St. Louis is an independent, freestanding, and ecologically self-sufficient zero-footprint city that recycles everything. It shares "open borders" with the Portland Arcologies, the Malibu Enclave, Singapore, Hong Kong, and the Helsinki Collective, but it is physically closed to the surrounding suburbs. Like a medieval European city it confers its own citizenship and uses walls and guarded gates to control access and commerce. In the "managed employment economy" of New St. Louis, all adults work. Vacancies are filled as residents in their later teens take a battery of tests (the Aptitudes) that match them up to appropriate jobs. The protagonist is a privileged wiseass slacker whose mom is on city council. He keeps putting off the Aptitudes until he has only one chance (too late for retakes) and finds that his only job is tending genetically modified pigs. His alternative is to lose his citizenship and be ushered out of the city with sixteen ounces of gold as a grubstake.

Benjamin Washington is no rebel. Tending pigs in a tightly regimented society is not a fun job, but it beats being tossed out into the "banged-up ring of suburbs" that NSL residents call "The Wilds." Nevertheless, he borrows the piggery's lorry and ventures outside as a favor to an ex-girlfriend whose new boyfriend is looking for *his* brother who has deliberately left NSL. "That's not a trip I'd want to take these days," his boss says when passing over the keys. On the way to St. Charles, they can manage I-70 if they don't go too fast (there is still a U.S. federal government, but it is stretched too thin to repair highways). They find the brother but run into angry locals who don't like their looks and punch the daylights out of Benji. A security guard pulls him out and tells him as he regains consciousness, "You got beat on is what happened. You New Louies are dumb as hell, you know that? Go out to a rave in the middle of The Wilds, and then you're surprised when the kids out there start taking a crowbar to your heads. Let me give you a little tip, townie: The kids out here in The Wilds, they don't like you. If you give them a chance to crack open your skull, they're going to do it" (200).

The underlying problem is economic disparity. Outside the walls, drought has created near-famine conditions. NSL is willing to provide some food assistance but won't share its technology, preferring to keep the outsiders dependent in their external ghetto. The city hires private security to deal with mounting protests outside the gates but sits smugly until "the battle of New St. Louis" takes places a week after Benji's adventure. Outsiders outfox the city's electronic identification system and steal genetically modified plants and seeds, leading to the start of a rapprochement between city and surroundings. Benji, meanwhile, is not much of a rebel—no Kuno or Alvin he. After his brief experience in the Wilds, he decides that escape is not worth the trouble and settles comfortably into the NSL equivalent of middle-class contentment.

The walls of New St. Louis are vulnerable to an angry suburban proletariat, but not the ramparts of Todos Santos in *Oath of Fealty* (1981) by Larry Niven and Jerry Pournelle. After a massive super-Watts riot has devastated South Central Los Angeles, European money has funded the construction of a vast city under a single roof. Modeled on the arcologies proposed by Paolo Soleri, Todos Santos is two miles square and rises a thousand feet from the ground. At the time of the story, sections of the framework are still being filled in with apartment modules. Its population stands 247,453, close to the design goal of 275,000. The arcology functions under the jurisdiction of Los Angeles, but just barely, using its huge economic clout to fend off most rules and regulations. It has made itself an integral part of the metropolitan economy through its purchases and by building its own subway that makes its three-mile-long shopping mall the downtown for all of LA.

So far, so good, but Todos Santos is also a virtual city-state and fiercely defended territory. Outsiders can spend their money at the mall, but they can't penetrate any farther without passing thick security checks. A wide surveillance zone where grass has grown over the bones of the old neighborhood reaches out from its walls. Beyond the green moat stretches block after block of "shabby houses and decaying apartments . . . a mockery to city government . . . houses filled with families without hope living on welfare—and on the leavings from Todos Santos" (22). Service entrances bear large signs reading "IF YOU GO THROUGH THIS DOOR YOU WILL BE KILLED," warnings that are enforced (reluctantly) with poison gas.

The plot revolves around efforts by environmental radicals to disrupt and sabotage the "termite hill" and its fierce, successful response. Niven and Pournelle, who have a reputation as extreme right-wingers, are actually more thoughtful than the thimble-size plot suggests. They understand that Todos Santos is a utopian experiment as well as a technical marvel. Because the story is told from the point of view of the capsule city's supersmart managers, readers want their self-defense to succeed. But the authors also understand that the arcology is like an elite private school that skims off the best, brightest, and most suitable applicants and leaves the rest of Los Angeles outside. The eco-radicals have a point that it consumes far more resources per capita than does a normal city. The idealistic deputy mayor of LA, who serves as the "worthy" antagonist, argues that Todos Santos is inexorably turning its back on common responsibilities, leaving the civic "middle" under more and more stress as fewer resources are available for social equity. He is, in effect, the voice for the Great Society, while Todos Santos epitomizes the privatizing ideology launched in the Reagan years, whose onset coincided with the book.

Todos Santos offers a conception of community that seems antithetical to the values of the libertarian authors. Outside is the world of amoral competition, crooked corporations, corrupt politicians, and ordinary people trying to survive among predators. "Isolation is what we're selling," says one of the leaders. People come to get away from crime and bureaucracy, to get independence. Inside is a world of shared values and expectations. "A hundred thousand eyes," muses an opponent, "but they're all looking inward. No privacy at all, and no interest in what goes on out here" (323). Todos Santos folks are low-keyed and trusting because they all share the same goals. People are polite. Informal mores and customs are more important than formal rules—a sort of idealization of small-town solidarity. It is "a city at peace with its police force. *Our* guards, *our* police, holding *our* civilization together." Is it an anthill, a utopia, or a commune with the petite bourgeoisie in place of hippies (229, 323, 120)?

From Los Angeles we can return to the heartland city of Detroit in To-bias Buckell's story "Stochasti-City" and Elizabeth Bear's story "The Red in the Sky Is Our Blood," both also set in the overlapping future of *Meta-tropolis*. Buckell's protagonist lives alone in the Wilds on the outskirts of Detroit, a suburbscape whose abandoned blocks are being reclaimed by nature. The high-rise core still functions as a business center, surrounded by some abandoned warehouses and a few nice suburbs within very short driving distance. "I didn't live there, though," says the narrator. "The fur-ther out you got, the longer it took to drive, the more gas it cost out where battery cars . . . and bikes couldn't easily get to, the rougher it got" (74). Tract houses have been abandoned, slumping slowly into the earth like old barns dragged down by blackberries or kudzu. The handful of people who are left can claim abandoned lots and buildings for mini-farms in an extralegal rearrangement of property. Buckell's Wilds are empty but not dangerous, with clusters of squatters who keep to themselves. Bear's heroine Cadie, on the run from the Russian mafia and a newcomer to Detroit, has avoided the Wilds. She has heard stories of "grocery stores and homes sacked and occupied," and she knows that people avoid sur-face streets in the Wilds if at all possible: "There were gangs out here, packs of the disenfranchised, squatters, and petty warlords" (145).

Buckell's and Bear's Detroit is no long stretch from the real thing. Since the urban crisis of the 1970s, the idea of planned shrinkage or urban tri-age has been on the table for policy makers to consider (although seldom to implement). It has been revived in recent years with "shrink to sur-vive" proposals for cities like Flint, Youngstown, and Detroit that would mean complete clearance of largely abandoned neighborhoods that have already been devastated by people whom urbanist George Galster calls "skippers" (those who scare people into selling cheap), "strippers" (who prey on empty buildings), "rippers" (who cheat desperate renters by claiming ownership of abandoned houses), and "burners" (who finish things off for fun or insurance payments). Urban planner Margaret Dewar has analyzed the changing neighborhood of Brightmoor in Detroit's northwestern corner. Once a fully populated neighborhood of blue-collar workers, it was more than half empty by 2010. Residents have appropriated the vacant lots for gardens, car parks, and buffer zones. They have carved hundreds of new pathways and dirt tracks across the empty landscape—essentially re-ruralizing in the twenty-first century a landscape that was urbanized in the twentieth.[11]

Both Bear and Buckell offer the depopulated Wilds as a setting for social experiment and reconstruction. In Buckell's version, the suburbs are peppered with Slumps, abandoned mid-rise apartment and office towers that were once Edge City nodes. Grassroots eco-revolutionaries liberate one of the buildings and turn it into a multistory self-sustaining garden-greenhouse and prepare at the end to take their vision of radical social change to other cities. Bear's eco-activists work on a smaller scale, mining trash piles and landfills ("giant plastic mines," 141) for materials to turn abandoned houses into small farms and miniature factories. They are not the ones who commandeer the skyscraper, but work for parallel goals as they develop cooperative low-visibility communities in the interstices of dying global capitalism.

Science fiction aside, there is an active subfield of planning for shrinking cities. Especially in Central and Eastern Europe, where national populations are stable or declining, there is wide interest in how to turn abandoned brownfield industrial lands into green space and how to preserve walkable cores, even with the continued development of low-density "suburban" corridors that one German geographer has designated the *Zwischenstadt*, or "city in between." In the United States, shrinkage has been a harder sell, even in the Great Lakes Rustbelt and in housing-bubble-blasted fringes of Sunbelt boom cities. Suburban areas do indeed house more and more poor people, but they are also vibrant centers for assimilating the millions of immigrants who keep the United States a growing nation. Most suburb rings balance poverty with polyglot progress.

Although forty- and fifty-page novelettes are not the place for extended exposition of post-capitalism and post-petroleum economies, *Metatropolis* may suggest an end point for traditional crabgrass chaos stories and a new beginning that spans rhetoric and reality. Scalzi, Buckell, and Bear are a generation younger than Mike Davis and Octavia Butler, and a decade or two younger than Neal Stephenson. In their hands, the future of middle-class suburbia is neither disaster nor an occasion for satirical glee. Theirs is not a complete vision by any means, with the multiple ethnicities and races of actual suburbs conspicuously absent, but it does suggest that we challenge rather than accept slumburb imagery. Instead, suburban collapse and abandonment is a necessary stage in social change, the winter that opens physical and institutional space for the spring of economic and environmental innovation.

CHAPTER SIX

SOYLENT GREEN IS PEOPLE!
VARIETIES OF URBAN CRISIS

Let the law but lift its hand from them for a season, or let the civilizing influences of American life fail to reach them, and if the opportunity offered, we should see an explosion from this class which might leave this city in ashes and blood.—Charles Loring Brace, *The Dangerous Classes of New York* (1872)

Thus, the cities of the future, rather than being made out of glass and steel . . . are instead largely constructed out of crude brick, straw, recycled plastic, cement blocks, and scrap wood. Instead of cities of light soaring toward heaven, much of the twenty-first-century urban world squats in squalor. . . . Indeed, the one billion city-dwellers who inhabit postmodern slums might well look back with envy at the ruins of the sturdy mud homes of Catal Hiiyiik in Anatolia, erected at the very dawn of city life nine thousand years ago.
—Mike Davis, *Planet of Slums* (2006)

American cities are going to hell in John Brunner's 1972 novel *The Sheep Look Up*, and it's their own fault, or at least the fault of unbridled American capitalism. It's not just suburbs that that are a problem. No, entire cities are offenses against the biosphere. Los Angeles freeways are permanent traffic tie-ups, the air is foul, and a report that the sun has been sighted through the acrid air is television news. Everyone wears filter masks outside. New York is no better, filled with muggers and supplied with tainted water that can turn the tiniest shaving nick into a festering sore. People in Manhattan carry umbrellas to be safe from caustic rain and dew: "Five minutes in the rain, umbrella or no umbrella, and if you don't go to the cleaners right away you need a new suit." Rivers catch on fire. The climax comes when an earthquake ruptures barrels of a military psychotomimetic stored in a Colorado mine shaft, allowing hallucinogenic drugs to seep into Denver's water supply and trigger mass psychosis in which tens of thousands of residents turn on each other in murderous and oblivious rage: "Denver from the air looks like the pit of a volcano. Gas stations, stores and private homes are going up in smoke. All the time, mingled with the roar of flame, one hears the crackle of shots. Sometimes that's the police fighting a rearguard action against the populace of a city which seems to have turned against them in the blink of an eye. . . . And the lava of this vol-cano—well, it's people. Tens of thousands of them, old and young, black and white, overflowing into the surrounding country" (404–5).

Brunner's take on Los Angeles and Denver was that of a cynical left-wing Englishman disgusted with American excess and with the poli-tics of the Vietnam War, but the trope of the city destroying itself from within was ready and waiting for his use. Cities have been careening toward imagined collapse for the last century and a half, as soon as peo-ple began to contemplate the effects of massive industrialization on the towns of Britain, Europe, and the United States. The specific concerns have changed over the generations, but the basic worry is the same—the fear that the accumulation of internal problems and contradictions will create an unmanageable crisis that pushes overgrown cities toward more and more desperate measures and then, perhaps, to disintegration amid social chaos. The result may be a violent revolution and war in the streets, or it may be a quiet catastrophe in which people cope with fewer and fewer resources.

Stories of resilience, marginal survival, and the disaster that comes with the failure of a long struggle are very different from common ca-lamity fiction that leaves cities in the rearview mirror. Atomic war, aster-oids, and all the myriad varieties of cataclysmic city-killing devices don't leave much to say about urban life. Plague in George Stewart's *Earth Abides*, thermonuclear bombs in Pat Frank's *Alas, Babylon*, and mutated plants in John Wyndham's *The Day of the Triffids* offer opportunities for individual effort and heroism, but the survivors make their new lives in small towns and rural refuges. As we shall explore in a later chapter, the cities themselves in these stories lie abandoned, zones of contamination and danger.

But what about cities where people hang around even as things get worse, where they muddle through in their daily lives and try to adapt their institutions and struggle to find technical solutions to growing problems? Sometimes the social center holds and cities survive until the next crisis. Sometimes all efforts to adjust prove futile, and things go from bad to worse to catastrophic. In the meanwhile, authors have the opportunity to explore some of the basic tensions of urban society—authoritarian or democratic politics, individual heroism or community action, institutional or technological change, large-scale or small-scale solutions.

Different generations of writers have identified favorite threats to urban survival, reflecting dominant worries among contemporary intellectuals and politicians. Rob Latham and Jeff Hicks have noted the way in which the tone of science fiction changed in the 1950s, as "utopian depictions of city life all but vanished and a host of new urban dystopias swarmed in to take their place," particularly around the trope of the overpopulated city and then around fears of pollution and environmental disaster.[1] If we take a longer view that reaches back before the techno-city era of the 1930s and 1940s, I suggest that we can see three broad concerns that have dominated particular eras. In succession from the later nineteenth century, these are the perils of fire, famine, and flood. In less metaphorical terms, they are the possibility of class warfare and revolution, the hazards of overpopulation, and the menace of environmental upheaval. In each case, the city creates its own crisis—through the polarization of wealth and the exploitation of the working class, through uncontrolled growth that stresses the city's physical and social systems, or through overconsumption that ruins the planet. These are tragedies in the formal sense, stories in which the city grows so rich, so proud, and so wasteful that it sets in motion the events that will carry it toward crisis and destruction.

FIRE

Jack London, adventure novelist and political radical, was also a writer with a distinctly negative take on the future of the early twentieth-century city. *The Iron Heel* is his novel about the rise of American fascism and class warfare. Published in 1908, it takes the form of a memoir/history written by eyewitness Avis Everhard, composed after the political disasters of the early twentieth century, rediscovered in 2632, and annotated by a future historian. London's dystopian story of his near future recounts how corporate capitalism seizes control of the state and how the resulting oligarchy presses its "Iron Heel" upon the working class. Much of the book is set-piece dialogues in which labor leader Ernest Everhard (Avis's husband) lectures the powerful and argues for socialist revolution, but it ends with a fast-paced description of the bloody suppression of the Chicago Commune after workers rise prematurely against the oligarchy in 1917 and are ground to dust.

The abortive revolution is seeded by the abject poverty created by untrammeled capitalism. Five years earlier, London had published *People of the Abyss*, his account of months in the vast teeming slums of East London. Exploring the same landscape that social scientist and reformer Charles Booth delineated through seventeen massive volumes in *Life and Labour of the People in London* (1892–1903), London borrowed his title from H. G. Wells's own depiction of poverty in the British metropolis in *Anticipations* (1901). London turned his eye to the residents of workhouses, the people of the streets, children, the unemployed, petty criminals and their victims:

> I went down into the under-world of London with an attitude of mind which I may best liken to that of the explorer. I was open to be convinced by the evidence of my eyes, rather than by the teachings of those who had not seen, or by the words of those who had seen and gone before. Further, I took with me certain simple criteria with which to measure the life of the under-world. That which made for more life, for physical and spiritual health, was good; that which made for less life, which hurt, and dwarfed, and distorted life,

was bad. It will be readily apparent to the reader that I saw much that was bad. Yet it must not be forgotten that the time of which I write was considered "good times" in England. The starvation and lack of shelter I encountered constituted a chronic condition of misery which is never wiped out, even in the periods of greatest prosperity.[2]

In *The Iron Heel* London fictionalized his experiences to describe American workers confined to miserable lives in the "great ghetto" of old neighborhoods that compound the worst of lower Manhattan and immigrant Chicago. Writing a decade before African Americans began to migrate in large numbers to northern cities, he was anticipating a white ghetto rather than a black ghetto, but the impacts of spatial confinement are the same: "The condition of the people of the abyss was pitiable. Common school education, so far as they were concerned, had ceased. They lived like beasts in great squalid labor-ghettos, festering in misery and degradation. All their old liberties were gone. They were labor-slaves. Choice of work was denied them. Likewise was denied them the right to move from place to place, or the right to bear or possess arms. They were not land serfs like the farmers. They were machine-serfs and labor-serfs" (302–3).

Prosperous corporations in London's near-future United States are able to satisfy and buy off the more skilled workers and split their interests from those of the unskilled populations of the urban core. The novel describes new suburban communities in language that anticipates the great labor-management bargain of post–World War II America that created what historian Lizabeth Cohen has called the "consumer's republic" and made possible the housing revolution that turned Ozzie and Harriet Nelson from traveling musicians to suburban householders. Here is Jack London's version, as channeled through Avis Everhard: "The members of the great labour castes were contented and worked on merrily. For the first time in their life they knew industrial peace. . . . They lived in more comfortable homes and in delightful cities of their own—delightful compared to the slums and ghettos in which they had formerly dwelt. They had better food to eat, less hours of labour, more holidays" (297).

London was well aware of the suburban trend and its positive reception by urban experts such as Adna F. Weber. Author of the magisterial study *The Growth of Cities in the Nineteenth Century* (1899), Weber took comfort in the capacity of suburbanization to ameliorate the ills of crowded cities. Writing in the *North American Review* in 1898, he argued that "the 'rise of the suburbs' is by far the most cheering movement of modern times. . . . The suburb unites the advantages of city and country both" to allow "the Anglo-Saxon race" to escape the "hot, dusty, smoky, germ-producing city tenements and streets."[3] In the world of *The Iron Heel*, the worker slaves left behind were presumably not Anglo-Saxons but Southern and Eastern Europeans, Mexicans, and others ranked on the lower rungs of the nineteenth-century racial hierarchy.

The elite have also suburbanized, to gated and protected communities, insulated by physical space and by their confidence in the rightness of the bifurcated city. The oligarchy, "as a class, believed that they alone maintained civilization. . . . Without them anarchy would reign. . . . I cannot lay too great stress [writes Avis Everhard] upon the high ethical righteousness of the whole oligarch class. This had been the strength of the Iron Heel" (300). In the paroxysm of the Chicago Commune, the rebels can attack downtown office towers, but "never once did they succeed in reaching the city of the oligarchs on the westside. The oligarchs had protected themselves well. No matter what destruction was wreaked in the heart of the city, they, and their womenkind and children, were to escape, unhurt. I am told that their children played in the parks during those terrible days, and that their favorite game was an imitation of their elders stamping upon the proletariat" (336).

Provoked into action before the anticorporate conspiracy can execute the sabotage and strategic actions of a carefully planned revolution, Chicago's undisciplined mobs face machine-gun-armed mercenaries who herd them toward Lake Michigan and slaughter them by the tens of thousands. Ernest Everhard described the awful first day of October 27, 1917 (coincidentally close to the October 25–26 dates of the Bolshevik Revolution in Russia), and then the end:

The next moment the front of the column went by. It was not a column, but a mob, an awful river that filled the street, the people of the abyss, mad with drink and wrong, up at last and roaring for the blood of their masters. I had seen the people of the abyss before, gone through its ghettos, and thought I knew it; but I found that I was now looking on it for the first time. Dumb apathy had vanished. It was now dynamic—a fascinating spectacle of dread. It surged past my vision in concrete waves of wrath, snarling and growling, carnivorous, drunk with whiskey from pillaged warehouses, drunk with hatred, drunk with lust for blood. . . .

. . . And why not? The people of the abyss had nothing to lose but the misery and pain of living. And to gain?—nothing, save one final, awful glut of vengeance. . . .

I lived through three days of the Chicago Commune, and the vastness of it and of the slaughter may be imagined when I say that in all that time I saw practically nothing outside the killing of the people of the abyss and the mid-air fighting between sky-scrapers. (326–27, 334)

In fiction and nonfiction, Americans had been worrying about urban class warfare since the New York draft riots of 1863 demonstrated the volatility of the immigrant working class and the bloody suppression of the Paris working class in 1871 showed the possibilities of open class warfare in modern cities. New York reformer Charles Loring Brace was certainly thinking about the Paris Commune, with its reported death toll of twenty thousand, when he wrote *The Dangerous Classes of New York* in 1872.[4] These were the unemployed, the homeless, the abjectly poor, the people with no stake in society—what Americans a century later would learn to call the underclass. Predicting a future of "ashes and blood" if nothing were done about the immiseration of the city, Brace was trying to prod New Yorkers to provide decent housing and join his scheme to resettle urban orphans on rural farms to break the influence of criminals and street gangs.

The next decade brought Josiah Strong's blockbuster *Our Country: Its Possible Future and Its Present Crisis* (1885). A Protestant clergyman who advocated for home missions, or church outreach work at home rather than abroad, he proclaimed that "the city has become a serious menace to our civilization" (172). He then proceeded to lay out his logic: American cities held special attraction for immigrants, and "because our cities are so largely foreign, Romanism finds in them his chief strength" (173). Not only were places like St. Louis and Philadelphia filling with Roman Catholics, but these unwanted immigrants were bringing a culture of saloons and intemperance. Cleveland, he reported, had a saloon for every 192 residents, Cincinnati one for every 124—worrisome statistics indeed, since "the demoralizing and pauperizing power of the saloons and their debauching influence on politics increase with their numerical strength." Working together, the factors of poverty, intemperance, and foreign religion made American cities hotbeds of socialism.[5]

> Here is heaped the social dynamite; here roughs, gamblers, thieves, robbers, lawless and desperate men of all sorts, congregate; men who are on any pretext ready to raise riots for the purpose of destruction and plunder; here gather foreigners and wage-workers; here skepticism and irreligion abound; here inequality is greatest and most obvious, and the contrast between opulence and penury the most striking; here is suffering the sorest. . . . Under such conditions smolder the volcanic fires of a deep discontent. . . .
>
> . . . But the supreme peril, which will certainly come, eventually, and must probably be faced by multitudes now living, will arise, when, the conditions having been fully prepared, some great industrial or other crisis precipitates an open struggle between the destructive and the conservative elements of society.[6]

Fears of urban disorder took concrete shape in U.S. cities in the form of imposing armories that still dot many urban centers. In the 1870s and 1880s, states reorganized their old, highly informal militias into increasingly professionalized predecessors of the modern National Guard. These middle-class organizations drew many of their early members and officers from Civil War veterans, and they needed large buildings to house arms and equipment. In the face of growing labor-management conflict—paralyzing railroad worker strikes in 1877 and 1886, the Haymarket bomb in Chicago in 1886, the Pullman Strike and the contingents of unemployed workers who tried to converge on Washington as Coxey's Army in 1894—civic leaders and guardsmen increasingly saw the new military units as tools for defending property, management, and civil order against unions and workers. Their hundreds of new fortresslike headquarters in the centers of growing cities were symbolic and practical reminders of middle-class fears of class warfare.[7]

The cataclysm that Brace and Strong saw in the offing, and that guard units stood ready to combat, was front and center in *Caesar's Column*, the apocalyptic novel that Ignatius Donnelly issued in 1890. Donnelly was a failed town promoter and an on-again, off-again politician, fairly successful in Minnesota as a Republican in the 1860s and 1870s, less so in trying comebacks as a Democrat and then Populist. He was also an impressively successful crackpot author. *Atlantis: The Antediluvian Continent* (1882) took Plato's myth seriously, with speculations that are still recycled in the twenty-first century. *Ragnarok: The Age of Fire and Gravel* (1883) anticipated Immanuel Velikovsky's *Worlds in Collision* by "discovering" the effects of a comet strike on Earth. *The Shakespeare Myth* in 1887 tried to use cryptographic analysis to prove that it was really Francis Bacon behind all those plays and poems. All the while Donnelly was becoming increasingly worried by the growing gap between capital and labor and helping to draft the 1892 platform for the Populist Party.[8]

Caesar's Column, initially published under a pseudonym and quickly selling tens of thousands of copies, was proto–science fiction rather than pseudo-science. It follows the standard utopian/dystopian trope of a visitor from afar who records his experiences and observations. In this case the visitor is Gabriel Weltstein, a wool merchant from Uganda who travels to New York by airship and writes a series of letters home. He finds a technologically spiffy city with subways under glass, televised newspapers, and unlimited electricity tapped from the aurora borealis. He also finds a city deeply riven by class divides. Through accident, he finds himself under the guidance of Max Pelton, one of the members of the Brotherhood of Destruction, who shows him the immense inequality engendered by the oligarchy that rules the United States.

Jack London, with a grasp of socialist theory, would posit a sophisti-cated resistance movement in *The Iron Heel* with a clear ideology and roots in organized labor—even if it falls short of its goals. Donnelly's revolutionaries are visceral rather than intellectual. Caesar Lomellini, the leader of the Brotherhood, is half Italian and half African American, telling ethnic markers that in contemporary racist thought connoted ani-mal instinct rather than reason. His revolution destroys the oligarchs but sheds rivers of blood and plunges the city of ten million into fiery chaos. Faced with the problem of disposing of tens of thousands of bodies, Lomellini has an inspiration:

> "Burn 'em up," said Caesar.
>
> "We can't," said the man; "we would have to burn up the city to destroy them in that way; there are too many of them; and it would be an immense task to bury them."
>
> "Heap 'em all up in one big pile," said Caesar.
>
> "That wouldn't do—the smell they would make in decaying would be unbearable, to say nothing of the sickness they would create."
>
> Caesar was standing unsteadily, looking at us with lackluster eyes. Sud-denly an idea seemed to dawn in his monstrous head—an idea as monstrous and uncouth as the head itself. His eyes lighted up.
>
> "I have it!" he shouted. "By G-d, I have it! Make a pyramid of them, and pour cement over them, and let it stand forever as a monument of this day's glorious work! Hoorrah!" (273–74)

Working in political polemic or fiction, Josiah Strong, Ignatius Don-nelly, and Jack London all focused on the American crisis in its largest cities, where immigration and industrialization seemed to be the tinder and kindling waiting for the spark of class conflict. In the era of the great fires in Chicago in 1871 and San Francisco in 1906, imagery of confla-gration was ever-present as "volcanic fires" and "ashes and blood." So we have a last glimpse of New York under the Brotherhood of Destruction: "Up, up, straight and swift as an arrow we rose. The mighty city lay un-rolled below us, like a great map, starred here and there with burning houses. Above the trees of Union Square, my glass showed me a white line, lighted by the bon-fires, where Caesar's Column was towering to the skies, bearing the epitaph of the world."

FAMINE

Before William and Paul Paddock published *Famine 1975! America's Decision: Who Will Survive?* (1967) and Paul Ehrlich wrote *The Population Bomb* (1978), J. G. Ballard penned the horrifying story "Billennium" for the January 1962 issue of *Amazing Stories*. "Billennium" formed a pair with Ballard's previous story "The Concentration City" from *New Worlds* in 1957. The earlier story highlighted the sheer scale of future cities in an overpopulated world, the latter the potentially appalling consequences for daily life.

"The Concentration City" takes place in an unspecified metropolis whose size is set in the opening lines that satirize American cities like Chicago with their infinitely extendable street grids:

> Noon talk on Millionth Street:
>
> "Sorry, these are West millions. You want 9775335th East."
>
> "Dollar a cubic foot? Sell!"
>
> "Take a westbound express to 495th Avenue, cross over to a Redline elevator and go up a thousand levels to Plaza Terminal. Carry on south from there and you'll find it between 568th Avenue and 422nd Street." (28)

The city of unspecified billions of people is subject to periodic collapses that can squash "half a million people like flies in a concertina" and undergoes constant redevelopment that carves miles-square gaps in the urban fabric. Despite the city's vast scale, engineering student Franz M. (a cousin of Joseph K.?) longs to find free, open space—a concept that his friends find absurd. He first experiments with the radical idea of a heavier-than-air flying machine by launching a model inside an arena buried deep within the city, then decides to ride the transit system to the end of the line. Ten days into his tedious trip, detailed over several pages, he finds that his train has reversed direction in a way that seems totally reasonable to everyone but him. It has *always* traveled east, they say, although Franz is convinced it was headed west when he embarked.

Like Charlie on the MTA, Franz cannot escape the endless loop. Ballard mixes in some left-wing politics—if there were free space outside the city, after all, the price of interior space would collapse and take real estate investors with it. Authority figures see it differently. Space—meaning the space of the city—is just like time, an ambient condition of reality that has no "outside." Someone must have built the city, insists Franz, someone must have laid the first brick. Nonsense: "It's always been here," the surgeon says. "Not these particular bricks and girders before them. You accept that time has no beginning and no end. The City is as old as time and continuous with it." Questions of physics aside, readers are left with images of the ultimately overgrown metropolis that is so vast as to be literally inescapable.

On the endless streets and levels of "The Concentration City," families can still occupy three-room flats. Not so in the future London of thirty million souls in "Billennium." The Malthusian pressure of population on food has required the government to halt the outward growth of cities in order to preserve every scrap of farmland, forcing the "internal colonization of the city." The streets are so thronged that pedestrians compact into a "lock" that holds everyone immobile, in one recent case trapping the protagonist Ward with seventy thousand others into a jam that does not clear for two days.[9] Housing is so tight that seven or eight people crowd into single rooms and landlords rent out broom closets. Ward's partitioned cubicle on a staircase is spacious for one person at 4.7 square meters, but, unfortunately for him, easily rounded up to 5 square meters—enough for him to be kicked out and the space rented as a double. Unexpected good fortune arrives when he knocks loose an internal partition to find an empty, forgotten room fifteen feet square! For the first month, Ward shares this fabulous luxury with one friend . . . who suggests inviting two women from work . . . who have relatives in need of housing . . . and Ward is back to only three square meters—thirty-two square feet—to call his own.

The context for "The Concentration City" and "Billennium" was both local and global. The stories appeared when Britain was struggling to overcome a severe housing shortage stemming from outmoded worker housing and the effects of the Depression and world war, leaving many to choose between tiny, tacky bed-sitters and clunky quick-built council housing. Beyond the sooty neighborhoods of Birmingham and Liverpool, however, was a larger fear of exploding global population. Pundits after 1945 took Germany's search for *Lebensraum* seriously as a cause of World War II and pointed with alarm to the doubling of the world's population between 1930 and 1960, even despite the massive casualties of war. World population was indeed riding the steeply rising segment of an S-curve, with upticks in the rate of change in the 1920s and 1950s. *Time* magazine made "That Population Explosion" its cover story for January 11, 1960.[10]

Time's story followed more than a decade of Malthusian warnings about exponential population growth ravaging the natural environment and outpacing food supply—often supported by reference to Aldo Leopold's landmark (and misleading) claim that the suppression of natural predators had allowed deer populations to explode and then crash disastrously from starvation in Arizona's Kaibab National Forest. The result was what we might call "nice eugenics," as distinct from the Nazi version. Population was growing fastest among the people of South America, Africa, and Asia, where it was producing horrifying object lessons like the "premature metropolis" of Calcutta—as much the world's favorite "shock city" in the 1950s as Manchester had been in the 1840s. The unfortunate solution seemed to be limits on those non-European peoples who were crowding the planet.

Two bestsellers encapsulated the problem in the late 1940s. Henry Fairfield Osborn Jr. wrote *Our Plundered Planet* (1948), reprinted eight times in its first year and translated into thirteen languages. President of the New York Zoological Society and cofounder of the Conservation Foundation, Osborn was part of the nation's northeastern establishment and worried about the pressure of population on forests, wildlife, and the American way of life. William Vogt, an ornithologist with the Pan American Union, published *Road to Survival* in the same year. It too was a great success, selected by the Book of the Month Club and condensed by *Reader's Digest*. A regular correspondent with Aldo Leopold, Vogt feared that the human drive for consumption coupled with exploding population threatened the resilience and sustainability of the natural world. He was very clear that medical interventions were making things worse. He wondered why the Truman Doctrine of intervention in the Greek civil war didn't include measures to reduce the "breeding of the Greeks" and criticized medical aid to poor nations that reduced the death rate without thought for how larger numbers would live. Writing for Americans and Europeans, he didn't apply the same reasoning to suggest withholding medical care to the peoples of the Atlantic world. The reasoning would lead a quarter century later to the Paddocks' explicit call for global triage in which some unfortunate nations would be left on their own to suffer population overshoot and famine like the Kaibab deer.[11]

John Brunner's *Stand on Zanzibar* (1968) is one of the canonical classics of science fiction, a conceptual prequel to *The Sheep Look Up* and a fictional presentation of the Osborn-Vogt dilemma. Overpopulation is the ever-present background noise for its kaleidoscopic narrative set in 2010. Population pressure makes housing tight and causes the United States to impose increasingly tight restrictions on childbearing. The title itself references global population: "If you allow for every codder and shiggy and appleofmyeye a space of one foot by two, you could stand us all on the 640 square mile surface of the island of Zanzibar." Brunner describes a New York with thirteen million people as a modest city: "It could not be compared with the monstrous conurbations stretching from Frisco to Ellay or from Tokyo to Osaka, let alone the true giants among modern megalopli, Delhi and Calcutta with fifty million starving inhabitants apiece . . . swarming antheaps collapsing into ruin beneath the sledgehammer blows of riot, armed robbery and pure directionless violence" (45). He continues with another page of scene-setting of crowded streets, homeless people, and sidewalks where people "thronged like insects."

This is essentially the same Manhattan that we visit in Harry Harrison's *Make Room! Make Room!*, a 1966 novel set in 1999 when the world's greatest city has reached thirty-five million. Harrison's narrative is a police procedural. Andrew Rusch is an NYPD detective who is assigned to solve the murder of a well-connected crook and political fixer. Through the oppressive August heat of a city feeling the effects of a global greenhouse effect, Rusch tracks a teenage tough through gritty streets and tenements, when he is not being called off the chase to help control protest demonstrations and riots.

New Yorkers inhabit a "billennium" metropolis. Poverty is extreme. Teams of humans survive yoked to carts that they haul through the streets. Pedicabs are the only taxis. There is no elbow room on the crowded streets and none in overcrowded apartments. People huddle in the doorways and under expressway pillars, squat in tenement stairways, and live in villages of derelict cars crowded into old parking lots. Thousands live on abandoned cargo ships moored in the East River. The welfare department has assigned "cavemen" to live in abandoned subway tunnels like Londoners during the blitz. Andrew Rusch shares a single partitioned room whose first occupant had been forced to share with him because of rising food prices. When the roommate dies, a family arrives to assert its legal claim to a space now too big for one person (the family had staked out the morgue to be first in line when a vacancy opened up).

Daily life revolves around water and food. Police guard metered public taps where householders line up every day to fill their jerry cans with brackish brown water. Only the rich can enjoy a shower and, occasionally, a few ounces of beef purchased from a black-market speakeasy. The most common food is weedcrackers made from algae and seaweed, supplemented by soy and lentil products like the especially luxurious soylent steaks. Even weedcrackers are getting expensive: "Supply and demand, supply and demand," says the man at the stand. "And I hear they have to farm weed beds further away" (60). Angry farmers blow up the Croton pipeline, continued saltwater intrusion destroys the Long Island aquifer, and drought kills crops around the country—leading to severe rationing and then a food riot reminiscent of eighteenth-century Paris.

Harrison's framework is explicitly Malthusian, channeling the arguments of Osborn and Vogt. There are too many people in New York, too many in the world.

Rusch's cranky, erudite roommate Sol Kahn sets him straight:

> Look, we live in a lousy world today and our troubles come from only one reason. Too goddamn many people. Now, how come that for ninety-nine per cent of the time that people have been on this earth we never had any overpopulation problems? . . . The reason . . . was that everybody was sick like dogs. A lot of babies died, and a lot of kids died, and everybody else died young. . . . They bred like flies and died like flies.
>
> I'll tell you what changed. . . . Modern medicine arrived. Everything had a cure. . . . Death control arrived. . . . People are still being born into the world just as fast—they're just not being taken out of it at the same rate. Three are born for every two that die. So the population doubles and doubles—and keeps on doubling at a quicker rate all the time. We got a plague of people, a disease of people infesting the world. (222–23)

Harrison wrote at a time of turmoil in American population policy, and he used *Make Room! Make Room!* as a contribution to the debates. In the novel, the government tries to hasten the demise of Eldsters by cutting back on welfare and medical care—although Congress would actually create Medicare in the same year that the book appeared. The food crisis in Harrison's New York is the occasion for inserting a debate between his characters about proposals to legalize birth control over church opposition, which is also the trigger for Sol's lesson in demographics. In fact, the Supreme Court had just affirmed the right of married couples to use contraceptives in *Griswold v. Connecticut* in 1965, although not extending the right to unmarried couples until *Eisenstadt v. Baird* in 1973.

Hollywood transformed *Make Room! Make Room!* into *Soylent Green* in 1973. The film retained the structure of a police procedural focused on Frank Thorn (Charlton Heston) and the setting of a hot, gritty city. The year is now 2022, and New York's population is forty million. As Vivian Sobchack notes, New York no longer soars on the screen—its buildings crouch low and crowded and drab.[12] Along with lots more bang-up action, the film retains the book's sense of claustrophobic poverty. A shop for the elite sells pitifully small amounts of fresh food from

In the New York City of *Soylent Green*, food riots require drastic measures. Variations on this image were incorporated into movie posters, the cover of the soundtrack album, and a reissue of Harry Harrison's source novel *Make Room! Make Room!* Courtesy MGM / Photofest © MGM.

behind locked screens. Commoners wear uniformly drab clothes, sleep in churches and on stairways, and riot over food. The murder victim is now a business executive who knows too much about the new wonder food soylent green, which has been introduced to replace soylent red and soylent yellow. At the climax Thorn follows the body of his friend Sol from a suicide parlor to a waste disposal site that turns out to be a food factory. As tens of millions of moviegoers know, soylent green is not made from plankton but from reprocessed corpses in a ghoulish cycle of sustainability—"It's people. Soylent green is made out of people! . . . Soylent Green is people!"

Soylent Green appeared at a very specific moment in the American love-hate relationship with New York. In popular culture the city of opportunity of the 1940s and 1950s was increasingly a place of dirt, drugs, and danger. From the mid-1960s to the mid-1970s, it was hard to find the affectionately portrayed city of *On the Town* (1949) and *Marty* (1955) on the big screen. From *Midnight Cowboy* in 1969 to *The French Connection*, *Panic in Needle Park*, and *Klute* in 1971 to *Taxi Driver* in 1976, filmmakers warned that New York was too big and too chaotic for anyone's good, including its own. In a nation confronted by urban crisis, it was not too hard to imagine a city eating itself.

FLOOD

In 1972, the group of economists and scientists who called themselves the Club of Rome issued a blockbuster report, *The Limits to Growth*. Using the most up-to-date computer modeling, the report came to Malthusian conclusions about natural resources: Global population growth and the incorporation of new nations into the world economy would place unsustainable pressure on the supply of minerals, petroleum, and other natural resources. The easy ores and oil fields had been mined and pumped, and prices were bound to spike as increasing demand met increasingly expensive supplies. The OPEC oil embargo of 1973–74 seemed like a political confirmation, anticipating the debates about the timing of "peak petroleum" that would continue into the twenty-first century. The Great Prosperity that had supported the growth of equitable consumer society in Western Europe, North America, and Japan ground to a halt with the deindustrialization and stagflation that marked the rest of the 1970s.[13]

Science fiction writers took note. The crisis of the 1970s shifted scarcity worries from the population demand side of the economic equation to the resource supply side (in part because the green revolution was muting fears of famine and because population growth was beginning to taper off with the demographic transition that has always accompanied urbanization). An undercurrent of scarcity made its way into the backdrops for new science fiction set in near-future America. Pamela Sargent's *Cloned Lives* (1976) depicted a year 2000 in which smart highways controlled automatic cars but suburbs were gradually going to seed and turn-of-millennium riots by Apocalyptics have left lasting scars. Gregory

Benford's *In the Ocean of Night*, published in 1977 and set in 2014, used a Los Angeles in which water is metered and charged by the flush, personal automobiles are rare, everyone has learned to practice fuel-conserving driving habits, and the burned-out remnants of "incidents" pepper the cityscape, complete with bullet-pocked walls.

Charles Platt in *Twilight of the City: A Novel of the Near Future* (1977), set in New York and environs in 1997–2000, novelizes the Club of Rome report. Increasing resource scarcity has led to a deeply bifurcated society and prompted Washington to impose drastic rationing with what is effectively an authoritarian coup. Things quickly spiral out of control. The American political and economic elite retrench to new walled cities in the Middle West and South, supported by a new peasant class who farm and serve in return for subsistence and security. New York partly empties out, and those who are left form an ad hoc government with a self-constituted militia. Within another year, however, the city falls further into anarchy. A gang of teens who resemble Mad Max understudies challenges the Peace Forces; the groups destroy each other in a final battle that leaves the city to a few remnant survivors. The future will be the slow reconstruction of society from small rural communities. The narrator describes the future in terms that could have come from E. F. Schumacher's manifesto for appropriate technology, *Small Is Beautiful* (1973).

> The city's dead. The little communities are growing and flourishing all around ... small towns with a few technological remnants, centered on agriculture, producing just enough to allow their children an education and to run a few simple services. ...
>
> People can't exploit other people so easily anymore. The basic resources are all gone in this part of the country: no more oil, no more easily smelted iron ore, no more metals outside of scrap metal in the garbage dumps. All there is is coal and wood for energy, and soil and water to grow food. There's room for cottage industries, now, but no real growth anymore. No way to get rich at someone else's expense. No way to build industrial empires. Things will stay small. They have to. (221)

Air pollution and resource exhaustion are creeping catastrophes that can tilt over to instant disaster, but global climate change has even greater potential for dramatic story lines because the effects are likely to be so visually compelling. Warming oceans and air increase evaporation, alter atmospheric circulation and rainfall, and generate storms and superstorms. John Barnes starts *Mother of Storms* (1994) with atomic detonations that fracture ocean clathrates to release huge volumes of methane—with the result of a planet-girdling storm that is a terrestrial analog of Jupiter's red spot. Stephen Baxter in *Flood* (2008) initiates an endless string of catastrophes with a huge storm that exacerbates the effects of rising seas and maximum tides to surge over the Thames Barrier and flood low-lying sections of London. The same thing happens in Richard Doyle's identically named *Flood* from 2002, and both draw on the real North Sea storm of 1953.

Drowned cities are mesmerizing. For two generations, underwater archaeology has been one of the fascinating staples of *National Geographic*. Amphorae from a Roman cargo ship, Spanish galleons beneath the Caribbean, the *Titanic* on the lonely ocean floor—all are images to stoke imaginations. Cecelia Holland opens *Floating Worlds* (1975) with a quick visit to the ruins of Manhattan, preserved for tourists within an undersea bubble. The author gives no backstory, and the action quickly moves to the surface of the Earth, Mars, and the gas giant planets, but the first two pages signal that we are in a very strange future. Even death by centimeters with gradual ocean-level rise brings memories of Atlantis. When the streets of Manhattan and London turn into canals, readers can enjoy long boat tours that defamiliarize the most familiar urban settings. Baxter in *Flood* takes his protagonists from the margins of the Thames spread kilometers wide to New York, swamped by the same rising seas: "The city's great buildings were an orderly forest of concrete and steel and glass, but you could see gaps in the forest, sprawls of rubble where buildings had fallen, often taking others down with them. . . . Boats prowled busily along the drowned streets" (153). If we are on the way to total disaster in Baxter's future, not so in Kim Stanley Robinson's *2312*, where New York is "an elongated Venice, a skyscraper Venice, a super Venice—which was a very beautiful thing to be. Indeed it was an oft-expressed cliché that the city had been improved by the flood" (92). Residents are coping very well, creating new streets from aerial plazas, skyways, catwalks, and suspended esplanades.

It is a short step from Robinson's still vibrant New York to more-troubled futures. In Donna McMahon's *Dance of Knives* (2001) the rising sea has made downtown Vancouver an island, isolated from the functioning mainland government. Crowded around the waterfront is a gang-plagued waterborne society something like the largely vanished floating cities of Hong Kong harbor. Across the continent in the year 2004, the Atlantic Ocean is slowly swamping Boston in David Alexander Smith's "Dying in Hull," which appeared in *Asimov's Science Fiction Magazine* in November 1988.[14] The town of Hull, on a long, narrow spit enclosing Boston Harbor on the southeast, has borne the brunt, its flatland houses are already half flooded, its government evaporated, most of its people gone. The "inland" city is still functioning, but the harbor is now a realm of youth gangs and pirates operating from Hog Island. Bostonians are talking about building a protective seawall, but Hull is too poor to save itself: "As the town of Hull sank, its houses had fallen to the Atlantic singly or in whole streets. These windward ocean-fronts, unshielded from the open sea, were the first to go. . . . Broken windows and doors were covered with Cambodian territorial chop signs of the Ngor, Pran and Kim waterkid gangs" (73).

Retired high school history teacher Ethel Endicott Cobb is one of the last remaining residents of Hull, stubbornly surviving in her ancestral home by navigating the flooded streets in her Boston Whaler to rescue food from abandoned houses and crossing the harbor to buy provisions with her pension check. The tone of the story is elegiac. Ethel contrasts her memories of two generations of students and their families with the realities of an inundated high school, wrecked houses, and former neighbors who have gone on to other lives. The past keeps sinking. Ethel rescues a photograph of one of her students from a sodden house, then has to fish it out of three feet of water when a waterkid grabs it and tosses it away. The story ends as she sits on her upper porch writing her will:

Today the ocean took my ground floor. One day it will take my house. It's going to reclaim South Boston and Dorchester and Back Bay. Folks will go on denying it like I've tried to, but it won't stop until it's through with all of us. . . .

After I'm gone, burn the place down. With me in it. At high tide so the fire won't spread. Nobody will bother you. Nobody else lives around here anyway. No one else has lived here for years.

22 K is a Cobb house. Always been a Cobb house. No squatters here. Give it all to the sea. (87)

Rueful melancholy also pervades Kim Stanley Robinson's story "Venice Drowned" (1981), set in a slowly dying city that has long symbolized regret and decline. Sometime after the unspecified changes of 2040 have raised sea levels by dozens of feet, the remaining Venetians have built new shelters on the roofs of the old city, and boats can pass in and out of the windows of San Marco. Carlo Tafur, to his personal disgust, makes his living from the new disaster tourism industry, ferrying visitors who want to dive the ruined churches and palaces. In the story, he takes two Japanese to the outlying island town Torcello, where only the ancient campanile of Santa Maria Assunta rises over the waves. After they strap on scuba gear and plunge down into the church, Carlo discovers to his dismay that his clients have a permit to salvage a great mosaic of the Madonna to reassemble in Japan—just one more of the treasures of Venice being salvaged from beneath the waves for collectors around the world.[15]

David Brin in *Existence* (2012) introduces Peng Xiang Bin and Mei Ling, who have shoresteaded in "a former beachfront mansion that now sloshed with the rising waters of the Huangpu Estuary" near Shanghai. While Mei Ling tends their child in the "hammock home" they have constructed on the roof and upper floor, Xiang Bin earns their money by diving for salvage from the flooded shoreline—"copper pipes, salt-encrusted window blinds . . . metal odds and ends"—that he sells to reclamation merchants. They are among hundreds of other shoresteaders, each staking a claim to a ruined beachfront mansion and the drowned landscape around it. The surviving and prospering city lies behind a seawall built to contain the new surf line, but already "with stains halfway up, from this year's high water mark" (54–55).

Shoresteaders and their petty salvage work are government policy to glean the last resources out of flooded territory. With the first evacuation in advance of the rising South China Sea, the buildings had been bulldozed and the easy salvage hauled away. Now shoresteading was the cheap way to persuade hundreds of desperate saps to strain their lungs and scrounge for anything of value left behind. Propelling his polystyrene raft with a single oar, Bin spots a new glitter from a mansion long since picked over, flips on his facemask, and dives to find that a recent collapse has revealed a storage room: "To Ziang Bin, almost anything down there would be worth going after, even if it meant squeezing through a narrow gap, into a crumbling basement underneath the stained sea" (59). He will find more than he wants or knows—an alien probe millions of years old that will thrust him into the center of global and galactic intrigue—but the haunting images of life on the social and physical margins of Shanghai remain.

The Chinese may pragmatically adjust to rising seas in *Existence*, but the government of Thailand in Paolo Bacigalupi's *The Windup Girl* (2009) is defiant. Bangkok is a low-lying river city veined by canals and only a few miles from the sea. Three generations after the collapse of the global petroleum economy, the world is a mess. Sea levels are still rising, courtesy of the fossil fuel orgy of the Expansion era, even though most energy now comes from the wind (travel is by dirigible and clipper ship) and from muscle power. Huge bioengineered megadonts power factories. Human workers pedal stationary bicycles to store energy temporarily in tightly coiled springs. Plagues have wiped out most natural food crops, leaving the world at the mercy of calorie companies that market disease-resistant strains of rice and wheat. New viruses and parasites mutate, disfigure, and kill faster than medical remedies can cope.

Thailand is resisting both the calorie companies and the ocean. It is one of the few nations that has preserved the capacity to maintain its own agriculture and aquaculture (the plot revolves around the efforts of an American "calorie man" to penetrate Thai seed banks and to overthrow its government). It has been fighting border wars with Vietnam and Cambodia over coal deposits. And it is also resisting the sea, building high dikes and pumping out the seepage: "It's difficult not to always be aware of those high walls and the pressure of the water behind. Difficult to think of the City of Divine Beings as anything other than a disaster waiting to happen. But the Thais are stubborn and have fought to keep their beloved city of Krung Thep from drowning. With coal-burning pumps and leveed labor and a deep faith in the visionary leadership of their Chakri Dynasty, they have so far kept at bay that thing which has swallowed New York and Rangoon, Mumbai and New Orleans" (7).

Bangkok is threatened not only by hovering flood, famine, and disease, but also by internal social and political fissures. Ethnic Chinese have arrived in the tens of thousands from Malaysia, refugees from genocidal ethnic cleansing, and have undercut the local labor market; ethnic violence simmers, waiting to explode. The Ministry of Trade contests power with the Ministry of the Environment, the former wanting to open the nation's borders and accommodate the calorie companies, the latter enforcing environmental laws and quarantines, sometimes by burning entire villages where a new pathogen is suspected. The Environmental Ministry's "white shirts" have turned into a bribe-taking, bullying police force. Every character is flawed. Opportunities for profit make the expat community brutal, manipulative imperialists. The cascading crises of the city make the local residents variously dishonest, venal, vengeful, self-destructively arrogant, and murderous.[16]

The end comes in fire and flood. The Trade Ministry stages a coup that brings in the Thai army to crush the Environment police in explosive street fighting that kills bystanders by the hundreds. The refugee quarter goes up in flames. Westerners intervene on behalf of Trade, eager for a new market and for the secret Thai seed bank, but their victory is short-lived. The remnants of the Environment police offer allegiance to the new regime but then turn on it by breaching the dikes and sabotaging the pumps. The Gulf of Siam engulfs Bangkok over the course of six days. The seed bank is saved, the government relocates, and the city empties of people. Its death atones for the excesses and sins that have made it corrupt, unmanageable, unlivable.

In *The Water Knife* (2015), Bacigalupi explores the flip side of global climate change in a near-future thriller about the politics of drought in the American Southwest. The action centers on Phoenix, overwhelmed by climate refugees from Texas and itself deprived of water by Nevada and California. The city is literally drying up. Poor people crowd around public water taps and squat in abandoned houses. Unofficial militias patrol the Nevada side of the Colorado River, killing any Zoners (Arizonans) and Texas refugees who try to escape the city's downward spiral. Water mafias have taken over the earlier eco-niche of Mexican drug cartels, and the states themselves are close to civil war, a semblance of order maintained only by federal enforcement of legal water rights (which can, of course, be stolen). The story in Phoenix ends in much the same way as in Bangkok, with open warfare erupting between Zoners and Texans, the protagonists barely escaping to try to rebuild their lives, and the city left to suffer from the sins of its deluded boosters who tried to outbuild the desert.

The Windup Girl is very much a twenty-first-century novel. Bacigalupi globalizes the sort of urban catastrophe that Anglo-American writers have usually kept close to home in New York, Denver, London, Chicago —or maybe Venice, as Europe's very own exotic city on the cultural margins.[17] In recent years, however, adventuresome science fiction writers have followed the pathways of the global economy to set novels in Vietnam (Linda Nagata, *Limit of Vision*), Shanghai (Neal Stephenson, *The Diamond Age*), Istanbul (Ian McDonald, *Dervish House*), Delhi (Ian McDonald, *River of Gods*), a new city surrounding Baikonur in Kazakhstan (Ken MacLeod, *The Sky Road*), and a city much like Alma Ata (Geoff Ryman, *Air*). These writers in their different ways are responding to the reality that the continuing urban explosion of the twenty-first century will be Asian and African. The United Nations in 2014 identified twenty-eight megacities with populations of ten million or more—sixteen in Asia, four in Latin America, three in Africa, and only five in all of Europe and North America.

The scope and compass of imagined urban catastrophe have expanded with the increasing prominence of non-Western cities in earthbound science fiction. In the nineteenth and early twentieth centuries, the crises of what I am calling "fire" stories are internal to European or American cities, products of their social and economic contradictions. They are part of the great effort to come to terms with the new phenomenon of industrial cities that spawned social science and scientific socialism as well as social science fiction. In "famine" stories from the post–World War II decades, the third-world problem of breakneck population-growth impacts is transposed to North Atlantic cities. In contrast, "flood" stories like *The Windup Girl* take the crises global, recognizing the ubiquity of technologies and the interconnectedness of economics and politics.

Neal Stephenson's sprawling novel *The Diamond Age* (1995) is an example that draws its narrative drive from ubiquity, interconnectedness, and the shifting balance between the West and the rest of the world. Asian societies have coalesced into expansive economic enterprises on the model of the overseas Chinese. Western societies have divided among a multitude of phyles, globe-spanning voluntary associations that are part tribe and part nation. There are Mormons, Afrikaaners, Maoist Senderos, the Distributed Republic (computer jockeys), Jesuits, Heartlanders (from the United States), Tutsis, and hundreds of others, but the great phyles are Atlantis, Nippon, Han (China), and Hindustan. Most of the Western phyles are second and third rank. Only Atlantis, a neo-Victorian phyle that offers loyalty to Queen Victoria II, is the semi-Western heir of nineteenth-century Anglo-American business values and drive. Otherwise, the power relationship of the nineteenth and twentieth centuries is inverted.

The neo-Victorians are experts in nano-engineering of products at all scales. Two of their largest companies manufacture artificial land with nanotech. Their new cities are strategically located in the global-Pacific economy to be the equivalent of "blessed places like Tokyo, San Francisco, and Manhattan. . . . each new piece of land possessed the charms of Frisco, the strategic location of Manhattan, the feng-shui of Hong Kong, the dreary but obligatory lebensraum of L.A." The choice of cities is deliberate: one Atlantic and three Pacific. This is a world in which the European frontier of North America, South Africa, or Australia has passed into history. "It was no longer necessary to send out dirty yokels in coonskin caps to chart the wilderness, kill the abos, and clear-cut the groves; now all you needed was a hot young geotect, a start matter compiler, and a jumbo Source [for the raw atoms needed for nanotech assembly]" (18–19).

The book reverses the normal American expectation of superiority to Asia. All the border crossers go the "wrong" direction, picking Asia over the United States. One of the leaders in the neo-Victorian meritocracy was born in Korea, raised in Iowa, became a nanotech whiz in Minneapolis, and then joined Atlantis to live adjacent to Shanghai. One of the judges of the Chinese Coastal Republic, consisting of Shanghai and adjacent trading zones, is a former Chinese American hoodlum from New York who has become a convert to the social discipline of Confucianism, and one of his assistants has emigrated from Austin, Texas. Another central figure is John Hackworth, a neo-Victorian engineer who is promoted from San Francisco to Shanghai after inventing chopsticks that play advertisements while you eat. He had enjoyed San Francisco "and was hardly immune to its charm, but Atlantis/Shanghai had imbued him with the sense that all the old cities of the world were doomed, except possibly as theme parks, and that the future was in the new cities, built [by nanotechnology] from the bedrock up one atom at a time" (71). Old cities, in this case, means European and American cities, not Asian.

The secondary plotline revolves full circle from "flood" (the environmental consequences of nanotechnology) to "fire" in the form of a military revolution that asserts Chinese nationalism against Western interests. The center of the action is Shanghai, a city divided between a small, traditionally governed enclave of the Celestial Kingdom and a Chinese Coastal Republic where the historic Bund is a vast shopping street with Western and Japanese stores. Residing on an adjacent nano-built island are the Western phyles, which use the Coastal Republic to access a huge Chinese interior that is still a great market for consumer goods. Chafing under Western technical and economic domination, China is seeking to develop its own technology that is more in tune with the essence of Chinese society. At the end, a new manifestation of Righteous and Harmonious Fists (Boxers) sweeps aside the warlords of interior China and drives the foreigners out of Shanghai. In so doing, the insurgents pave the way for China to adopt productive technologies suitable to its needs and to cut itself off from dependence on the West. The end result is the twenty-first-century negation of Pacific ambitions that animated Europeans and Americans for two centuries—which is also the outcome of Bacigalupi's novel when the Thais frustrate the calorie corporations by flooding and abandoning Bangkok to reestablish themselves independent of Western influence.

CHAPTER SEVEN

KEEP OUT, YOU IDIOTS!
THE DESERTED CITY

Danforth refused to tell me what final horror made him scream out so insanely. . . . We had snatches of shouted conversation above the wind's piping and the engine's buzzing as we reached the safe side of the range and swooped slowly down toward the camp, but that had mostly to do with the pledges of secrecy we had made as we prepared to leave the nightmare city.—H. P. Lovecraft, "At the Mountains of Madness" (1936)

"Such an abandoned metropolis must hold many secrets. We must be wary here."—Larry Niven, *Ringworld* (1971)

D oors hang open and swing in the wind. Vehicles, familiar or alien, rust in the streets. Towers in the city center speak of past glories—there may even be abandoned museums—but nobody is around. Stranded travelers or explorers comb through the ruins, looking for loot to help them survive or clues to the nature of a lost civilization. Don't linger! the reader wants to shout. Don't imagine that you can safely spend the night on an upper floor of a "downtown" tower. Mutated rat-things are lurking among the ruins, or devolved ape-things, or automated robotic protectors, or automated traps and snares set millennia ago. The next pages will be very exciting.

They certainly are exciting in Justin Cronin's best-selling vampire apocalypse novel *The Passage* (2009). Secret government science experiments gone horribly wrong loosed a vampire-making virus on the world.

Nine out of ten North Americans died, while one out of ten turned into madly driven, flesh-devouring, infectious "virals" that gobble up "everything with hemoglobin in its veins and a heat signature between 36 and 38 degrees, i.e., 99.96 percent of the mammalian kingdom" (305). Only handfuls of people survived in paramilitary units and in fortified compounds from which it is safe to venture only during the day and well armed. Now, in the year 92 A.V., scouts from a compound in the San Jacinto Mountains of Southern California tap the abandoned city of Banning for useful supplies.

> Peter could discern, through a haze of airborne dust, the long, low shape of the Empire Valley Outlet Mall. Peter had been there plenty of times before, on scavenging parties; the place had gotten pretty picked over through the years, but it was so vast you could still find useful stuff. The Gap had been cleared out, and J. Crew too, as had the Williams-Sonoma and the REI and most of the stores on the south end near the atrium, but there was a big Sears with windows that offered some protection and a JC Penney with good exterior access so you could get out fast, both still containing usable things, like shoes and tools and cooking pans. (289)

Yes, shoes and cooking pans, and also books from the public library on the north end of town near the mall. The symbolic search for knowledge in the deserted city is the mistake. A book-loving caretaker of an isolated power station associated with the compound has made one too many trips to the library, which has been reinhabited by virals. Infected himself, he has assaulted his coworkers. Three scouts and one power station survivor return to check out the library and inadvertently call forth the vampires who have been sheltering in its basement. Their numbers are too great, their movements too fast. They capture/infect/kill one of the four, drive the others in wild flight to safety.

Not too long after, the survivors of the Banning library encounter set off with four others on a trek to Telluride, Colorado, to find the secret government laboratory that spawned the infection. On their way, they reach the "vision of towering ruins" (519) that is Las Vegas. They are looking for fuel for their Humvees, but twilight lowers as they try to navigate streets choked with rubble and abandoned military vehicles. The buildings are monumental, with strange names like Luxor and Mandalay Bay. Some are "burned, empty cages of steel girders, others half collapsed" (522), but one is still intact. With night arriving and the airport out of reach, they take refuge on the fifteenth floor of what turns out to be the "Milagro Hotel and Casino." They are just settling in for a watchful night, peering out over the ruined city, when the window shatters and a viral swoops in to snatch one of the party. It's a trap: "All those blocked streets, they led us right here" (530). They try to make it out of the building. There are virals everywhere, blocking the exits, chasing them through the hotel toward a narrow, oh-so-narrow escape.

DISASTERVILLE

Abandoned cities have been science fiction staples for a century. On journeys of discovery or flight, our heroes come upon an empty city whose people and civilization have vanished like those of Banning and Las Vegas. For Cronin's protagonists and for other explorers and refugees, deserted cities hold out the lures of pre-disaster supplies, possible shelter, and lost knowledge. The vacant shell can be an American city after atomic warfare or strange places on alien worlds. Empty cities instantly supply the sense of estrangement that is central to the science fiction experience. In the hands of Anglo-American writers, they also draw on a thick heritage of antiurban writing and rhetoric. If we think that cities are bad for us, it's not a bad idea that they die, and it's not unexpected that they are as troublesome in death as in life.

A generation before *The Passage*, Stephen King had already nominated Las Vegas as the city of death in his blockbuster catastrophe novel *The Stand* (1978). After mutated influenza escapes a bio-research lab and wipes out the overwhelming majority of North Americans, survivors slowly sift across the continent, pulled like iron filings to two magnetic poles—Las Vegas and Boulder. Survivors who are attracted by worldly power converge on Las Vegas, that seemingly most artificial of cities. Repopulated Vegas becomes the center for a new empire in the far western states (there is a shadow of Mordor in the geography, with Las Vegas situated within the rings of mountain ranges that create the Great Basin of Nevada and adjacent states). The bad guys, led by the supernaturally evil Randall Flagg, create a place of rigorously enforced rules and order guided by objective thought. To come near the city is either to accept demonic fascism or die. Flagg is "the last magician of rational thought, gathering the tools of technology" (919), tools that eventually destroy the city through the providential detonation of a nuclear warhead.

Boulder is the bucolic alternative to the perversity of Las Vegas. Here come those who are immune to the call of power but not to the attractions of community. They find a relatively blank slate because most residents seem to have tidied up and left town before the plague hit. There are a few dozen newcomers at first in what they call the Free Zone, then a few hundred by the time their first Colorado winter closes in the town, then something like eleven thousand by the following April. They buckle down to the nitty-gritty of reconstituting civil society. Residents come together for town meetings at the Chautauqua Auditorium—a real place located where the town gives way to mountain parks and one that harks back to earlier American traditions of community. They restore symbols of solidarity by reaffirming the Declaration of Independence and the Constitution. They create a steering committee and hold town meetings. They organize work groups to scavenge for supplies in Denver and repair the power plant. At the end of the novel, the Zoners of Boulder are free to set their own course—which involves hiving off new settlements before the town grows dangerously into a city again.

Boulder stands on the "good" side of a small-town/city divide in Anglo-American culture that sees far more virtue in the countryside and village than in the metropolis. In the indictments of critics from Thomas Jefferson to W. T. Stead in *If Christ Came to Chicago* (1894) and Lincoln Steffens in *The Shame of the Cities* (1904), cities are bad for individual bodies and for the body politic. As reservoirs of disease they destroy individuals, and as cesspools of temptation and degradation they pollute souls. The lurid "prostitute's confession," supposedly penned on her deathbed by one who had once been an innocent maid from the country, was one of the nineteenth century's popular and titillating genres. No one escapes the snares of the city, for the extremes of wealth corrupt the morals of the rich at the same time they grind down the poor, whose dependency on a fickle market undermines the very basis of democracy. Jefferson sounded all the alarms when he wrote Benjamin Rush on September 23, 1800, that "I view great cities as pestilential to the morals, the health and the liberties of man." He was finding the bright side of a yellow fever epidemic that had killed thousands of Philadelphians.

Stephen King's Boulder is literally a town of ghosts when the refugees and trekkers arrive, a place where houses and shops stand empty and machinery waits for someone to flip the on switch. In the world of western American ruins, it is a cousin to Rocky Mountain ghost towns whose nostalgic dereliction is easily domesticated into backcountry attractions. There may possibly be ghosts behind the creaking doors of abandoned mills and cabins, but that eerie noise is likely the wind, or the skittering of a scavenging raccoon, and it's an easy jaunt back to the ski resort condo after a day of exploring.

Howardsville, Colorado, or Highland City, Montana, or Shaniko, Oregon—low-key tourist destinations all—stand in contrast to the apocalyptic scenery of the real ghost cities of nuclear technology. In the former Soviet Union and now in Japan are nuclear catastrophe zones where the shells of old cities remain to be slowly reclaimed by struggling vegetation. Okuma on the coast of Honshu is a hollow reminder of the Tōhoku earthquake and Fukushima nuclear plant meltdown. The Chernobyl disaster in Ukraine turned Pripyat from a modern model city for nuclear facility workers into an empty shell where soldiers stripped furnishings from apartments and buried them along with precious automobiles in the equivalent of mass graves—creating what is now a marginal site for schadenfreude tourism.

The city destroyed by atomic warfare—rather than atomic power and weapons production—is a commonplaces of science fiction, taking its place alongside cities destroyed by preatomic armies, earthquakes, tidal waves, fires, rising sea levels, meteors, volcanoes, asteroids, and comets. Mike Davis in *The Ecology of Fear* and Max Page in *The City's End* have inventoried the multiple ways in which novelists and filmmakers have ruined Los Angeles and New York.[1] Imagined bombardments by German battleships or by Soviet bombers are simple variations on a theme. So are earthquakes triggered by overbuilding in "The Tilting Island" (1909) and the feral creatures stirred by environmental degradation and urban renewal in the 1981 film *Wolfen*. The same tropes and images also recur over the decades—silent streets wandered by the last survivor, the shattered remains of the Statue of Liberty, the last couple contemplating the Adam-and-Eve option, skyscrapers toppling to earth or drowned by a rising sea. Eric Drooker's cover of the *New Yorker* for May 23, 2011, depicts the New York Public Library lions festooned with vegetation in a green shade like a temple lost in the Amazonian jungle.

What is telling is not only the glee with which we imagine the destruction of these symbolic cities, but also the possibility of refuge. If survivors can reconstitute a semblance of normal life, they will do it in the countryside and small town. In Pat Frank's 1959 best-seller *Alas, Babylon*, atomic war destroys Miami, Tampa, and Jacksonville, but civilization survives in the small town of Fort Repose. This is a Florida of four million people rather than today's eighteen million, with Walt Disney World yet unbuilt, leaving elbow room to regain some of the survival skills of nineteenth-century farmers. Because they are still close to the land—fishermen, recreational hunters, and farmers—the people of Fort Repose do a pretty good job of imitating their great-grandparents. With strong leadership from former military officers, they organize a barter economy and fight off a relatively tame set of highwaymen who are actually crooks from Las Vegas stranded in Florida. Civil society frays around the edges, but holds. Fort Reposers are sorry about the deaths of tens of millions, often bitterly sorry, but they are also pleased that they have themselves remained true to rural America. They realize that the nation should never have become so centralized and dependent on cities and the economic efficiencies that they offer, and that the postwar world may actually be a healthier place.

DANGEROUS VISITS

The catastrophe story's exodus sets the scene. Depictions of abandoned cities follow in tales set decades or millennia later about the temptation and dangers of tentative and problematic returns. They are an especially useful feature for adventure trek stories, supplying episodes to mix with environmental challenges, inadequate supplies, and hostile natives. Making their way across a strange planet or a postapocalyptic Earth, adventurers have already suffered dangerous weather, daunting landscapes, failing equipment, and dwindling food. Now they come upon a deserted city that offers the enticements of refuge and shelter . . . the attractions of goods and supplies . . . the lure of forgotten knowledge.

Larry Niven's Ringworld novels offer good examples. Exploring the amazing world-construct in *Ringworld* (1970), Louis Wu and companions encounter two distinct cities. In the sequel *The Ringworld Engineers* (1980), Wu encounters two more. Interspersed with other challenges, these deserted cities are part of the variety pack of quick-turning action scenes that have given the series its enduring popularity (along with the really cool starting premise of a Dyson Ring, of course).

In the first book, humans Wu and Teela Brown and nonhumans Speaker-To-Animals and Nessus come across a ruined city. Designed to hover high in the air, it has fallen from the sky when the Ringworld power supply failed in a catastrophe long past. People still live around its margins, going out to work fields in the day, sheltering in the ruins at night. They turn out to be dangerous because Wu does not match up with their expectations of how he, as presumably one of the Engineers who built Ringworld, should behave. The travelers have to fight their way out. The temptation to explore the empty city in search of information is compelling—the city gives them a map of their section of the vast world—but it's also dangerous.

In *The Ringworld Engineers*, Wu encounters another abandoned city. It had been built tall, with towers and floating buildings. Now it lies in ruins, another casualty of the literal fall of the cities. One building remains relatively intact. Inside are a group of Machine People who have been traveling to trade (they are so named because they maintain alcohol-powered machinery). Laying siege are vampires who exude a pheromone that makes sexual desire override all self-control. The vamps get close enough to entice and entrap all but one of the Machine People. Wu can't help exploring the city, only to find himself caught and crazed as well. The one Machine People survivor manages to save him, and they set off on new chapters of adventures. The abandoned city was a trap, despite being an interesting and intriguing place to explore (135–42).

Abandoned cities can be dangerous even when they are empty of terrestrial and extraterrestrial vampires. Automated defenses still operate centuries after the city has emptied. Laser cannon shoot exploring planes out of the sky. Sensor systems call up armed robots. Andre Norton's explorers in *Star Rangers* (1953) are a group of galactic patrol members crashed on a strange planet. They find an empty city to explore but come face to face with robotic guards.

> He could see the patroller now. It was at the far end of the block. The flashing lights on the buildings played across its metal body. But the sergeant was almost sure that it was unlike the ones known to galactic cities. The rounded dome of the head casing, the spider-like slenderness of the limbs, the almost graceful smoothness of its progress, were akin more to the architecture of this place.
>
> Its pace was steady and unhurried. It paused before each doorway and shot a spy beam from its head into the entrance. Manifestly it was going about its appointed task of checking the security of each portal. . . .
>
> Was it relaying back to some dust-covered headquarters an alarm?
>
> But its arms were moving—
>
> "Kartr!"
>
> Night sight or no night sight, Kartr had not needed that shout from Rolth to warn him. He had already seen what the patroller held ready. He hurled himself backward, falling flat on the floor of the hall, letting momentum carry him in a slide some distance along it. Behind him was a burst of eye-searing flame, filling the whole entrance with an inferno. Only his trained

muscles and sixth sense of preservation had saved him from cooking in the midst of that! . . .

"Are you hurt? Did he get you?" . . .

"The bag of bolts? I scragged him all right—a blast hole right through his head casing and he went down. He didn't reach you?"

"No. And at least he's told us something about the civilization they had here." The sergeant surveyed the blaze behind him with critical distaste. "Blow a hole in a city block to get someone. Wonder what they would have thought of a stun gun." (285)

Perhaps because automated defenses are such an easy complication to drop into the action, Larry Niven decided to have fun thinking up a variation to stymie his Ringworld explorers. As they explore an empty city, Louis Wu and Speaker-To-Animals are dismayed to find their fly-cycles taken over by remote control and flown into a cavernous building where they are trapped, suspended in space and dangling upside down. They have unknowingly violated some ancient traffic laws and activated a traffic control system that flies them directly to a detention facility, presumably intended when the city was active to be where they would pay off a fine for reckless driving. Now they are abandoned to eternal captivity in "an airborne Sargasso Sea" with the bones of earlier captives littering its distant floor . . . until they are released by a half-crazed survivor of a ramship crew who herself has been stranded on Ringworld for decades too long.

Even more dangerous than robotic defenses is the reinhabited city, the deserted city reinfested or repopulated with the wrong kinds of things or people. Whether it was built by humans or by some other race, whether it has been emptied by nuclear, viral, zombie, or vampire apocalypse or by the simple passage of time, any nice people who might have survived the disaster and decay have stayed away. Only nasty people and things have come back to haunt the ruins and threaten the traveler/explorer.

Knowledge is what draws Fors into an abandoned city in Andre Norton's *Star Man's Son: 2250 A.D.* (1952). Scattered tribes inhabit North America three centuries after nuclear holocaust. There are proud, horse-mounted, nomadic plains people, dark-skinned farmers moving up from the south, and the Star Men whose mission is to explore abandoned places and add to knowledge. The latter are the descendants of technicians and scientists who had been preparing a voyage to the stars. Now they seek out scraps of information: "Many times around the evening fires had the men of the Eyrie [the Star Men] discussed the plains below and the strange world which had felt the force of the Great Blow-up and been turned into an alien, poisonous trap for any human not knowing its ways. Why, in the past twenty years even the Star Men had mapped only four cities, and one them was 'blue' and so forbidden" (6–7).

Fors is the son of a Star Man and a plains woman. Born a mutant, with white hair and night sight, he is frozen out of any chance to become a Star Man himself. He therefore takes off on an adventure of exploration. In due course he finds a city: "This was one of the cities, the great cities of huge sky-reaching towers! . . . His city—all his . . . an untouched storehouse waiting to be looted for the benefit of the Eyrie. . . . Libraries—those were what one was to look for—and shops, especially those which had stores of hardware or paper. . . . Hospital supplies were best of all" (38). The city seems largely intact, perhaps the victim of disease after the nuclear war. It holds ruined buildings and a museum that has not yet been ransacked. But lurking in the shadows and cellars are subhuman and cruel Beast Things that drive Fors from the city. In one explanation, they are offspring of city dwellers and invading soldiers caught in radiation, creating children so mutated as no longer to be human. In another, they are the result of failed experiments to combine human and rat genetic material. "Whichever theory was true, the Beast Things, though they aroused revulsion and instinctive hatred among the humans, were also victims of the Old Ones' tragic mistake, as shattered in their lives as the cities had been" (132).

George Allan England's serialized postapocalyptic novel *Darkness and Dawn* from 1912–14, a full half century before Norton's book, uses the Rip Van Winkle plot to introduce a deserted city. After thousands of years, an engineer and a stenographer awaken high in the Metropolitan Life Tower (the world's tallest building from 1909 to 1913). They find themselves the only humans left in New York. Like other visitors to the future city, they explore its shops and streets as they struggle to survive and fall tastefully in love. Allan is strong and capable, Beatrice strong but happy with standard gender roles. The publisher sold the story as "Romance, Mystery, Adventure," although critic Nick Yablon in *Untimely Ruins* explores England's socialist background and reads the story as an explicitly anticapitalist revolutionary allegory that uses the postapocalyptic setting as a way to make readers think about alternatives. More to our point, the deserted city is reinfested by mutated ape-men who cross over from New Jersey, forcing Allan and Beatrice first to fight for their lives and then to flee to the isolated countryside far from the enticing but dangerous city.[2]

Allan and Beatrice are the literary ancestors of Robert Neville in Richard Matheson's novel *I Am Legend* (1954) and its several film adaptations as *The Last Man on Earth* (1964) with Vincent Price, *The Omega Man* (1971) with Charlton Heston, and back to *I Am Legend* (2007) with Will Smith. The setting shifts from Los Angeles to New York for the most recent film, but the basic premise stays the same. A plague has killed nearly all human beings, turned some variously into vampires, albino mutants, or infected virus-monsters, depending on the version, and left behind scientist Robert Neville to live a barricaded life in the depopulated city. He searches for a cure, encounters the undead, and comes up with a solution that holds out hope for humankind, but only at the cost of his own life. The setting gets eerier with the successive versions: Matheson's hero has to contend with vampire hordes from the get-go, but Will Smith spends substantial screen time with only his dog for companionship in the empty streets before encountering the infected. Whatever the details, surviving/saved humans end the story by escaping the dangerous city, just as George Allan England imagined generations earlier.

The infestation can be much less gruesome than mutated Beast Things, devolved ape creatures, and viral mutants. Even when physically normal, humans who have reinhabited cities are likely to be impure of heart. The power-hungry denizens of Stephen King's Las Vegas have plenty of cousins who are susceptible to recatching the urban disease of domination and empire building and doing the wrong things all over again. Kim Stanley Robinson in *The Wild Shore* (1984) extrapolates a future in which the neutron bombing of the United States has left a scattering of farming and fishing villages along the Southern California coast, connected to near neighbors by occasional trading fairs. Trouble comes up the coast from San Diego, where a petty dictator has consolidated power in the ruins of Mission Valley. His agents offer a tempting deal—connection to a larger political unit by a railroad that is slowly pushing northward in return for a modicum of taxes. When the villagers of San Onofre travel south to see for themselves, they find a society that is already corrupted by power and embarked on the seductive path of industrialization. There are not yet dark, satanic mills on the San Diego mesas, but the villagers can see them coming and want nothing to do with the emerging empire.

LOST CITIES

In *Ringworld* and *The Stand*, *The Wild Shore*, and *The Passage*, and in many other exploration stories, the abandoned city is one episode in a longer narrative arc of a survival journey or a bildungsroman. In the closely related lost city/lost world genre, however, the deserted city is the whole point. The somewhat truncated "century of lost cities" in European/American exploration stretched from the 1840s to the 1920s. At the start of that era, American diplomat John Lloyd Stephens stumbled across the Mayan cities of Copán, Chichen Itza, and Palenque, and British adventurer A. H. Layard directed early excavations at the site of Nineveh. Archaeologists and travelers continued to bring abandoned cities to the European attention through the excavation of genuinely lost sites like Knossos and Mohenjo-Daro and the description of cities like Angkor, Great Zimbabwe, and Machu Picchu that were known locally but still had to be "discovered," meaning added to the mental maps of Europeans and North Americans.

With all that discovering going on, and with Europeans energetically carving out colonial empires in Africa and southern Asia, underwriting and dominating the development of Latin America, and attempting the same in China, writers of adventure fiction met the growing challenge of expanding geographical knowledge by inventing places. Adventures of European expansion began to feature unknowable or impossible locales to supplement real Pacific islands, frozen tundras, and wild outbacks. Travel romancers around the turn of the twentieth century invented undiscovered islands in the wild ocean, hidden Antarctic valleys conveniently heated by volcanism, cave cities, secret Himalayan sanctuaries, and unexplored plateaus in Amazonia, and then peopled them with atavistic animals or unexpected colonies of surviving Phoenicians, Vikings, Israelites, and Crusaders.

Science fiction added a twist to what were basically alternative histories. In the standard lost-city narrative, white Europeans or Americans discover a lost society of other white people, or perhaps honorary white people such as Israelites who can be assimilated within the ruling race, or perhaps a nonwhite people who happen to have a white boss like She Who Must Be Obeyed. In contrast, there are no people of any skin color in the City of the Old Ones that an American scientific expedition discovers hidden behind a towering mountain range in the interior of Antarctica in H. P. Lovecraft's "At the Mountains of Madness." Lovecraft wrote the novella in 1931 and finally sold it to *Astounding Stories* in 1936. The details of the expedition are plausible. Richard Byrd had famously overflown the South Pole in a Ford Trimotor plane in 1929, so Lovecraft gave his scientists airplanes to carry them inland from the Antarctic coast over unknown territory. There are lots of details about logistics and base camps and geological poking and prodding. Indeed, the story moves at the pace of a glacier as particulars are added for verisimilitude and hints are dropped that something very bad is in the offing for these adventuresome Americans. The narrator is one of the few survivors, returned with a warning for the world.

What is the warning? There is a fantastic deserted city in the heart of Antarctic, and *you don't want to go there!* It is incredible, a place cobbled together from remembered fragments of archaeological digs—a bit of Knossos, a bit of Mesa Verde, a bit of the stone cities of the Incas. Lovecraft offers plenty of perhaps unneeded detail.

> Here, on a hellishly ancient table-land fully twenty thousand feet high, and in a climate deadly to habitation since a prehuman age not less than five hundred thousand years ago, there stretched nearly to the vision's limit a tangle of orderly stone which only the desperation of mental self-defense could possibly attribute to any but conscious and artificial cause. . . .
>
> . . . This Cyclopean maze of squared, curved, and angled blocks had features which cut off all comfortable refuge. . . . Only the incredible, unhuman massiveness of these vast stone towers and ramparts had saved the frightful things from utter annihilation in the hundreds of thousands—perhaps millions—of years it had brooded there amidst the blasts of a bleak upland. . . .
>
> For boundless miles in every direction the thing stretched off with very little thinning; indeed, as our eyes followed it to the right and left along the base of the low, gradual foothills which separated it from the actual mountain rim, we decided that we could see no thinning at all except for an interruption at the left of the pass through which we had come. . . . The foothills were more sparsely sprinkled with grotesque stone structures, linking the terrible city to the already familiar cubes and ramparts which evidently formed its mountain outposts. These latter, as well as the queer cave mouths, were as thick on the inner as on the outer sides of the mountains.
>
> The nameless stone labyrinth consisted, for the most part, of walls from ten to one hundred and fifty feet in ice-clear height, and of a thickness varying from five to ten feet. It was composed mostly of prodigious blocks of dark primordial slate, schist, and sandstone—blocks in many cases as large as 4 × 6 × 8 feet—though in several places it seemed to be carved out of a solid, uneven bed rock of pre-Cambrian slate. The buildings were far from equal in size, there being innumerable honeycomb arrangements of enormous extent as well as smaller separate structures. The general shape of these things tended to be conical, pyramidal, or terraced; though there were many perfect cylinders, perfect cubes, clusters of cubes, and other rectangular forms,

and a peculiar sprinkling of angled edifices whose five-pointed ground plan roughly suggested modern fortifications. (42–44)

The attraction is knowledge. This is a scientific expedition, and the narrator muses that "ingrained scientific habit may have helped; for above all my bewilderment and sense of menace, there burned a dominant curiosity to fathom more of this age-old secret—to know what sort of beings had built and lived in this incalculably gigantic place." But the quest for knowledge is dangerous, and some cities are better left unexplored. The first people to come near the city discover remarkably well-preserved alien creatures, which they try to dissect. When the narrator arrives the next day—he and his companions fly over the high range and land in the city itself—everyone is dead. There are writings and pictographs on the walls that tell a story of an elder race that preceded humans by millions of years. The empty halls echo with strange noises and reek with fetid odors. Drawn by insatiable curiosity, the explorers delve deeper into the city through downward-leading tunnels and passageways and tunnels and subterranean halls and still more tunnels. Portents become more portentous, until the explorers find themselves fleeing for their lives from a ravening creature that rises from deeper down. It's a shoggoth, one of the servant creatures that had rebelled against the Elder Race and helped to bring their city to ruin. It's an amalgam of giant garden slug, Arrakian sandworm, tunnel boring machine, and lamprey eel . . . and definitely bad news.

"At the Mountains of Madness" lies at the extreme for deserted city stories with its over-the-top horror and utterly fantastic premise. It straddles the margin between science fiction and fantasy, but it also contains key elements of the type. The explorers are off on their own. The abandoned city is physically fascinating, and it offers the promise of knowledge—knowledge that turns out not to be worth the cost.

In one comparative framework, stories like "At the Mountains of Madness" belong in the same category with slasher/horror films. Sitting in the theater, we want to shout at that attractive girl on the screen: "Don't go there! Don't go down those dark basement stairs! Keep out of that neglected attic! Don't take the back-alley shortcut—stick to the well-lit main streets! And for heaven's sake, don't spend the night in that deserted cabin in the woods!" Sitting in our chair, late at night in a pool of light from a single lamp, we mutter the same thing, wondering why Lovecraft's protagonists, and their many pulp literature cousins, plunge into the deserted city without adequate reconnaissance and then keep going, farther and farther, deeper and deeper.

There is a difference, however. The doomed teenager is motivated by idle curiosity and perhaps by a dare. For most science fiction explorers, the empty city entices with the promise of the practical. They poke around because they are curious, but curious with a purpose. The deserted city may have stores of food or medicine, or maps of the new planet, or clues to the cataclysm that drove away its inhabitants. These are left-brain attractants, in keeping with the rational problem-solving ethos central to the science fiction genre. For writers as different as Cal Tech graduate Larry Niven and New England curiosity H. P. Lovecraft, cities are containers of readable objective history, weird or curious as it may be.

LIFE AMONG THE RUINS

Pat Murphy cleverly turns the deserted-city story inside out and upside down in *The City, Not Long After* (1989). She posits a late twentieth-century plague that has killed the vast majority of Americans. Survival rates were marginally higher in small towns and rural areas, where an agricultural economy is slowly recovering, but San Francisco is an abandoned city. Now, sixteen years (the title's "not long after") after the great die-off, roughly a hundred San Franciscans are scattered in random hotel suites, houses, and shops, rattling around in the spaces where more than seven hundred thousand people once lived. There is rudimentary trade between the city and Marin County farmers, but someone who ventures in without preparation will find empty streets, abandoned and scavenged automobiles with the remains of their occupants, slowly crumbling buildings, burgeoning vegetation, and streams that have surfaced from their culverts and pipes to reclaim their natural paths between the hills.

It looks like we may be in the traditional territory of *I Am Legend*, but no, those hundred city-dwellers are right-brain people, a mix of eccentrics and artists who use the city itself as an inspiration for poetry and music and a canvas for installation art and performance art. A neo-Mayan collective has repainted the Trans-America tower. Mirrors and glass have turned several blocks into a shimmering Garden of Light. One San Franciscan is a tattoo artist. Another collects human skulls, polishes them with floor wax, and arrays them with carefully picked artifacts taken from the skull's original surroundings: "A pair of wire-rimmed bifocals, an empty whiskey decanter, a naked plastic doll with curly blond hair and baby-blue glass eyes, a hash pipe, a Bible, a lace glove" (63). Others construct giant wind chimes or weld life-size human figures whose hinged jaws chatter in the breeze. A man who has decided he is a machine rather than human makes other solar-powered devices to roam the city, like mechanical spiders, rats, and dogs. Danny-boy, who has grown up knowing only the city of art, persuades dozens of his fellows to paint the Golden Gate Bridge blue for the sheer pleasure of watching its transformation. The city's "mutants," in short, are defined not by vampirism but by compulsions to create.

Danger lies not inside the city but outside, where a former army officer is re-creating a territorial state in the Central Valley. With political pressure and a small army, he has cobbled together Sacramento, Modesto, Fresno, Stockton, Chico, and smaller towns into an authoritarian polity that suppresses dissent in the name of order and patriotism. San Francisco is both an attraction and a thorn in his side. It offers resources, and it also challenges the concept of strength through unity. Murphy draws General "Fourstar" Miles as a cross between Elmer Gantry and General Jack D. Ripper: "There are those who would forget our heritage, cast aside our traditions. . . . A selfish few hoard the resources of the city of San Francisco, scorning our offers of friendship and alliance. . . . They revel in anarchy, squandering the treasures of the past, delighting in unnatural acts that are an abomination in the eyes of man and God"

(33–34). He is a shadow of Randall Flagg, without magical powers but speaking the same language.

The plot is simple. Jax is a half-wild young woman from the Valley. When her mother dies after abuse by the soldiers, she flees to San Francisco to warn of the coming invasion. She meets Danny-boy and they slowly fall in love—not surprising, given that they are the only teenagers in the city. The San Franciscans slowly realize the invasion threat is real and decide to resist by nonviolent guerrilla actions. In effect, they stage performance art that steadily demoralizes the invaders, who number only 150 because post-disaster California is still thinly populated. Danny-boy saves Jax by killing General Miles and dies in turn, the leaderless soldiers are happy to decamp from the weird city, and San Francisco returns to its own version of normal.

Writing in the 1980s, Murphy was recognizing and defending San Francisco's reputation for difference. In the background is the Haight-Asbury scene of the mid-1960s, political turmoil at San Francisco State University in 1968, the emergence of the Castro as a gay neighborhood, the assassination of Harvey Milk in 1978, and the HIV/AIDS epidemic in the early 1980s. In this context, in which many other Americans viewed San Francisco as the antithesis of order, the book makes an obvious political argument that San Francisco's difference is liberating rather than dangerous—hence the rant by General Miles. However, it also makes a larger statement about cities as the centers of creativity. From her early years, Jax treasures a snow-globe paperweight that contains a miniaturized downtown San Francisco—a direct statement that San Francisco and other cities are vast artifacts and works of art. When the globe accidentally shatters, Jax realizes that she must take her own part in the ongoing creation process along with all the active artists and eccentrics.

Pat Murphy's reversals on the abandoned-city plot directly undercut the common science fiction preference for country over city, for frontiers over the presumed stasis and stability of urban centers, for individual adventurers over individuals embedded in the social networks of the metropolis. As the war approaches, Danny-boy tells Jax what a city is good for: "We're good at showing people a view of the world that they've never seen before. We're good at making people uneasy. We're good at convincing people to see things differently" (179). What the outsiders discover in Murphy's abandoned city is not old lore but new ideas, not vampires or shoggoths but new creations, not danger and death but refuge from war.

CHAPTER EIGHT

MARKET AND MOSAIC

The Gebiet is a preserve where no rules apply, and no punishments are inflicted. Ordinary people can do what they want down there.
—Cordwainer Smith, "Under Old Earth" (1966)

Nighttown pays no taxes, no utilities. The neon arcs are dead, and the geodesics have been smoked black by decades of cooking fires. In the nearly total darkness of a Nighttown noon, who notices a few dozen mad children lost in the rafters?—William Gibson, "Johnny Mnemonic" (1981)

The city reeked. But today was market day down in Aspic Hole, and the pungent slick of dung-smell and rot that rolled over New Crobuzon was, in these streets, for these hours, improved with paprika and fresh tomato, hot oil and fish and cinnamon, cured meat, banana and onion. The food stalls stretched the noisy length of Shadrach Street. Books and manuscripts and pictures filled up Selchit Pass, an avenue of desultory banyans and crumbling concrete a little way to the east. There were earthenware products spilling down the road to Barrackham in the south; engine parts to the west; toys down one side street; clothes between two more; and countless other goods filling all the alleys. The rows of merchandise converged crookedly on Aspic Hole like spokes on a broken wheel.—China Miéville, *Perdido Street Station* (2001)

Where do you go for sex, drugs, and rock and roll? Where can you buy anything you want? Where do the striving artists and musicians hang out? Big cities have districts on the fringe for marginal people, often on the literal edge of downtown. Science fiction cities are full of informal districts whose residents make their own rules. Sometimes we visit these marginal neighborhoods as a simple plot de-

vice. Sometimes we find the explosive violence that seethes in an unequal society—see *Blade Runner* (1982) or Alastair Reynolds's *Chasm City*
(2001). When night turns back to day, the bars shut down, or maybe
switch from wine to coffee. The squares and sidewalks come alive. The
urban jungle reemerges as urban bazaar, a teeming marketplace of goods
and ideas where we can wander past food carts, encounter a traveling
carnival, listen to a political harangue, and sip a drink at a sidewalk café.
Here we can encounter the thriving, stimulating city celebrated by Jane
Jacobs—the best of Greenwich Village and the Left Bank.

The theorist of the marginal district in science fiction is Samuel R.
Delany. In *Trouble on Triton* he coined the term "unlicensed sectors" for
these districts on the edge. Vice and crime, to be sure, but also artistic
expression can flourish where rules don't apply. The unlicensed sector
has twisting back ways and dark alleys, but Delany presents it as creative
and alive. It is home to political dissidents (or at least their leaflets and
graffiti) and to artists like street theater troupes. Here is the rationale
embedded in the novel:

> At founding, each Outer Satellite city had set aside a city sector where no
> law officially held—since, as the Mars sociologist who first advocated it had
> pointed out, most cities develop, of necessity, such a neighborhood anyway.
> These sectors fulfilled a complex range of functions in the cities' psycholog-
> ical, political, and economic ecology. Problems a few conservative, Earth-
> bound thinkers feared must come, didn't: the interface between official law
> and official lawlessness produced some remarkably stable *un*official laws
> throughout the no-law sector. . . . Today it was something of a truism: "Most
> places in the unlicensed sector are statistically safer than the rest of the city."
> To which the truistic response was: "But not *all*." (8)

The ordered disorder of the unlicensed district in Delany's imagined
city Tethys relates to the work of sociologist Peter Langer, who has identified "images" or structuring concepts that implicitly guide how urban sociologists understand the ways in which city dwellers organize and deal
with their diversity. He suggests that scholars interested in analyzing

how individuals within cities work and interact often choose between city as "bazaar" and city as "jungle."

> The city as bazaar imagines the city as a place of astonishing richness of activity and diversity unparalleled in nonurban areas. It is a market, a fair, a place of almost infinite exploration and opportunity, a center of exchange. The richness of opportunity of the city exposes each individual to a variety of experiences and fosters the development of unique combinations of social affiliations and lifestyles.
>
> The city as jungle sees the city from the group up as a densely packed, intricately intertwined, potentially dangerous place. Its diverse species crowd each other, search for their own place in the sun, and battle each other for room to develop and reproduce. Niches are cultivated and defended, and it is perilous to stray too far from familiar paths. Paradoxically, this rich, lush growth is precariously based, and it can easily be turned into a wasteland.[1]

These images overlap with several critical efforts to create typologies of science fiction cities. The disorderly, unlicensed city is often at the top of the list. John Gold identifies the Noir City as a distinct science fiction type, a place of menacing shades and shadows that foretells a dystopian future. Brian Stableford describes the hostile, impersonal, and physically oppressive city as one of the genre's most common urban tropes. Vivian Sobchack offers a variation on the same type, using "Trashtown" as the name for the city or district that is vibrant, cluttered, and beyond the edge of propriety. Noir City or Nighttown embodies the urban jungle, while Trashtown points to the city as bazaar, and both are enormously attractive to fiction writers. Trashtown is more seductive than a Tidytown like underground Topeka, and far more likely to offer instant plot twists because of the sheer variety of people, places, and activities that it implies. Nighttown is far more dramatic than Quiet-summer-afternoon-town.[2]

The essence—the essential life—of a city is not the physical container but the people it contains. Cities are where deals go down, ideas blossom, lovers arrange trysts, and conspirators hatch plots. Science fiction storytellers would be lost without the inescapable settings of the bustling marketplace and the crowded tavern or bar—both places where a variety of goods and services can be found and where anybody can put in an appearance, meaning trouble and plot complications can be just around the corner. Delany's Tethys, for example, is "pretty much modeled on New York," although with a population closer in size to San Francisco and partaking of elements from naturally evolving unlicensed sectors like Soho in 1960s London, North Beach in San Francisco, the French Quarter in New Orleans, and the Quartier Latin in Paris.

Cities are physical and cultural devices for making connections. What they do best is act as exchanges and marketplaces that facilitate the swapping of commodities and ideas. The trades can be dangerous and illicit transactions among people with different levels of power, like pimps and prostitutes, or drug dealers and high school teens, or many other denizens of Nighttown. Cities are also settings for legitimate trade in literal shops and markets and provide the places where individuals encounter and sometimes talk with each other. The stage may be as limited as the local sidewalk (see the 1985 movie *Smoke*) or the "third place" of coffee shop, laundromat, bowling alley, video arcade, or corner bar "where everybody knows your name."[3] These are the foundation stones of what the political philosopher Jürgen Habermas has called the "public sphere," the realm of civic discourse that is essential to liberal society where people of different backgrounds interact, learn to work together, or, sometimes, come into conflict.

Exchange requires difference. Individuals with wants and desires have to be matched with people who have the capacity to supply what is needed. The result has been geographic fragmentation and segmentation that balances the public spaces of exchange. Preindustrial cities were divided by religion, ethnicity, and occupation. Industrial-era rail transportation allowed cities to grow and spread and sort by class as well as race, creating cities that are social mosaics, a sometimes uneasy confederation of subareas and neighborhoods. In the ambiguous heterotopia of Triton, residents of the city of Tethys distribute themselves among a dazzling array of common interest living units, apartment blocks sorted by politics, age, sexual preference, class (how many slots are you from the top?), and other dimensions of everyday life. Delany himself summarizes the city as a "collection of communes and co-ops, with family units at the outer rim and singles in the inner city, with the social interplay between a licensed and an unlicensed sector," and comments that its "government structure will have to be at least as rich and imaginative and plural as the life structure of its citizens"—a challenge of political creation that he decided not to cram into the novel, but an underlying assumption nevertheless.[4]

WHERE THE ACTION IS

The first issue of Ron Randall's comic book series *Trekker* follows bounty hunter ("trekker") Mercy St. Clair through the streets and alleys of New Gelaph. The initial action finds her starting her search for a smuggler at Vlatz Bar, in a rundown storefront on the sleazy side of town: "Volcano Alley is a choking den of filth. The air is thick with sweat and steam. There is no safety in shadow or in light."[5] Randall knew that there is nothing like a visit to a tavern or bar to get a story going, and most readers would rather follow a protagonist into a sleazy, ill-lit, and perhaps illicit dive where a fight is about to erupt than into an upscale wine bar where customers are sedately swirling their glasses of pinot noir.

Science fiction writers oblige. John Shirley opens *City Come A-Walkin'* (1980) at the end of a long night in a smoky rock club in the wrong part of San Francisco. The breakneck action in the Japanese animated film *Akira* (1988) kicks off in a basement biker bar on an already rundown street in the reconstructed Neo Tokyo of 2019. Pat Cadigan's *Tea from an Empty Cup* (1998) kicks off in a dark, pulsing video parlor (well, actually a virtual reality parlor). Samuel Delany's Nebula-winning *Babel-17* (1966) starts in a bar adjacent to a spaceport. The jacket blurb for the original Ace paperback sets the stage: "The commander of the Earthpeople's Alliance journeyed into the bizarre depths of Transport Town to seek Rydra Wong, the cosmic poetess whose mind could perceive the meaning of all the world's tongues." And, of course, trouble comes looking for Luke Skywalker in Chalmun's Cantina early on in *Star Wars*.[6]

Trekker bounty hunter Mercy St. Clair confronts an informant in Vlatz Bar in the seedy district of New Gelaph, the kind of setting beloved by writers of science fiction adventure and science fiction noir. Courtesy *Trekker*, illustrations and story © 1987 by Ron Randall, originally published by Dark Horse Comics.

William Gibson seemingly took out a patent on science fiction noir with his pioneering cyberpunk fiction from the 1980s. His 1981 story "Johnny Mnemonic" kicks off in the Drome, "a single narrow space with a bar down one side and tables along the other, thick with pimps and handlers and an arcane array of dealers" (1). The location is Nighttown, part of the vast Boston-Atlanta Sprawl. The same atmosphere pervades *Neuromancer*, Gibson's immensely influential debut novel from 1984. This putative grandfather of cyberpunk novels opens in a bar in the Chiba district of the Tokyo Sprawl. As the protagonist Case shoulders his way into the Chatsubo, he overhears a drug-abuse joke and then seats himself at the bar between a whore and a visiting African naval officer before accepting his beer from a bartender with a surplus Russian prosthetic for one arm. "The Chat" is part of Night City, "a narrow borderland of older streets" with no official name but unofficially tolerated, a place shuttered and inert by day but thronged at night with patrons of its bars, arcades, yakatori stands, massage parlors, and the cybernetic equivalent of tattoo parlors where enough money could buy body modifications and enhancements.

> Night City was like a deranged experiment in social Darwinism, designed by a bored researcher who kept one thumb on the fast-forward button. Stop hustling and you sank without a trace, but move too swiftly and you'd break the fragile surface tension of the black market. . . . Biz here was a constant subliminal hum, and death the accepted punishment for laziness, carelessness, lack of grace, the failure to heed the demands of an intricate protocol. . . .
>
> . . . But he also saw a certain sense in the notion that burgeoning technologies require outlaw zones, that Night City wasn't there for its inhabitants, but as a deliberately unsupervised playground for technology itself. (7, 11)

Blade Runner (1982), another canonical and extensively analyzed science fiction landmark from the early 1980s, has its own bar scene set in Taffey's Snake Pit, where bounty hunter Rick Deckard visits halfway through the film. It is a dark, menacing, but also intriguing place— women in retro fashions, pipes being puffed and joints smoked, masked dancers swaying to techno-beat music, and drinks with snakes in them (well, probably tequila worms). The *Blade Runner* version of Los Angeles circa 2019 has, of course, become the inescapable embodiment of science fiction noir. The entire film *looks* like how we expect Night City to look, and it is the look that captures our imagination. The scenes were shot in good part on a dressed-up version of an Old New York Street set on a Burbank movie lot, with the designers adding slick futuristic elements to the substrate of a gritty street. Dim lighting, omnipresent rain, and drab color palate underscore the noir detective story line, and Andrew Milner has pointed out the direct echoes of noir detective cinema in clothing, liquor, tobacco, and voice-over.[7] In effect, *Blade Runner*'s design and cinematography added visual sophistication and "futurism" to the early urban jungles of *Soylent Green* and *Escape from New York*, and these films fixed expectations for three more decades of near-future science fiction cinema.

Blade Runner's Los Angeles is structured around a contrast of high and low, light and shadowed, spare and crowded, repeatedly drawing direct references to *Metropolis* and inverting the surface aesthetic of techno city.[8] The corporate ziggurat of the overworld looms over a surface world of densely packed and bustling streets, looking vaguely like a massive 1940s radio-phonograph console. Flames inexplicably vent from the tops of towers. Searchlights zigzag the sky but seldom penetrate the claustrophobic streets. The opening minutes indelibly set the scene, as Norman Klein point outs, with "that breathtaking pan, from the stoking fires into the brooding skyline, across to the pyramid of the Tyrell Corporation, back to the horizontal loops of flying pods, and finally down into the morass of Asian fast-food stalls on the street level." In this dual city, the Tyrell Corporation, which has hired detective Deckard to find and terminate renegade androids, pulls the strings from its soaring headquarters tower. In director Ridley Scott's backstory, Tyrell is one of four supercorporations that bestride the future worlds "where the poor get poorer and the wealthy get wealthier." The mood, to quote science fiction master Robert Silverberg, is "oppressive and scary" as we find ourselves trapped in "one of the ultimate urban nightmares . . . dark, menacing, congested, dominated by those immense ponderous towers that crouch like monsters upon the land."[9]

Blade Runner may be LA's "official nightmare," as Mike Davis claimed in *Ecology of Fear*, but look again and notice the intense vitality of the streets.[10] The city of 2019, compounded from fragments of New York, Milan, and Hong Kong, is disordered, heterogeneous, and active. Taffey's Snake Pit is interesting as well as edgy. The streets teem with vitality, the Asian faces suggesting its attractions for entrepreneurial immigrants. The streets are both a jungle (this is a noir detective story) and a bazaar that combines the feel of Asian street markets and the tawdry Times Square of the 1970s. Klein notes that many Los Angeles residents found a scene in which Deckard (Harrison Ford) grabs lunch at an outdoor market to be appealing rather than offputting or threatening, and the entire pulsating mishmash of food carts, sushi bars, and discount retailers that line *Blade Runner* streets match one of the standard twenty-first-century

Looming over future Los Angeles like a vast ziggurat in the film *Blade Runner*, the headquarters building of the Tyrell Corporation epitomize the film's contrasts between skyscrapers and streets, light and darkness, power and people. The design echoes *Metropolis*, from more than half a century earlier. Courtesy Warner Bros. / Photofest. © Warner Bros.

prescriptions for vitalizing bland American cities. As Stephen Rowley puts it, "If vibrancy and vitality are what we are after, there is a lot to like about this fictional Los Angeles of 2019. It has plenty of street-level convenience retailing and restaurants. The nightlife looks fantastic. There is either a good public transportation system, or everything is pretty close together. . . . It abounds, then, in the kind of qualities that Los Angeles lacks but which have led to the rehabilitation of New York in the public imagination as an exciting, attractive place to live."[11]

Katsuhiro Otomo's *Akira* reproduces the visual structure of *Blade Runner*, along with its choice of 2019 for its future. Audiences enjoy frantic horizontal motion through the streets of Neo Tokyo, but the action is framed by vast lighted buildings that serve the elite at the top and the middle class in well-patrolled and manicured middle levels. The riffraff get the streets, visually overpowered by buildings that blot out the sky, which is never seen in the course of the film. The government headquarters building looms and lowers like the Tyrell Corporation building.

(*Above*) Harrison Ford as
Rick Deckard pauses at a
streetside food-stall bar in
the midst of his hunt for replicants in *Blade Runner*. Courtesy Warner Bros. / Photofest.
© Warner Bros.

(*Right*) Like Lemmy Caution
(Eddie Constantine) in the
advertising poster for *Alphaville*, biker gang leader Sho-
taro Kaneda stands in front of
the Neo-Tokyo skyline in the
Japanese film *Akira*. Courtesy
Streamline Pictures / Photofest. © Streamline Pictures.

From Fritz Lang's classic *Metropolis* to *Blade Runner, Akira*, and the *Star Wars* epic, vertically divided cities have become an easy cliché for science fiction films, where the visual contrast of heights and depths packs a lot of scene-setting punch and provides the visual armature for class division and conflict. Take Coruscant, that city of never-ending skyscrapers with thousands of levels overlooking the streets and the undercity. In *Star Wars II: Attack of the Clones* (2002), Obi-Wan Kenobi leaps from a high window and sails through the urban canyons, first clutching a flying droid and then rescued by Anakin Skywalker's air speeder. As the chase scene unfolds, the viewer drops dizzyingly through the city to crash finally on the street—where Obi-Wan and Anakin face a cacophony of colors and sounds like *Blade Runner*'s LA streets—but with multiple species. In the recent Star Wars 1313 video game, players plunge groundward like Obi-Wan to find themselves in subsurface district 1313, a place of vice, crime, and exciting adventures.

A more fully developed twenty-sixth-century analog of street-level Los Angeles and Neo Tokyo is the setting for Alastair Reynolds's *Chasm City* (2001). During its three-hundred-year Belle Époque at a critical nexus of the space lanes, the planet Yellowstone had boasted "cities as fabulous as a dream, and Chasm City the mightiest of them all" (206). Perched on the edge of a caldera that opens on the great rift that gives the city its name, it has benefited from easy access to energy and to the breathable atmosphere that rises from the rift to be contained under eighteen interlocking biodomes known as the Mosquito Net. By the time the book opens in the 2510s, however, a nanotech virus has devastated the magnificent city. The "melding plague" disrupted machinery, melted buildings into new and fantastic shapes, and killed humans who had nano implants by setting off uncontrolled distortion of their tissues. The survivors are a bifurcated society. In the Canopy, the remnant elite have reconstructed a dissolute society on the tops of the warped and deformed skyscrapers. Thousands of meters below the "oddly textured cloud deck" (367) of the Canopy is the Mulch, a "carpet of slums" (237) that wraps around the bases of the towers.

Decadent boredom is the mark of the Canopy. The food is exquisite, the drugs are powerful, the fashions extreme. Many of its residents have artificially extended life spans that force them to find stranger and stranger satisfactions. They can manipulate the shapes of their bodies at whim—zebra-striped skin is a mild example, a head elongated to insect shape more extreme. Daredevils bungee jump into the chasm, where a leap that lasts ten seconds too long means death from toxic clouds. Others hunt marked humans through the Mulch darkness. The Game began with the excuse of executing criminals but now exterminates innocent victims while audiences follow the action.

The Mulch is different entirely. It lies in shadow under a continual drip of rain, like the LA of *Blade Runner*. Deep puddles and small lakes make some of the lower part uninhabitable. Shanties cling to the lowest levels of the looming towers, "encrustations of structures lashed against the footslopes" of towers, the vertical shantytowns having acquired their own "parasitic layer of encrustations in the form of ladders, staircases, horizontal landings, drainage conduits, trellises, and animal cages" (411–12). Haphazard construction makes the Mulch "less a district of the city than a stratification" covering a few stories above the scummy, black pools (237). Where the Canopy has a twenty-sixth-century version of a high-end shopping mall with bars and boutiques, the Mulch has a market of individual vendors that clusters around its Grand Central Station (steam trains are the highest technology that can survive at the planet's surface). Most Mulchers get around on foot, by rickshaw, and occasionally in a methane-powered vehicle. The population is a mix of criminals and ordinary folks "who live by their wits rather than their credit ratings" (234).

Like the world of *Blade Runner*, the "down" city is more interesting and vibrant than the "up," and no more dangerous—just dangerous in different ways. The Mulch may be "twisted roads and floods, and barnacled slums" (367), but on those twisted streets we hear "street musicians, criers, muezzins, vendors, and animals" (412). What we see are food stalls, outdoor puppet theater, bakeries, and a scrum of people. The central market is "a densely packed bazaar: a motley city of tents and stalls, through which passed only the narrowest and most twisting of passageways. . . . Stalls had been built or piled above one another. . . . There were several dozen vendors and many hundreds of people" (200). Kids tout the services of this business and that. As one person from the lower city says, "Canopy, they never do favor" (246), but outsiders can find at least some helpful people among the Mulchers, as long as they understand the intricate and informal market-based democracy.

Cordwainer Smith highlighted that capability in his stories of the underpeople in the future Earth of the Instrumentality, where undercity districts are capable of growth and self-determination. In "Under Old Earth" (1966) the surface city is Earth Port, where the Lords of Instrumentality live. Down below are the Gebiet and Bezirk. Both are perfectly good German words, the first for "region or land" and the second for "administrative district," although the Bezirk/berserk link is obvious and made explicit in the story. They are, however, unlicensed districts where the laws of above are not applicable and anything goes. "This is the Gebiet, where all laws have been lifted, and down below and over yonder is the Bezirk, where laws have never been" (210). As one of the Lords comments, "We let them have the Gebiet, beyond our own jurisdiction. We gave them the Bezirk, to do with as they pleased" (214). Although there is trouble down below, there is also potential for social organization, a point that is clearer in "The Ballad of Lost C'Mell" (1962). The underpeople of the Gebiet and Bezirk have been genetically engineered from cats, dogs, and other animals, some in special form and many looking like and interacting just like humans. They are, in other words, a caste. They may live out of necessity in different/lower parts of the city, but have the ability to organize to gain substantial rights in the course of the story.

The redemption of Nighttown is explicit in "The Dead Lady of Clown Town" (1964). The story takes place in the dual city of Kalma on Formalhaut III. The upper city is run for humans, with animal people and robots (some with animal brains or essences) as servants. A secret door leads to the undercity, which exists, apparently unknown or disregarded, under the larger platform that supports the upper city. As in Chasm City, the social difference is explicitly mapped onto a megastructure metropolis: "She was looking from the New City to the Old City. The New City rose on its shell out over the Old City, and when she looked 'indoors' she saw the sunset in the city below" (125). And, "She could see where the great shell of the New City of Kalma arched out toward the sky; she could see that the buildings here were older, less harmonious than the ones she had left. She did not know the concept of 'picturesque.' Or she would have called it that" (126).

The fully human Elaine accidentally finds herself in the lower city, where she meets the genetically engineered underpeople, who have lived in isolation except when the Lords occasionally send robots to spread disease and control the population. Long ago the lower city took the self-deprecating name Clown Town. Elaine's presence helps to trigger a revolt in which she supports the underperson leader D'Joan. The revolt fails, and D'Joan (Joan of Arc) is burned at the stake, but the action has sown the seeds of change by challenging the foundations of a regime based on self-satisfaction and inequality.

The Mulch and Clown Town demonstrate the power of social organization and self-direction even in impoverished places. The Mulch is dirty and poor and precarious, but its residents are capable of mutual help as well as predatory relations. The people of Clown Town may be underpeople and exiles, but they have developed a caste consciousness and organized themselves in ways parallel to the social structures that ethnographers find in superficially chaotic squatter communities. They have the same sort of crude democracy that researchers have observed in the shantytowns of Lima, the favelas of Rio de Janeiro, and the slums of Nairobi.[12]

LITTLE WORLDS

A city is "a mosaic of little worlds that touch but do not interpenetrate," in the justly famous words of early twentieth-century sociologist Robert Park. That formulation, based on a reading of Chicago in the 1910s and grounded on sociological studies of industrial cities such as Charles

Booth's *Life and Labour of the People of London* and W. E. B. Du Bois's *The Philadelphia Negro*, has influenced models of urban society for close to a century.[13] Even recent theorists like geographer Edward Soja, who tries to break out of the framework by asserting that Los Angeles is different, end up cutting the same materials into different shapes and assembling a variation on old patterns. Indeed, the image of a mosaic restated the verbal map of Manhattan that journalist Jacob Riis offered in 1890 in the investigatory classic *How the Other Half Lives*:

> A map of the city, colored to designate nationalities, would show more stripes than on the skin of a zebra, and more colors than any rainbow. The city on such a map would fall into two great halves, green for the Irish prevailing in the West Side tenement districts, and blue for the Germans on the East Side. But intermingled with these ground colors would be an odd variety of tints that would give the whole the appearance of an extraordinary crazy-quilt. From down in the Sixth Ward . . . the red of the Italian would be seen forcing its way northward along the line of Mulberry Street to the quarter of the French purple on Bleecker Street and South Fifth Avenue, to lose itself and reappear, after a lapse of miles, in the "Little Italy" of Harlem, east of Second Avenue. Dashes of red, sharply defined, would be seen strung through the Annexed District, northward to the city line. On the West Side the red would be seen overrunning the old Africa of Thompson Street, pushing the black of the negro rapidly uptown, against querulous but unavailing protests, occupying his home, his church, his trade and all, with merciless impartiality.[14]

Riis understood something that Park, who actually knew better, left out of his famous formulation: Because a great city is in constant flux, its little worlds do, in fact, constantly interpenetrate. Residents compete for housing, as with Italians moving into an African American neighborhood in Riis's example. They navigate the same streets and use the same parks and public spaces—sometimes sharing them amicably and sometimes falling into violent conflict. Behind the life of streets and neighborhoods is our understanding of cities as sets of subcultures. The sheer size of cities provides a critical mass of individuals with specialized backgrounds or interests. Ethnic groups are large enough to support specialized businesses. Gays and lesbians have the numbers to support their own institutions. Model railroaders and Lhasa apso fanciers can form clubs. As sociologist Claude Fischer has stated, the subcultural theory of urbanism suggests that the very heterogeneity that many classic urban theorists feared and criticized for disrupting social harmony actually creates new types of social cohesion that simultaneously draw together people with common interests throughout a metropolis while reinforcing the distinctiveness of its subareas.[15]

M. John Harrison's description of the fantastic medievalesque city Viriconium in a group of linked stories published from 1971 to 1984 draws, perhaps inadvertently, on subcultural theory. He largely populates the city, the setting for three novels and several stories, with members of two subcultures—artists and street gangs. Each group requires urban numbers. Street gangs (and revolutionary movements) need a mass of disaffected youth to supply recruits; strength of numbers allows the person who would be an isolated thug and bully in a small town to gain membership in a community of the like-minded. Artists need a set of critics, collaborators, collectors, and gallery owners interested in their genre. The story "Luck in the Head," for example, presents the poet Ardwick Crome as someone who defines himself by his stance and standing within artistic debates, content as long as his work is subject to recognition and even savage critique.

Nowhere is this vibrancy of the heterogeneous city more prominent than in the work of Londoner China Miéville, a master of the multifarious city in twenty-first-century speculative fiction. Running through his many books is the trope and theme of the dual city whose disparate halves are unknown or sometimes unknowable to each other. Close to home, as it were, *King Rat* (1998) introduced both a dual character in Saul Garamond, human-seeming but part rat in genetic heritage, and the literal underground London of sewers, tubes, and conduits for the city's nonhuman underclass. *Un Lun Dun* (2007) is a young adult fantasy in which teenage girls enter a complex under-London through book stacks rather than a rabbit hole or looking glass, but with similar results. In *Embassytown* (2011) the human characters live in a ghetto or colonial concession within a larger indigenous city that tolerates their presence as a trading enclave similar to the Dutch toehold in Japan's Nagasaki harbor in the seventeenth century and foreign concessions in nineteenth-century Chinese coastal cities. The city is divided by physical barriers to movement between the Host world and human enclave that cannot be breached without special breathing equipment and by the fact that only a tiny handful of humans can communicate across the species divide, for, in another duality, the Ariekei always speak simultaneously in two streams of sound.

The City and the City (2009) is set in a version of southeastern Europe after the collapse of the Soviet empire, where the city of Beszel retains the aura of shabby socialism and Ul Qoma is plunging into nouveau capitalism.[16] The two fully articulated cities exist literally side by side, some blocks in "crosshatched zones" having buildings from the two cities standing adjacent to one another. But in this strange place, there is no direct interaction. Residents of each city must deliberately ignore the other; they learn as children to disregard and unsee (untrained tourists regularly transgress the boundary between the two realities to the disgust of the authorities). In effect, Miéville takes divided Belfast, Jerusalem, and Cold War Berlin and follows the logic of their situation.[17] What people unsee are cultural differences, since the language is the same and there don't seem to be deep ethnic differences. Unseeing itself is a clear metaphor for our inability to understand and empathize and even notice people outside our comfort zone, whether homeless people, or Ralph Ellison's Invisible Man.

With this context, we can reconsider Armada, the city built on the bones of old boats that is the setting for *The Scar*, this time to view it not as a vast whole that wheels slowly around the ocean but as an assembled bricolage, a 3-D collage of pieces linked by historical happenstance and "tethered together in a weave of chains and hinged girders. Each vessel was a pontoon in a web of rope bridges." Each ship that makes up the assemblage is its own neighborhood, creating the variety of a land-based city: "There were slums and mansions in the bodies of tramp merchant ships, and built tottering across sloops. There were churches and sanatoria and deserted houses" (80). The city has cheap neighborhoods and expensive neighborhoods. There are temples, an asylum, a university. Armadans come from multiple human cultures and multiple nonhuman races. They have sorted themselves into districts and built "all the institutions of any city on land, devoted to learning and politics and religion, only perhaps in harder form" (173). Semiautonomous ridings enforce variations of local law in different sections (the term references the old English and colloquial Canadian political geography, and also districts that ride on the sea).

Armada is riven by politics, brought to a head by the polarizing scheme of the two charismatic and crazed leaders of Garwater Riding ("the Lovers") to risk the city by capturing and harnessing a huge sea creature. Behind-the-scenes maneuvering leads to a rare meeting of the city's Senate, where each of eight ridings has one vote. The debates change no minds, even as the minority in the five-three decision complain bitterly that they are still in the dark about the ultimate purpose of the hugely expensive gamble. Resentment simmers, led by the civilized vampirs of Dry Fall riding (whose influence is limited because of their nocturnal lives). As the voyage to the Scar reaches its climax, the vampirs lead a desperate mutiny in an effort to divert the Ahab-like Lovers from their quest: "Armada was tearing itself apart. Bellis heard gunshots and saw a flickering of flames where Dry Fall met Garwater. A human mob was approaching, and there were running fights between them and the Garwater sailors. It was not now the city against the vampir alone—as news of the rebellion spread, those who opposed the Lovers' plans had to come out to fight. Hotchi slammed their spines against men; cactacae hurled their great bulks against each other in ugly combat" (565). The rebellion fails and the city settles into an uneasy peace blanketed by "a traumatizing uncertainty, a rancor. . . . This had been a civil war. . . . People were numbed and blasted by it" (583–84).

Armada is factionalized by species and politics, but it simultaneously has the cultural vibrancy and variety of a great city grown over time: "But the city had not been bounded by the ships' existing skins. It reshaped them. They were built up, topped with structures; styles and materials shoved together from a hundred histories and esthetics into a compound architecture" (80). Gaps between the tethered ships turn into markets where shop boats decked out with banners crowd and jostle as stallholders hawk their wares. Armada would please urban theorist Leonie Sandercock, who has argued the importance of what she calls "mongrel cities" where "difference, otherness, fragmentation, splintering, multiplicity, heterogeneity, diversity, plurality prevail." She admits that many may find such uncertainty and boundary crossing disturbing, but asserts that "it is to be celebrated as a great possibility: the possibility of living alongside others who are different, learning from them, creating new worlds with them, instead of fearing them."[18] She could indeed be describing Armada, which one character describes to another:

> Culture? Science? Art? Bellis, do you even understand where you *are*? This city is the sum of *hundreds* of cultures. Every maritime nation has lost vessels to war, press-ganging, desertion. And they are *here*. They're what built Armada. This city is the sum of history's lost ships. There are vagabonds and pariahs and their descendants in this place from cultures that New Crobuzon has never so much heard of. . . . Their renegades meet here and overlap like scales, and make something new. . . . The oldest vessel here is more than a thousand years old. . . . Nobody knows the population of Armada, but it's hundreds of thousands at least. Count all the layers and layers of decks; there are probably as many miles of street here as in New Crobuzon. (103)

New Crobuzon is Armada's mirror city, the other half of another complementary pair. New Crobuzon is stationary, where Armada is mobile. Armada lives explicitly by piracy; New Crobuzon captures new resources through formal military conquest and annexation. The floating city receives refugees from New Crobuzon, and New Crobuzon makes war on Armada. The different species of Armada enjoy a rough equality, whereas humans dominate New Crobuzon, relegating other species to residential ghettoes (semi-insectoid khepri, eagle-like garudas) and low-paying jobs as laborers and wage workers (vegetation-derived cactacae, amphibious vodyanoi). New Crobuzon is tightly regulated, but Armada authorities are tolerant of social diversity: "In New Crobuzon, what was not regulated was illicit. In Armada, things were different. It was, after all, a pirate city. What did not directly threaten the city did not concern its authorities" (395).

A supporting player in *The Scar*, New Crobuzon is the omnipresent star in *Perdido Street Station* (2001), where it first appears. Indeed, the plot of that novel is simpler than the city in which it is set. Scientist Isaac Dan der Grimnebulin takes on simultaneous quests to save his lover Lin (a khepri female with the body of a human woman and the head of a scarab beetle) from a crime lord, to help a crippled bird-person of the garuda species regain flight, and to save the city from escaped slake-moths, mysterious creatures who are sucking sentience from the city. The quests take him through the city's slums, markets, trash heaps, and neighborhoods to the Perdido Street Station itself, New Crobuzon's transportation hub and headquarters for the powerful militia who keep their thumb on the city. The climax is a successful struggle against the slake-moths that requires Isaac to orchestrate the efforts of multiple individuals and species.

The book opens in the public city at the Aspic Bazaar, where "all distinctions broke down" in "a blaring mess of goods, grease and tallymen." The city's residents animate its streets, markets, and cafés. Action in Perdido Street Station moves among public streets and markets, private workspaces, and "third places" where strangers can meet and interact as equals. Isaac's efforts take him to the notorious Moon's Daughters pub, whose "clientele consisted of the more adventurous of the city's bohemians: artists, thieves, rogue scientists, junkies and militia informants jostling under the eyes of the pub's proprietor, Red Kate" (66–67). Later the same evening he heads to the far more cheerful Clock and Cockerel to meet Lin and her crowd of artists, and everyone ends the night at Bombadrezril's Unique and Wonderful Fair, whose food, balloons, carnival rides, and games of chance bring out a crowd in which "bankers and thieves mingled to ooh, scandalized and titillated" (82). In *The Scar*, Tanner Sack, a refugee from New Crobuzon to Armada, remembers a favorite part of his old city—the shoe market with shouting vendors in a tiny square in Pelorus Fields, the small cafés that lined the street, with their regular clientele. "When he had no work and a little money, he might spend hours in the ivy-covered Boland's Coffees, arguing and idling with Boland and Yvan Curlough and Sluchnedhser the vodyanoi, taking pity on the mad Spiral Jacobs and buying him a drink" (336).

These New Crobuzoners are enacting the role of public space as articulated by design critics and social commentators like Richard Sennett, who argue that community identities are best formed, promoted, and defended in shared spaces. This is not the passive observation celebrated by Walter Benjamin with the image of the flaneur who wanders the streets of Paris, but rather the creation of meaning by the active participation that is required for community life. Michel de Certeau opened his chapter about "Walking in the City" in *The Practice of Everyday Life* (1980; translated 1984) by contrasting the view of Manhattan from the top of the World Trade Center with the everyday experience of the sidewalk. He argues that abstract plans do not create cities. Instead, "the ordinary practitioners of the city live 'down below' . . . they are walkers, *Wandersmänner*, whose bodies follow the thicks and thins of an urban 'text' they write without being able to read it." Walking the city is both a literal activity and shorthand for the routines and actions of daily life. Myriad individuals generate the meaning of urban space by moving through it, using it, and filtering it through their own perceptions and imaginations in ways beyond control and discipline. De Certeau offers a democratic—even utopian—vision in which the city emerges from the networks and interactions of individuals going about their lives.[19]

Readers quickly grasp that New Crobuzon, with its population somewhere in the millions, is a transfigured version of London—both the Victorian city and the late twentieth-century city in which Miéville grew up—spiced, he says, with a touch of Cairo and maybe New Orleans. We are, very deliberately and explicitly, in a made-up world that is the very opposite of Tolkien's Shire—urban, grubby, and complex rather than rural, cutesy, and socially one-dimensional. The map that accompanies the book shows an oval-shaped city spanning two sides of a river, not far from the sea, and divided into districts that echo the boroughs of London. The map also resembles the top view of the cerebral cortex, split into hemispheres by a river and with the patterns of neighborhoods looking like a view of the brain's gyri or ridges, perhaps to emphasize the role of the city as a place of constant information generation and exchange. Fans have abstracted the transit system of street railways and aerial tram lines and reproduced them as a separate map that mimics the famous map-diagram of the London Underground. The city has neighborhoods of brick and timber-frame houses that are reminders of older London, and newer soaring structures, particularly the vast Perdido Street Station itself with a topping spire.

New Crobuzon is a rich amalgam of neighborhoods sorted by class, lifestyle, and species, but also under continual pressures of change. There is something like a central business district near the great central station, with a confusion of carts and pedestrians, elegant stores, specialty shops, law offices, and organizational headquarters. Khepri cluster together in slum-like Creekside and more respectable Kinker. Glasshouse is a cactacae ghetto, named for the giant greenhouse that these sentient cactus-like beings need for climate control. Left-leaning Bohemians and artists prefer Salacus Fields and the even edgier Howl Barrow. Meanwhile, "progressive academics held court in cafés and bookshops" in the well-scrubbed and respectable Ludmead district. The elite live in Flag Hill, Canker Wedge, and Nigh Sump, but they've abandoned Petty Coil because of the encroachment of smoky industry, leaving its ancient buildings to entrepreneurial craftsmen. The striving middle class of shopkeepers, lower managers, and skilled factory workers live in Sheck. The poor live in crowded but relatively safe Flyside, hoping to avoid the lawless slums of Spatters.

Much of New Crobuzon is a mix of races and classes swirled together like a marble cake. Lin's apartment building houses "petty thieves and steel workers and errand-girls and knife-grinders" (15). Some neighborhoods like Aspic are cosmopolitan and tolerant. Riverskin was a mixed area with humans alongside "small colonies of vodyanoi by the quiet canal, a few solitary outcast cactacae, even a little two-streeted khepri hive . . . a shop run by a hotchi family . . . their spines carefully filed blunt so as not to intimidate their neighbors," and even a homeless Llorgiss (509). Residents of Sheck, in contrast, jealously guard their humanness by making it uncomfortable for any khepri out after dark.

That is just the start of a social geography as complex as London or Chicago. The book is filled with journeys by foot and by cab through the city and back and forth across its bridges, designed in part to allow the author to show off the variety of the city. The evil crime boss Mr. Motley, who is himself constructed from bits and pieces of many individuals and species, offers a tribute to New Crobuzon early on:

> And what of the city itself? Perched where two rivers strive to become the sea, where mountains become a plateau. . . . New Crobuzon's architecture moves from the industrial to the residential to the opulent to the slum to the underground to the airborne to the modern to the ancient to the colorful to the drab to the fecund to the barren. . . . This is what makes the world, Ms. Lin. I believe this to be the fundamental dynamic. Transition. The point where one thing becomes another. It is what makes you, the city, the world, what they are. . . . The zone where the disparate becomes part of the whole. The hybrid zone. (41)

Hybridity has been a hot topic in social and cultural analysis in recent decades, and Miéville makes it an inescapable entry point for thinking about New Crobuzon. The city is full of hybrid creatures, sometimes natural like the khepri and sometimes remade with grafts from other individuals (usually as frightful punishment). Cosmopolitan in the extreme, the city itself is a hybrid with its clashing neighborhoods and members of six races sharing its confines (or in Leonie Sandercock's terminology, a mongrel city par excellence). Cultural hybridity implies vigor, creativity, the merging of differences into something new and stronger. The hybridity shows itself not only in the eclectic mix of architecture, the multiplicity of neighborhoods, and the variety of immigrant and "racial" groups but also in their continual interaction. The Perdido Street Station itself is where everything comes together. It a place with permeable edges whose "architecture oozed out of its bounds" (616). It functions "practically" a bit like the converging rail lines at London's Clapham Junction, but it is also the place where the action of the novel comes to a boil in "a climactic battle among slake-moths, criminal and government forces, a giant spider who straddles states of being, and Isaac and his mates."[20]

Perdido Street Station is very much a political novel. Christopher Palmer argues that the author is "exploring whether the diversity of New Crobuzon can feed collective collaboration."[21] The plot revolves around efforts to connect and mobilize what amounts to a political coalition, albeit one for direct action rather than electoral contests. Given Miéville's strongly left-leaning politics, it is not surprising that Palmer can read the peril posed by the slake-moths as a metaphor for devouring capitalism. The challenge for Isaac is to persuade groups and individuals on the margins to forgo differences and work together against repressive power for a practicable end.

Miéville himself has said that dialectic analysis lies at the heart of his thinking. In his interpretation, dialectic is about dynamic change, recognizing that difference is the basis for creativity that transcends difference. The focus is on "blurred interstices, gray area, hard cases—but *as part of a social and historical totality.*" Dialectics is "about *movement,* dynamism, tendencies within an overall, comprehensible, and total system. . . . This is obvious in my fiction in that the social tensions and contradictions that drive plot are generally endogenous—I try to avoid the sense of a static system. Modernity, history, is always-already-in-transition."[22] New Crobuzon characters build new things out of the old and discarded, especially the Construct Council that assembles itself out of electronic junk into a sentient mechanical creature, and Isaac himself, who builds his crisis engine out of the same junk.

Communication and interaction are central to both the city and the story of *Perdido Street Station.* In the opening pages Miéville tells us that "parasites, infection and rumour were uncontainable" in a city where everything and everyone connected (9). Not long afterward, Isaac describes himself as "the main station for all the schools of thought. Like Perdido Street Station . . . all the trainlines meet there—Sud line, Dexter, Verso, Head and Sink Lines; everything has to pass through it. That's like me. That's my job. That's the kind of scientist I am" (50). The climactic actions to save the city require Isaac to integrate fragments of information and knowledge and to plan and manage cooperation among disparate groups of humans, other species, the Construct Council, and a really strange being that hops among different dimensions. With victory over the slake-moths, the basics of the city don't change—neither its physical form nor its social complexity. At the end, Miéville reaffirms the city in its resilience and variety: "the vastness of New Crobuzon, this towering edifice of architecture and history, this complexitude of money and slum, this profane steam-powered god" (710).

THE CREATIVE CITY

In *Perdido Street Station*, Lin makes her sculpture alone, but at the same time as part of a supportive community that energizes her art. She abhors the conformity of traditional khepri art, where many sculptors often collaborate on a single project as, in effect, crafters working from a blueprint. To Lin that sort of work represents "dedication and community, and bankrupt imaginations" (20). She breaks away from Kinkin, the respectable and dull khepri ghetto, to live in Salacus Fields, a neighborhood full of artists. She makes herself part of a multispecies coterie of artists and intellectuals—a human art critic, a cactacae cellist, "painters and poets, musicians, sculptors. . . . This was Lin's milieu" (76). The city itself fuels her personal rebellion and the individualistic art that earns her a lucrative and ultimately deadly commission to create a statuary portrait of Mr. Motley.

Lin's work illustrates sociologist Howard Becker's argument that art is created not by isolated individuals but rather within "art worlds" that include everyone who makes the production and consumption of art possible. An art world for the visual arts is a network of people who cooperate and compete as they provide materials, practitioners, critics, patrons, galleries, and customers for a particular art type or style. A comparable music world would span composers, publishers, performers, critics, performance venues, people who make and repair instruments and equipment, and audiences for particular types of music, from classical to bluegrass to indie rock.[23]

Lin also exemplifies the way that the inherent variety of the mosaic city and the necessary interactions of the marketplace city are the preconditions for creativity. *The Triumph of the City: How Our Greatest Invention Makes Us Richer, Smarter, Greener, Healthier, and Happier,* by the crackerjack economist Edward Glaeser, makes an eloquent case for cities as the keys to originality and innovation.[24]

Cities are creative because they hold a critical mass of people who can share and critique one another's ideas, but just as important are their fluid social arrangements where the stale hand of custom trembles and weakens—where, as Karl Marx put it, "all that is solid melts into air, all that is sacred is profaned." For some, of course, for the sacred to be profaned—for established values to be undercut and disregarded—is a prospect to be fought at all cost. There is underlying continuity between English Tories in the nineteenth century who lamented the rise of a non-deferential, liberal, secular society and a mid-twentieth-century sociologist like Louis Wirth, whose 1938 essay "Urbanism as a Way of Life" argued that dense, heterogeneous cities by their very nature led to competitive and discordant lives. Invert the negative judgment and the same argument shows why Paris, Vienna, and New York have been the capitals of modernity in art and social thought where orthodoxies struggle to survive. "The great prosperity of contemporary London and Bangalore and Tokyo," writes Edward Glaeser, "comes from their ability to produce new thinking. Wandering these cities—whether down cobblestone alleys or grid-cutting cross streets, around roundabouts or under freeways—is to study nothing less than human progress."[25]

In the previous chapter we saw Pat Murphy's take on artists in the city, with San Francisco as the natural and nurturing home of eccentric creativity. The most fully realized district in Viriconium is the Artists' Quarter. Off in the galaxy, Melissa Scott's city of Burning Bright may be mundane in layout and technology, but it is another example of a metropolis that offers the critical mass to support different kinds of creative work. It is home to enough role-playing computer gamers to refine a particular type of performance art and attract participants from other planets. Community celebrations bring out street musicians, and residents deck themselves in elaborate costumes. On each year's climactic night, illuminated boats clog the harbor and barges parade past spectators bearing giant animated puppets that are simultaneously political commentary and specialized artistic expression. "There is nothing quite like our Carnival, not anywhere in human space," says a proud resident (185).

The tension between cultural conservatism and urban innovation sets the story line for John Barnes's *A Million Open Doors* (1992), where a technology of instant interstellar transfer opens the stultified social Darwinesque theocracy of Caledony to outside influence. Among the vanguard delegation sent by the Thousand Cultures to prepare for the transition is Girout, whose own culture values poetry, music, and romantic posturing. To earn his keep in Caledony, where everything has a price and everyone has to pay his own way, Girout sets up a school in the capital city Utilitopia where he teachers martial arts, music, painting, and drama, introducing young Caledonians to an unknown realm of artistic expression. The results are explosive. When the students put on their own night of performances at their Occasional Mobile Cabaret—songs, poetry, stand-up routines, a one-act comedy—they provoke the authorities, who see making art as political protest. The authoritarian crackdown succeeds in the short term, for Barnes is realistic about the likely balance of power; but political ferment in the more open-minded city, where Caledony's misfits and nascent artists have congregated, slowly subverts the bureaucratic order and its commitment to a narrow set of values and behaviors.

In *Virtual Light* (1993) and *All Tomorrow's Parties* (1999), William Gibson epitomizes the city as creative milieu by positing a transformed San Francisco–Oakland Bay Bridge, which accretes a spontaneous squatter town after an earthquake renders the bridge unusable.[26] This is neighborhood difference taken to the extreme, even in highly differentiated San Francisco. Over the years, the squatters have built and bolted and glued all sorts of secondary structures to the frame of the bridge, created their own social rules, and managed their own barter economy. There has been no plan, just the synergy from individual actions and choices. The inhabited bridge has "a queer medieval energy," a description that links the improvised community to Lewis Mumford's celebration of the medieval commune as an alternative to the industrial city. Michael Beehler has inventoried the descriptions that Gibson applies: piecemeal, organic, patchwork carnival, formless mass of stuff, not to mention kaleidoscope and state fair midway.[27] The bridge has become a physical expression of the social variety that fuels creativity:

> Its steel bones, its stranded tendons, were lost within an accretion of dreams: tattoo parlors, gaming arcades, dimly lit stalls stacked with decaying magazines, sellers of fireworks, of cut bait, betting shops, sushi bars, unlicensed pawnbrokers, herbalists, barbers, bars. Dreams of commerce, their locations generally corresponding with the decks that had once carried vehicular traffic; while above them, rising to the very peaks of the cable towers, lifted the intricately suspended barrio, with its unnumbered population and its zones of more private fantasy. (*Virtual Light*, 25)

Gibson offers a political message that the masses can be trusted to do the right things, in contrast to corporate capital, which is trying to destroy the old city for profit. In classic storytelling pattern, misfits and underdogs come together around bicycle messenger Chevette Washington to battle the forces of wealth and power. As Gary Westfahl writes, the novels "display genuine respect for uneducated, working-class individuals, valorizing their energetic determination to survive . . . and endless ingenuity in adapting to and thriving in challenging circumstances."[28] It is also possible to mobilize the theories of Michel Foucault, for the people of the bridge are contained within a larger disciplinary society that limits and tries to commodify the bridge itself as a tourist attraction. In resisting, the bridge community, through its hybridity, shows glimmerings of heterotopia as an alternative to corporate pseudo-utopia.[29]

The bridge is a place of art and creativity as well as a social escape valve. Residents live in a salvaged world where even yellow recycling tubs are repurposed. A jam maker heats her kettle with a scrounged propane ring. A furniture maker pieces together wood from abandoned or demolished houses. The border between craft and art is indefinable. A metalworker lays the drive chain from a motorcycle on the forge, to be beaten into a blade of "strangely grained Damascus" (*All Tomorrow's Parties*, 79). At night the bridge glows with scrounged and recycled lights. To a Japanese anthropologist, it is a place of discovery and magic: "Fairyland. Rain-silvered plywood, broken marble from the walls of forgotten banks, corrugated plastic, polished brass, sequins, painted canvas, mirrors, chrome gone dull and peeling in the salt air" (*Virtual Light*, 25, 62–63).

The authenticity of the bridge contrasts with the artificiality of its milieu. Its inward-looking spontaneity is the opposite of the carefully crafted "reality" television shows that permeate mainstream media. The damaged but reborn bridge contrasts with the damaged and propped-up Transamerica Tower, the late twentieth-century symbol of the corporate transformation of San Francisco. The action in *Virtual Light* kicks off when Chevette steals a pair of virtual reality glasses that show investor plans for remaking the city with a grid of huge eighty-story towers marching over the hills, ensnaring the city in a carefully designed and managed future that would realize the Corbusian fantasy of a fully programmed high-rise city.[30]

Gibson thus situates the bridge as a continuation of culturally daring San Francisco. Chevette, who arrives in San Francisco from suburban Oregon, is blown away by the excitement of the bridge. Her friend Tessa, a cinematographer from LA, loves the bridge because it is "interstitial," a word that Gibson consciously takes from the realm of cultural studies. Another character describes it as an "autonomous zone." It functions like the urban Bohemias of earlier centuries, the places "where industrial society went to dream." It is populated by a cross-section of the bad and the good, drug addicts and thieves, but also eccentrics and dropouts and artists. It is a metaphor for the excitement and risks of art. "The bridge is no tourist's fantasy," Chevette thinks. "The bridge is real, and to live here exacts its own price." At the same time, it is "a world within the world, and, if there be such places between the things of the world, places built in the gaps, then surely there are things here, and places between them, and things on those places too" (*All Tomorrow's Parties*, 174, 80–81).

Gibson draws on the historical precedents of bustling arcaded bridges in Paris, London, Italy, but even more on the model of Trashtown. Samuel Delany, to come full circle, argues that "Junk City" is a modern addition to the counterpoised images of Brave New World and New Jerusalem, which he finds in work by W. H. Auden. In a literal sense, Delany describes Junk City as the dead cars in suburban driveways, the furniture dumped on the street corner, the junky apartment interiors crammed with outdated electronics. But junkyards can be refuges for misfits, and junk itself the raw materials for new creations: "Junk City has its positive side: it's the Lo Teks living in the geodesic superstructure above Nighttown in Gibson's 'Johnny Mnemonic.' You can even see it presaged a bit among those who enjoy the urban chaos in my own *Dhalgren*—or the un-licensed sectors in the satellite cities of *Triton*."[31] The junk heaps of New Crobuzon give birth to an unprecedented machine intelligence. The detritus of San Francisco ends up as art on the Bay Bridge, found in the gaps and in the places between the gaps. Far more than they need sleek shopping malls and office parks, artists and start-up businesses need spacious and cheap spaces like Isaac Dan der Grimnebulin's live-in laboratory. Cities cut off their own futures when they try to spiff up and gentrify every tawdry commercial strip. Novelist Salman Rushdie puts it well: "*Mélange*, hotchpotch, a bit of this and a bit of that is *how newness enters the world*."[32] A city can be a creative milieu even when it looks its worst, and sometimes because it looks its worst.

CITIES THAT WILL WORK

Whether in London's ornate arcades or Rio's fractious favelas, whether in the high-rises of Hong Kong or the dusty workplaces of Dharavi, our culture, our prosperity, and our freedom are all ultimately gifts of people living, working, and thinking together—the ultimate triumph of the city.

—Edward Glaeser, *The Triumph of the City* (2011)

T
he growth of cities commonly marks the progress of intelligence and the arts." The author of this pithy sentence was George Tucker, one of the founding faculty members of the University of Virginia. A politician and writer who appreciated cities as engines of improvement, he was one of those public intellectuals who act as a commentator and synthesizer for a generation, well known in their lifetimes but rapidly fading from memory as issues change and their contributions look broad rather than deep. If he were working in the twenty-first century, he would be an op-ed columnist and blogger. In his own time, he was an essayist, pamphleteer, and novelist. *The Valley of Shenandoah* (1824) unsuccessfully imitated the novels of Walter Scott. *A Voyage to the Moon* (1827) was proto–science fiction that used the premise of a fantastic voyage to satirize contemporary society.

Born in Bermuda, educated at William and Mary, and resident of Richmond and Lynchburg, Virginia, Tucker served three undistinguished terms in Congress and then had a stroke of fortune when Thomas Jefferson asked him to be professor of moral philosophy at the brand-new University of Virginia. He lectured there from 1825 to 1845 and ended his career in Philadelphia, writing and publishing a four-volume history of the United States. Before and after Charlottesville, Tucker kept his pen busy with philosophical essays, political and economic commentary, a laudatory biography of Jefferson, a four-volume history of the United States, and, most importantly, *Progress of the United States in Population and Wealth for Fifty Years, as Exhibited by the Decennial Census* (1843).

Tucker believed in American-style progress, with scientific discovery fueling economic development and allowing the development of human capacities. His 1822 essay "On Density of Population" argued that people in concentrated numbers, not isolated Jeffersonian farmers, are necessary to advance science and the arts and stimulate the economy through competition. His 1843 book acknowledged urban problems but celebrated urban potential: "If these congregations of men diminish some of the comforts of life, they augment others; if they are less favourable to health than the country, they also provide better defenses against disease, and better means of cure. . . . They are more prone to innovation, whether for good or evil. . . . Whatever may be the good or evil tendencies of populous cities, they are the result to which all countries, that are at once fertile, free and intelligent tend."[1]

Tucker's rhetorical antithesis is not only an early stab at urban social science but also a framework for revisiting the different types of science fiction city. Anticipations of the future offer stimulating and creative cities, as well as cities that are dystopian or just plain dull. On one side of the balance are exciting techno cities and awe-inspiring cities as vast machines. On the other side are cities under social and environmental stress and the several possible outcomes of their crises—collapsing feral suburbs, confining and deadening carceral cities, and abandoned cities that almost always hold more menace than opportunity.

Pessimistic visions of the urban future draw on a social and political imagination with deep roots in Western social science. The astonishing growth of industrial cities in the nineteenth century generated a dozen variations on theories of contrast that argued that there had been a transition from the old days—often the *good* old days of community and stability—and the new age of destabilizing, alienating, and disorderly urban society. In different versions, folkways give way to stateways, primary relationships to secondary relationships, *gemeinschaft* to *gesellschaft*, deeply rooted culture to deracinated civilization, and, of course, feudalism to capitalism—the theorists, in order, are William Graham Sumner, Georg Simmel, Ferdinand Tönnies, Oswald Spengler, and Karl Marx.

As a great disturbing cause of social change, cities are characters in their own right, tragic protagonists whose flaws make downfall inevitable—at least that is the standard assumption behind many narratives of both the urban present and the urban future. Because cities create and exacerbate economic and social disparities, they create contradictions that can lead to bloody revolution. Their imperative to grow makes them the flash points for crises of overpopulation. Their exaggeration of consumerism makes them the founts of environmental disaster. If they are societal death traps, as so many critics in the European-American tradition have agreed, the interesting question is precisely what disease will kill them.

Optimistic versions often start with the physical rather than the social city, letting design take flight. For a century from the mid-1800s to mid-1900s, the aesthetic of the technological sublime captivated Western society. It meant sleekness, speed, and power—machines as fast as speeding bullets and more powerful than locomotives. Europeans and Americans celebrated vast railway stations shedded over with steel and glass, ocean liners, streamlined trains, and sleek rockets. They marveled over electric dynamos and cities wreathed in incandescent light, world's fair towers from the Eiffel Tower to the Space Needle, soaring bridges and mighty dams—"And on up the river is Grand Coulee Dam / The mightiest thing ever built by a man," wrote Woody Guthrie in "Roll On, Columbia." One of the stars of the 1939–40 New York World's Fair was the General Motors Futurama, with its anticipation of a nationwide freeway system. Another was *The City*, a film made by the American Planning Association, with music by Aaron Copland and narrative by Lewis Mumford. It contrasts dark, reeking Pittsburgh and pitiless, crowded New York with a vision of the future city that begins with electricity surging from Hoover Dam, follows with a two-engine airliner soaring over the continent, and ends with a fresh, clean Garden City suburb made possible by good planning and up-to-date technology.

As the era of megaprojects has waned with the evaporation of communist ambitions and the rise of neoliberal ideologies of government frugality, the future increasingly looks like the best place for grand and grandiose city-building thought experiments. Science fiction offers the opportunity to unleash architectural and engineering imaginations—hence a nearly seamless connection between design utopians like Buckminster Fuller and Paolo Soleri and scores of science fiction cities.

Positive and negative swirl together in the mosaic and marketplace city, where daylight and noir interpenetrate, where bazaar and jungle are close relatives. Until war comes, Tethys is a pretty interesting and compatible place to live—an ambiguous heterotopia, according to Delany's subtitle. Through all its turmoil, New Crobuzon remains a fascinating city of multiple species, multiple neighborhoods, multiple human languages, and multiple politics. It is certainly a reconfigured version of the London of *Bleak House*, but it is also a city that gestures to the different London of William Wordsworth's "Composed upon Westminster Bridge":

> This City now doth, like a garment, wear
> The beauty of the morning; silent, bare,
> Ships, towers, domes, theatres, and temples lie
> Open unto the fields, and to the sky;
> All bright and glittering in the smokeless air.

Nor is every city under stress doomed to spectacular collapse. It is easy to imagine a troubled city dying and collapsing, but there is an alternative plotline in which characters manage to cope with inconvenient truths and mounting crises rather than fall victim to cataclysm. What if we imagine a future city as embedded in a formal comedy, a story in which crisis is resolved and social order restored? Then we want to explore the fabric of everyday life and the processes of political change.

How do city people cope and fail as individuals and communities? Do they create new institutions or rely on existing governments? Can grass-roots innovation prevent a slide into anarchy?

Despite the appeal of disaster journalism, comedy in urban history is actually more common than tragedy. Modern cities are immensely resilient. San Francisco, Tangshan, and Kobe after earthquakes, Chittagong and New Orleans after hurricanes, and hundreds of cities after devastating bombing and war—the impulse is to rebuild to preserve the cultural capital of special places, utilize the remaining physical capital, and protect the financial capital invested in real estate. City planners Lawrence Vale and Thomas Campanella have summarized the components of urban recuperation. Restoration and rebuilding require outside investment, to be sure, but also depend on the ability to use a city's surviving infrastructure and institutions. Indeed, urban disasters reveal the resilience of government in managing the emergency and guiding reconstruction. As planner Kevin Lynch put it in *Wasting Away* (1990), "A city is hard to kill, in part because of its strategic geographic location, its concentrated, persisting stock of physical capital, and even more because of the memories, motives, and skills of its inhabitants."[2]

Nicola Griffith opens and closes *Slow River* (1995) on the banks of the Humber in the gritty English industrial city of Hull, a superficially implausible choice for a resilient city.[3] The Humber is "sleek and implacable" (4), not exactly Wordsworth's Thames that glides at its own sweet will, but still a force that has nurtured civilization and generations of history. It frames a dark and disturbing story about fragmented identity and childhood sexual abuse in a near-future city that borrows its atmosphere from Victorian noir and might lead us to expect the worst. The protagonist Lore van de Oest is the daughter of a powerful industrial family who escapes a stage-managed kidnapping to awaken in a lonely alley naked, bleeding, and without her personal identify chip. She is functionally reborn, saved by an information thief and sex worker who helps her assume first one and then a second new identity that she lives for three years before confronting her family and unmasking the corruption at its heart. As she slowly heals, the river that has shaped the city helps her to reshape herself: "I would spend the rest of my life by the river," she thinks at the end, "being visible" (342).

There is a lot that sets the novel apart, particularly for the early 1990s. Most of the strong characters, including Lore, are lesbians. Their relationships, ranging realistically from domestic to damaging, appear in the narrative as expected and straightforward—Griffith won the Lambda Literary Award for science fiction as well as the Nebula Award. In a decade of speculation about cyberspace and nanotech, the book's future technology is the science of sludge. There is not an abundance of science fiction in which chemistry is the scientific pivot, but the van de Oest fortune comes from a monopoly on the modified bacteria and enzymes that digest and purify the vast flows of wastewater that course under every city. Lore herself, brought up with the specialized knowledge, takes a grunt-level job in a sewage treatment facility as part of her self-definition.

Lore moves among the different social strata of modern urban society —the rich, the working class, the underworld. Talking with friends, she explores the rain forest as a metaphor for the city. She doesn't see the imaginary jungle of predatory chaos, but rather the layering of ecological niches from canopy to forest floor: "The jungle isn't just one place, you know—it's a dozen, all in layers. . . . Don't you see? Everything works in layers, jungles, cities, people. Each layer has its predator and prey, its network of ally and foe, safe place and trap. Its own ecosystem" (212–13). Griffith reiterated the same idea in a commentary on the book, stating that her definition of a city is "a place with a large enough population to *have* different layers. . . . Every citizen will know a different layer, will bend before a different social wind." Using a metaphor appropriate for *Slow River*, she described points of social contact as the "irrigation arteries" of a city and continued that "it is from such intersections of different nutrient streams that the energy and the art of a metropolis are born."[4]

Griffith's city is robust as well as complex. The plot subjects the city to environmental stress but not to the sort of environmental disaster that SF loves. Sabotage damages the delicate functioning of the treatment plant where Lore works, threatening to flood the city with toxic effluent, but quick action by dedicated workers salvages the operation, with emergency responders mobilized as needed. As Griffith commented soon after publication, "Much science fiction of the nineties destroys some aspect or other of the city. I did not want to do that. I wanted to keep as background the city as I have seen it, as a reader might recognize it. So the city in *Slow River* hovers continually on the brink of disaster . . . [but] I posit a technological advance that adds a bit of hope to the mess."[5] The result is a resilient city to frame the growing strength and resilience of the central character. The resilience extends to Lore as the story closes with the affirmation of social stability, with her partial reconciliation with fragments of her family and her bonding with a coworker as a likely permanent couple: "We walked hand in hand down the street. When I met my family again, I would introduce them to both of us" (343).

Resilience in an even more stressed urban community forms the backdrop for Nalo Hopkinson's debut novel *Brown Girl in the Ring* (1998). The plot has parallels to *Slow River*, focusing on a young women who must come to terms with her family heritage and her own identity, in this case as a Caribbean Canadian who has to accept spiritual gifts and powers that will mark her as different from most of her peers. Hopkinson sketches a future Toronto whose inner city has been abandoned by government and corporate capital (modeled, she says, after Detroit). In the face of neglect and poverty, residents improvise. Some join drug-dealing gangs, but others recycle abandoned spaces, develop a barter economy, and look after each other. In one corner of "the Burn," the "three pastors of the Korean, United, and Catholic churches that flanked the corners had joined forces, taken over most of the buildings. . . . They ministered to street people with a firm hand, defending their flock and their turf with baseball bats when necessary" (10). The optimistic ending has the provincial premier promising no-interest loans for the Burn's grassroots entrepreneurs. Perhaps micro-enterprise will thrive and grow, and the city regenerate.[6]

Kim Stanley Robinson's "Science in the Capital" trilogy (2004–7) uses a wider perspective to depict an entire city where social institutions fray but hold under the stress of climate disaster. As he did in earlier books like *Pacific Edge* and his Mars trilogy, Robinson explores the ways in which personal lives and civic lives interact, and he takes the ordinary seriously. The action builds slowly, especially in the first volume (tellingly titled *Forty Signs of Rain*), with much attention to commuting, child care, working out at the health club, processing NSF grant applications, and other quotidian routines. The books intercut the crisis of global climate change with the struggles of managing a family with two kids and two high-achieving professionals. Protagonists are National Science Foundation scientists and a senatorial staffer who try to make scientific institutions and government *work* to cope with global climate change and its impacts, and dozens of pages describe committee meetings and bureaucratic strategizing that actually get things done. The setting is Washington, described inaccurately as a "swamp" but otherwise depicted as an ordinary multiracial city.

By taking Washington seriously as a functional community rather than an aberration, Robinson challenges a knee-jerk reaction among many Americans and highlights his long-standing commitment to the importance of civic life. The books extend his repeated argument that utopia is a process rather than an end state—"utopia is when our lives matter," as one of his earlier characters says. Critic Robert Markley comments that "throughout the trilogy, scientific procedures—collecting data, testing hypotheses, and rewarding successful pilot projects—offer a utopian model of the ways in which politics should work. . . . One of the few novelists to take seriously rather than satirically the bureaucratic processes in and through which we live, Robinson describes at length meetings at the NSF devoted to deciding what grants to fund and what projects to prioritize. . . . In large measure, the arc of the trilogy depends on Frank and his fellow scientists keeping this 'necessary survival strategy' in mind as they go about their work."[7]

Forty Signs of Rain (2004) is the build-up book. We start with a summer city where temperatures are higher than normal . . . always in the nineties and just bearable. For perspective, Robinson introduces envoys from Khembalung, a nation of Tibetans displaced by politics and nature to a tiny island nation in the Bay of Bengal that is under real threat from rising oceans. The climax is a weather event that floods much of Washington via the Thames scenario: huge rains, plus high tides, plus storm surge from a hurricane up the coast combine meteorological forces, so that water coming downstream meets the backed-up Potomac. Rock Creek floods out the zoo and forces release of animals. Much of the Mall and Tidal Basin are flooded so that the monuments and museums are islands in the flood—the high-water mark on the Lincoln Memorial is twenty-three feet above normal river level.

The overt "heroic" action comes from Frank Vanderwal, a University of California–San Diego professor on loan to NSF—and is subtly undercut. In the first book he does some derring-do when he uses climbing skills to break into the NSF building at night to try to retrieve an intemperate resignation letter, only to find it no longer there. In the second, after signing up for a second year with NSF, finding no apartments available in a city recovering from flood, and deciding to live in a treehouse in Rock Creek Park, he tries out "paleolithic life with good dental care." He interacts with a group of homeless men who camp out and a group of ferals who play Frisbee golf through the park, live in squats, and salvage food from dumpsters. He also knows that he is playing, unlike the homeless Vietnam veterans with whom he interacts and tries with partial success to help. In the second and third books, Frank's efforts to help a girlfriend escape the toils of a secret spy agency are well meant but do as much harm as good—heroics are better left to the pros.

The driving action in *Fifty Degrees Below* (2005) is the continuing effect of global warming. Big chunks of the Antarctic icecap begin to slip loose into the sea. Melting of Greenland and north polar ice sends a flood of freshwater into the North Atlantic to stall the Gulf Stream circulation and triggers sudden climate change in Europe and North America—to a regionally isolated cold climate even as the whole world is warming (the scientifically plausible scenario also driving the dreadful film *The Day after Tomorrow*). Winter starts cold, and then—suddenly—temperatures plunge by thirty, forty, fifty degrees Fahrenheit. The summer's flood has increased Washington's homeless population by thousands. Now when temperatures plunge from North Woods cold to Antarctic cold in a single

night, people die, in much the same pattern as sociologist Eric Klinen-
berg described in *Heat Wave: A Social Autopsy of Disaster in Chicago*. In
the summer of 1995 in Chicago and in Robinson's near-future winter,
the vulnerable are the old, the homeless, and the socially isolated, partly
because they lack money and physical resources, partly because they
fail to access support systems. "The cold snap went on. The jet stream
was running straight south from Hudson Bay. The wind strengthened
and added to every already-existing problem—fire, frostbite, trees down,
power lines down. It began to seem like street work and polar emergency
work were what he had always done" (429).

By the end of the second book, Washington has muddled through the
first new winter with rolling brownouts and overstressed emergency services, avoided a direct hit from a Sandy-like hurricane that devastates
New Jersey and New York, seen the election of a scientifically literate
president, and girded for a new winter. In the process, we observe civic
institutions that work. First-responders and hospitals are stressed, but
they function. People turn out to help. Hundreds of volunteers coordi-
nate an effort to monitor escaped zoo animals. Park rangers and work
crews are upbeat as they clear downed trees and direct citizens who
pitch in until their workplaces reopen.

Over the next year (*Sixty Days and Counting*, 2006) conditions incre-
mentally worsen. The new winter is as hard as before, with fuel short-
ages and random blackouts the new normal, and the summer brings
severe drought that of course makes people wish for some snow and ice.
Ships of the nuclear navy are moored at coastal cities to provide supple-
mental electricity. Corners of Washington are dotted with empty houses,
burned out or abandoned after the flood.

Nevertheless, catastrophe doesn't come. A massive international effort
to resalt a key segment of the North Atlantic restarts the Gulf Stream.
Work starts to mitigate rising oceans by pumping seawater into dry ba-
sins in Central Asia and North Africa. As the Antarctic ice shelf slides
into the surrounding seas, another pump system moves water to refreeze
in the center of the continent. Bioengineered lichen increases the carbon
uptake of the Siberian forest in a risky but apparently successful experi-

ment by the Russians. These "terraforming" projects—one of Robinson's favorite thought experiments—are possible because corporations and nations can work together. The new president proceeds to implement environmental survival strategies (his "sixty days" comparable to Franklin Roosevelt's one hundred days). International organizations function, and even China calls on American assistance when its ecology collapses.

By Robinson's own description, the trilogy is intended as a comedy. Neither the protagonists nor the world are brought low by fate. Instead, wobbling institutions move back toward a center like a ship righting after nearly capsizing. The quashing of the secret agency that has been spying on Frank and his girlfriend is anticlimactically easy. Even conservative climate deniers in Congress are scared straight by the climate impacts in their districts. As in the most traditional of comedies (and paralleling the end of *Slow River*), social order is upheld with the continued strength of one marriage and prospects for three more, including Frank and his friend and the president and his science adviser. Robinson recognizes that cities may sometimes be responsible for their own dissolution by fire, famine, flood, or abandonment, but that they also have tightly woven social relationships and the social capital that is the source of resilience. Thick civic and social networks support short-term survival and long-term innovation. Rebecca Solnit in *A Paradise Built in Hell* convincingly argues that it is elites who panic in civic emergencies and ordinary folk who cope and cooperate. She demonstrates the capacity of communities to improvise and sustain social institutions under enormous stress, whether in the wake of the Halifax explosion of 1917, the Mexico City earthquake of 1985, or Hurricane Katrina.[8]

So Washington survives, like Mexico City and New Orleans. So will its other peers. Despite Kipling's lines, London, New York, and Tokyo are unlikely to become one with Nineveh and Tyre. Modern cities benefit not only from internal strength but from the sometimes maligned global economy that allows them to draw resources from vast distances far more effectively than premodern places that succumbed to conquest or climate change. Robinson understands the power of social and psychological ties that bind residents to their cities, and he also understands the scale of third-millennium society. Swan Er Hong's determination to rebuild Terminator in 2312 mirrors the determination of New Orleans to rebuild after Katrina, but success also depends on the engagement of her city and planet with the multiglobal solar system economy.

Interesting cities are complex cities—places of possibility intertwined with the problems created by change. New Crobuzon is endlessly fascinating, and Samuel Delany's Tethys remains intriguing. In the realm of television SF, the distributed city of *Battlestar Galactica* and the teeming space station metropolis of *Babylon 5* support richer stories than do the thin communities of the *Star Trek* universe. Harlan Ellison made underground Topeka a cultural monoculture—stable but repellent. Future Bangkok in *The Windup Girl* is unstable, dangerous, and ultimately doomed, but dynamic and absorbing in the meanwhile until disaster hits from outside. As science fiction writer Kathleen Ann Goonan writes: "Cities are, simply put, places where we come together to survive, where the symbiosis and mix of many humans becomes heady and elixirlike, leading to new intellectual, artistic, and emotional realms; leading also to the decay which occurs when old forms—physical and social—are no longer viable but still remain."[9]

Kim Stanley Robinson shares George Tucker's insight that cities are a necessary component of economic and social development—that "populous cities . . . are the result to which all countries, that are at once fertile, free and intelligent tend." Readers who follow the settlement of the Red Planet in Robinson's sweeping Mars trilogy see the growth of Sheffield as a port city comparable to San Francisco, Burroughs as an industrial city like Denver, Serenzi Na as a mining town like Butte, Bradbury as a smaller agricultural city like Grand Junction. As Martian society becomes more complex, flight to the outback provides escape but no solutions to conflict. The way to work through problems is to build civil society through conversation and dialogue, face to face in the taverns and hallways and meeting rooms of Martian cities.

NOTES

NOTES TO INTRODUCTION

1. V. Gordon Childe, "The Urban Revolution," *Town Planning Review* 21 (April 1950): 3–17; Michael E. Smith, "Sprawl, Squatters, and Sustainable Cities: Can Archaeological Data Shed Light on Modern Urban Issues?," *Cambridge Archaeological Journal* 20, no. 2 (2010): 229–53.

2. Samuel R. Delany, "A Future Narrative of Cities," *ParaDoxa* 2, no. 1 (1996): 27–28.

3. Gary K. Wolfe, *The Known and the Unknown: The Iconography of Science Fiction* (Kent, OH: Kent State University Press, 1979).

4. Lewis Mumford, *The Story of Utopias*, originally published in 1922, remains a literate introduction. Ruth Eaton, *Ideal Cities: Utopianism and (Un)Built Environment* (London: Thames & Hudson, 2002), highlights the associated visual imagination. Also see Frank E. Manuel and Fritzie P. Manuel, *Utopian Thought in the Western World* (Cambridge, MA: Belknap Press of Harvard University Press, 1979), and Françoise Choay, *The Modern City: Planning in the Nineteenth Century* (New York: George Braziller, 1969).

5. Frank Lloyd Wright, *The Disappearing City* (New York: W. F. Payson, 1932); Le Corbusier, *The City of To-morrow and Its Planning* (New York: Payson & Clarke, 1929); Robert Fishman, *Urban Utopias in the Twentieth Century: Ebenezer Howard, Frank Lloyd Wright, Le Corbusier* (Cambridge, MA: MIT Press, 1982).

6. Bruce Sterling, "The Virtual City," *ParaDoxa* 2, no. 1 (1996): 46–47; Robert Rydell, *World of Fairs: The Century-of-Progress Expositions* (Chicago: University of Chicago Press, 1993). Also see Rob Latham and Jeff Hicks, "Urban Dystopias," in *The Cambridge Companion to the City in Literature*, ed. Kevin R. McNamara (New York: Cambridge University Press, 2014), 166–67.

7. Paolo Soleri, *Arcology: The City in the Image of Man* (Cambridge, MA: MIT Press, 1969). The book is big enough to cover an entire coffee table. At about the same time, engineers George Danzig and Thomas Saaty offered a presumably serious model for a similar superstructure in *Compact City* (San Francisco: W. H. Freeman, 1973).

8. Carlo Aiello, *Evolo Skyscrapers* (Los Angeles: Evolo, 2012) and *Evolo Skyscrapers 2* (Los Angeles: Evolo, 2014).

9. Jon Adams and Edmund Ramsden, "Rat Cities and Beehive Worlds: Density

and Design in the Modern World," *Comparative Studies in Society and History* 53 (October 2011): 727–28.

10. Melvin Webber, "Order in Diversity: Community without Propinquity," in *Cities and Space*, ed. Lowden Wingo Jr. (Baltimore: Johns Hopkins University Press, 1963), 23–56; Barry Wellman, *Networks in the Global Village* (Boulder, CO: Westview, 1999); Rainie Harrison and Barry Wellman, *Networks: The New Social Operating System* (Cambridge, MA: MIT Press, 2012).

11. Andrew Lees, *Cities Perceived: Urban Society in European and American Thought, 1870–1940* (New York: Columbia University Press, 1985).

12. Morton White and Lucia White, *The Intellectual versus the City: From Thomas Jefferson to Frank Lloyd Wright* (Cambridge, MA: Harvard University Press, 1962).

13. In *Notes on the State of Virginia* (1784), Jefferson wrote: "The mobs of great cities add just so much to the support of pure government, as sores do to the strength of the human body. It is the manners and spirit of a people which preserve a republic in vigour. A degeneracy in these is a canker which soon eats to the heart of its laws and constitution."

14. Claude Fischer, *To Dwell among Friends: Personal Networks in Town and Country* (Chicago: University of Chicago Press, 1982).

15. Edward Glaeser, *The Triumph of the City: How Our Greatest Invention Makes Us Richer, Smarter, Greener, Healthier, and Happier* (New York: Penguin, 2012), 74.

16. Richard Florida, *The Rise of the Creative Class* (New York: Basic Books, 2002); Peter Hall, *Cities in Civilization: Culture, Innovation, and Urban Order* (New York: Pantheon, 1998); Peter Hall, "Creative Cities and Economic Development," *Urban Studies* 27 (April 2000): 639–49.

17. R. Buckminster Fuller, *Critical Path* (New York: St. Martin's, 1981).

18. John B. Calhoun, "Population Density and Social Pathology," *Scientific American*, February 1962, 139–48. Jon Adams and Edmund Ramsden discuss the impact of Calhoun's ideas on architectural theory in "Rat Cities and Beehive Worlds."

19. Nicola Griffith, "Layered Cities," *ParaDoxa* 2, no. 1 (1996): 36.

20. Carl Abbott, *Frontiers Past and Future: Science Fiction and the American West* (Lawrence: University Press of Kansas, 2006). For an example, I have argued that SF writers have consistently utilized and depicted Colorado as a place of refuge and survival because of the way that the state in the later nineteenth and earlier twentieth century epitomized the mountain West in the national imagination. Carl Abbott, "Rocky Mountain Refuge: Constructing Colorado in Science Fiction," *Science Fiction Studies* 39 (July 2012): 221–42.

21. Brian Attebery and Veronica Hollinger, eds., *Parabolas of Science Fiction* (Middletown, CT: Wesleyan University Press, 2013), vii.

22. Grounded in specific American experience, these two middle chapters on suburban and urban crisis trace a historical trajectory as writers in different decades respond to the changing world around them. The other chapters are structured synchronically as variations on a theme.

23. This distinction is similar to Henri Lefebvre's differentiation between the "representation of space" or "conceived space" and space as both everyday experience and imaginative experience ("representational space" or "lived space"). The former refers to space as conceptualized and ordered from the top down by scientists, planners, technocrats, and bureaucrats, the latter to the individual experiences that respond to, reimagine, and remake ordered spaces. At roughly the same time these theorists were writing, journalist Jonathan Raban in *Soft City: A Documentary Exploration of Urban Life* (London: Harvill, 1974) made the similar point that large cities are places whose openness and plasticity give individuals the freedom to shape their own lives.

24. Anthony Duckworth-Smith sums this point up nicely in *Future Histories: Post-Urban Design* (Perth: Australian Urban Design Research Center, 2015): "The city, its form and substance are backdrops: what matters are the setting for the experiences and actions of those trying to reshape or redefine their lives" in the often strange places of the future.

25. The structure of each chapter roughly follows the same trajectory, starting with straightforward examples of the urban type and ending with work that reflects with greater nuance on character and community. Chapter 1 opens with the perky topic of personal aircars and ends with J. G. Ballard's vision of a high-rise condo tower as the ultimately horrifying technological feat. Chapter 4, "Utopia with Walls: The Carceral City," starts with young adult fiction and concludes with Harlan Ellison's classic "A Boy and His Dog" and Molly Gloss's subtle *The Dazzle of Day*. Chapter 7 on deserted cities opens with horror/thrillers by Justin Cronin and Stephen King but ends with Pat Murphy's upbeat reversal of the deserted-city trope in *The City, Not Long After*.

26. An imposing body of scholarship in both science fiction studies and history explores the genealogy and theory of dystopia in speculative fiction. Starting places are Latham and Hicks, "Urban Dystopias," for a clear introduction; Tom Moylan, *Scraps of the Untainted Sky: Science Fiction, Utopia, Dystopia* (Boulder, CO: Westview, 2000), for a key entry in SF scholarship; and Frederick Jaher, *Doubters and Dissenters: Cataclysmic Thought in America, 1885–1914* (London: Free Press, 1964), for a pioneering work of intellectual history.

27. John Stuart Mill, *Principles of Political Economy with Some of Their Applications to Social Philosophy* (1848), book 3, chap. 17.

CHAPTER 1. TECHNO CITY; OR, DUDE, WHERE'S MY AIRCAR?

1. The magazine genre goes back to the nineteenth century and flourished from the 1930s to the 1960s. In the career of Hugo Gernsback, the border between popular science and science fiction blurred, as he published both genres in his pulp *Science and Invention*.

2. Examples of real-life efforts to create these sorts of devices are in Daniel H. Wilson and Richard Horne, *Where's My Jetpack? A Guide to the Amazing Science Fiction Future That Never Arrived* (New York: Bloomsbury, 2007).

3. My use of "techno city" bears a family resemblance to Robert Fishman's use of "technoburb" and "techno-city" in *Bourgeois Utopias: The Rise and Fall of Suburbia* (New York: Basic Books, 1987). His technoburbs are outlying metropolitan communities that offer the full range of housing types, employment, commercial facilities, and public facilities as found in traditional central cities; techno cities are the multi-nodal metropolitan regions, such as Los Angeles, that contain multiple technoburbs.

4. Alison Sky and Michelle Stone, *Unbuilt America: Forgotten Architecture in the United States from Thomas Jefferson to the Space Age* (New York: McGraw-Hill, 1976).

5. Robert Fishman, "Detroit, Linear City," in *Mapping Detroit: Land, Community, and Shaping of a City*, ed. June Manning Thomas and Henco Bekkering (Detroit: Wayne State University Press, 2015), 77–78.

6. Christopher Rand, *Los Angeles: The Ultimate City* (New York: Oxford University Press, 1967); "Self-Sufficient Structures Carry a Metropolis across New Jersey," drawing included in Warren Young, "What's to Come," *Life*, December 24, 1965, 143–67; Sky and Stone, *Unbuilt America*, 113–15, 190–91.

7. Tyler Cowan, *The Great Stagnation: How America Ate All the Low-Hanging Fruit of Modern History, Got Sick, and Will (Eventually) Feel Better* (New York: Dutton, 2011); Peter Thiel, "The End of the Future," *National Review*, October 3, 2011; Neal Stephenson, "Innovation Starvation," *Wired*, October 27, 2011, http://www.wired .com/2011/10/stephenson-innovation-starvation/all/.

8. Ferriss's drawings of the actual Rockefeller Center look very much like his imaginary city, save that the edges of the buildings are drawn more precisely. See his architectural renderings in the Columbia University Archives: http://library .columbia.edu/locations/avery/da/collections/ferriss.htm.

9. Hugh Ferriss, *The Metropolis of Tomorrow* (New York: Washburn, 1929); Joseph Corn and Brian Horrigan, *Yesterday's Tomorrows: Past Visions of America's Future* (Baltimore: Johns Hopkins University Press, 1984), 15, 42–43. Bertolt Brecht shared Lang's excited impression of towering New York in "The Late Lamented Fame of

the Giant City of New York," written after the stock market crash and before Brecht had actually visited.

10. Witold Rybczynski, "Dubai Debt," *Slate*, January 13, 2010, http://www.slate .com/articles/arts/architecture/2010/01/dubai_debt.html.

11. Baran Ornarli, "Forty-Five Incredible Futuristic Scifi 3D City Illustrations," *Inferno Development*, June 19, 2010, http://www.infernodevelopment.com/45-incred ible-futuristic-scifi-3d-city-illustrations, and Cameron Chapman, "100 Imaginative Cities of the Future Artworks," *Hongkiat*, http://www.hongkiat.com/blog/cities-of -future-artworks/.

12. King's was "one of many similar extrapolations of the skyscraper city, imagined and drawn even before the Woolworth Building or Empire State Building," such as William Robinson Leigh's "Visionary City," drawn in 1908 for magazine publication. Corn and Horrigan, *Yesterday's Tomorrows*, 34.

13. The setting is continued in *City of Hope and Despair* (2011), and *City of Light and Shadow* (2011).

14. Rob Latham, "The Urban Question in New Wave SF," in *Red Planets: Marxism and Science Fiction*, ed. Mark Bould and China Miéville (Middletown, CT: Wesleyan University Press, 2009), 178–95.

15. Gary Westfahl, *William Gibson* (Urbana: University of Illinois Press, 2013), 37; Latham, "Urban Question," 178–79.

CHAPTER 2. MACHINES FOR BREATHING

1. Asteroid cities are a variation on the space station city, constructed in the hollowed center of an asteroid whose rock provides the same protection from radiation and encapsulation of atmosphere as space-station steel. The hollow asteroid is often imagined as a nonurban landscape of farms and villages that line the interior surface of a cylinder, as in *Dark Lightning* (2014), John Varley's homage to Robert Heinlein's *The Rolling Stones* (1952). In M. J. Locke, *Up against It* (2011), however, an urban habitat for two hundred thousand is improbably suspended and spun up for gravity inside the cavernous core of the asteroid 25 Phocaea.

2. Sky and Stone, *Unbuilt America*, 99.

3. Trantor has an interesting literary history. The Foundation trilogy is one of the classic reads of science fiction. Chronologically linked stories that had originally appeared in *Astounding* from 1942 to 1950 contained brief mention of Trantor as imperial capital and then as a city in rubble after the fall of the empire. Asimov pulled these stories together as *Foundation* (1951), *Foundation and Empire* (1952), and *Second Foundation* (1953). He wrote "The Psychohistorians" in 1951 specifically as the first section of *Foundation* to introduce his epic of galactic history and, in-

cidentally, the city-planet. When Asimov returned to the Foundation universe in the 1980s with prequels and sequels, Trantor reappeared with more details and occasional inconsistencies.

4. Catherine L. Ross, ed., *Megaregions: Planning for Global Competitiveness* (Washington, DC: Island Press, 2009).

5. Constantinos Doxiadis, "Ecumenopolis: Tomorrow's City," 1968, http://www.doxiadis.org/.

6. Oswald Spengler, *The Decline of the West* (1918–23; New York: Random House Modern Library, 1965), 246–47.

CHAPTER 3. MIGRATORY CITIES

1. Simon Stadler, *Archigram: Architecture without Architecture* (Cambridge, MA: MIT Press, 2005); Peter Cook, *Archigram* (New York: Princeton Architectural Press, 1999); Sorkin quoted in Design Museum, http://design.designmuseum.org/design/archigram/.

2. Rory Stott, "A Walking City for the 21st Century," November 3, 2013, http://www.archdaily.com/443701/a-walking-city-for-the-21st-century/ArchDaily.

3. *Le Transperceniege* specifies 1,001 cars, which would make a rather ungainly train eighteen kilometers long, which is six times the longest bulk freight train and more than ten times the longest passenger train as of 2014.

4. Because the term is still in the process of settling firmly into urban planning, there are some alternative applications for "distributed city" that emphasize devolution from large-scale metropolitan systems to small-scale and localized planning. Australian environmentalist and "green urbanist" Peter Newman argues for a model of distributed cities in which energy systems, utilities, and transportation have been decentralized to avoid disastrous system-wide crashes—an idea that Kim Stanley Robinson embodied in *Pacific Edge* nearly a quarter century ago. Michael Blowfield and Leo Johnson in *Turnaround Challenge: Business and the City of the Future* (2013) use "distributed city" to emphasize the importance of scattered, small-scale innovation nodes that can network from places as different as Nairobi and Austin. It is an appealing idea in its own right, but Cory Doctorow stole their thunder with his depiction of the New Work in *Makers* (2009).

5. Fosco Lucarelli, "Mikhail Okhitovich and the Disurbanism," July 14, 2012, http://socks-studio.com/2012/07/14/mikhail-okhitovich-and-the-disurbanism/.

6. Jay Lake, personal e-mail, November 15, 2013. Distributed cities have a parallel in Rem Koolhaus's description of junk cities as places constituted from bits and chunks of the modern landscape accreted into a chaotic whole. Rem Koolhaus, "Junkspace," *October* 100 (Spring 2000): 175–90.

7. Herodotus, *History*, book 8: 61.

CHAPTER 4. UTOPIA WITH WALLS: THE CARCERAL CITY

1. A whole subgenre of the-future-is-already-here communications thrillers is premised on the ability of heroes and villains to manipulate information flows to pursue or frustrate political and economic power grabs. When science fiction writers like William Gibson in *Pattern Recognition* (2003), *Spook Country* (2007), and *Zero History* (2010), Walter John Williams in *This Is Not a Game* (2009) and *Deep State* (2011), and Cory Doctorow in *Little Brother* (2008) take on stories of electronic spying, commercial espionage, and political mobilization via the Internet, it is not clear whether they are writing contemporary fiction, "speculative fiction of the very recent past" (in Gibson's words), or science fiction set in a very near future. In any case, the cities are the cities we know: Istanbul, Jakarta, London, Moscow, Los Angeles. They are cool, exciting settings for action-packed stories, but they are the same places that we could visit ourselves, and fiction has a hard time staying ahead of real hackers, whether employees of the Chinese military or members of a hacking collective like Anonymous.

2. Forster refers to his underground city as a hive or honeycomb, and cities with similar settings, such as in Isaac Asimov's *Caves of Steel*, discussed later in this chapter, are sometimes grouped as "hive stories." See Jon Adams and Edmund Ramsden, "Rat Cities and Beehive Worlds: Density and Design in the Modern City," *Comparative Studies in Society and History* 53 (October 2001): 722–23; Eric S. Rabkin, "The Unconscious City," in *Hard Science Fiction*, ed. George E. Slusser and Eric S. Rabkin (Carbondale: Southern Illinois University Press, 1985), 31.

3. *The Collected Tales of E. M. Forster* (New York: Knopf, 1947), vii.

4. Some critics do read Lys as superior to Diaspar—pastoral communism contrasted to revitalized technocracy (Tom Moylan, "Ideological Contradiction in Clarke's *The City and the Stars*," *Science Fiction Studies* 12 (July 1977): 150–17). Others have pointed out how closely Diaspar resembles the New Jerusalem described in Revelation 21–22, down to twelve exit tunnels for the twelve gates (Thomas P. Dunn and Richard D. Erlich, "Environmental Concerns in Arthur C. Clarke's *The City and the Stars*," in *Aspects of Fantasy: Selected Essays from the Second International Conference on the Fantastic in Literature and Film*, ed. William Coyle (Westport, CT: Greenwood, 1986), 204–5.

5. C. J. Cherryh's story "The Only Death in the City," which leads off *Sunfall* (1981), directly mirrors the setup of *The City and the Stars*. Future Paris has been sealed inside high walls for so many centuries that inhabitants have forgotten the outside. Residents effectively live forever, being repeatedly reincarnated with their memories intact. Disturbance comes when someone is actually born a new soul with no memories or knowledge of the millennia-old customs that allow society

to function. This time, however, stasis muffles change and self-incarceration is unbroken.

6. Wolfe, *Known and the Unknown*, 88, 89, 93.

7. The follow-on television program did follow Logan and Jessica after their flight, but only by turning into a simple series of future adventures outside the city.

8. Harlan Ellison, "A Boy and His Dog," in *The Essential Ellison*, ed. Terry Dowling (Omaha: Nemo Press, 1987), 923.

9. Ibid., 928.

10. Joanna Russ, "'A Boy and His Dog': The Final Solution," *Frontiers: A Journal of Women's Studies* 1 (Autumn 1975): 153–62.

11. The historical Millerites were a religious movement in upstate New York who expected the Second Coming for October 1844, but it is also an apt term for the *Dusty Miller*'s people. Although they are not waiting for the millennium, they are very much engaged in finding a new heaven and new earth.

12. Drew Mendelson's *Pilgrimage* (1981) is an amalgam of the spunky kids, moving city, and carceral city tropes. A vast, self-contained city of twenty-five million people inhabiting 113 levels reaching two miles into the sky has been creeping across the landscape of Earth for thirty thousand years as the guild of Structors continually dismantle the rearmost sections and reconstruct new sections in front. The original inhabitants were folks who were afraid to head for the stars, building the city as a refuge that they have become unable to leave because of inbred agoraphobia. Three teenagers, chafing at the need to choose permanent careers and worried that the city seems to be sliding into chaos, set forth on a truth-seeking trek through the vast city. They have adventures along the way, including a time on an automated boat crossing a lake that has accumulated under the city—for some reason without their clothes, hence allowing some tits and ass on the paperback cover. The book is essentially a rewrite of *The City and the Stars* in a glacially moving city.

13. Jo Walton, "Quakers in Space: Molly Gloss's *The Dazzle of Day*," Tor.com, http://www.tor.com/blogs/2009/12/quakers-in-space-molly-glosss-lemgthe-dazzle -of-daylemg/.

CHAPTER 5. CRABGRASS CHAOS

1. Scott Donaldson, *The Suburban Myth* (New York: Columbia University Press, 1969), ranged over both academic and popular writing. Becky Nicolaides focuses on key intellectuals such as Lewis Mumford in "How Hell Moved from the City to the Suburbs: Urban Scholars and Changing Perceptions of Authentic Community," in *The New Suburban History*, ed. Kevin Kruse and Thomas Sugrue (Chicago: University of Chicago Press, 2006).

2. Peter Blake, *God's Own Junkyard: The Planned Deterioration of America's Landscape* (New York: Holt, Rinehart and Winston, 1964), 106–7.

3. Charles Abrams, *The Language of Cities* (New York: Avon, 1971), 60.

4. Boyle's novel is discussed in Carl Abbott, "Real Estate and Race: Imagining the Second Circuit of Capital in Sunbelt Cities," in *Sunbelt Rising: The Politics of Space, Place, and Region,* ed. Michelle Nickerson and Darren Dochuk (Philadelphia: University of Pennsylvania Press, 2011), 265–89.

5. Mike Davis, *City of Quartz: Excavating the Future in Los Angeles* (New York: Verso, 1990), 110, 111.

6. Edward Blakely and Mary Gail Snyder, *Fortress America: Gated Communities in the United States* (Washington, DC: Brookings Institution, 1999); Evan McKenzie, *Privatopia: Homeowner Associations and the Rise of Residential Private Government* (New Haven, CT: Yale University Press, 1996).

7. Rebekah Sheldon frames the novel's setting within the rise of neoliberal capitalism; see Sheldon, "After America," in *The Cambridge Companion to American Science Fiction,* ed. Eric Carl Link and Gerry Canavan (New York: Cambridge University Press, 2015), 206–18.

8. Rob Kitchin and James Kneale, "Science Fiction or Future Fact? Exploring Imaginative Geographies of the New Millennium," *Progress in Human Geography* 25 (March 2001): 27.

9. Alex Schafran traces the new representation of suburban dystopia in the media and academia and the resulting "discursive mishmash" in "Discourse and Dystopia, American Style," *City: Analysis of Urban Trends, Culture, Theory, Policy, Action* 17, no. 2 (2013): 130–48.

10. Timothy Egan, "Slumburbia," February 10, 2010, http://opinionator.blogs.nytimes.com/2010/02/10/slumburbia/.

11. George Galster, *Driving Detroit: The Quest for Respect in the Motor City* (Philadelphia: University of Pennsylvania Press, 2012); Margaret Dewar and Robert Linn, "Remaking Brightmoor," in *Mapping Detroit: Land, Community, and Shaping of a City,* ed. June Manning Thomas and Henco Bekkering (Detroit: Wayne State University Press, 2015), 143–65.

CHAPTER 6. SOYLENT GREEN IS PEOPLE! VARIETIES OF URBAN CRISIS

1. Latham and Hicks, "Urban Dystopias," 168–71 (quote 168). Joan Dean has noted the dominance of overpopulation worries in science fiction films of the 1970s. Joan F. Dean, "Between *2001* and *Star Wars*," *Journal of Popular Film and Television* 7, no. 1 (1978): 16–17.

2. Jack London, *People of the Abyss* (1903), author's preface, www.sonoma.edu/writings/peopleoftheabyss.

242 NOTES TO CHAPTER 6

3. Adna F. Weber, "Suburban Annexations," *North American Review* 166 (May 1898).

4. The actual number is now estimated at between six thousand and ten thousand.

5. Josiah Strong, *Our Country: Its Present Crisis and Its Possible Future* (1885; Cambridge, MA: Belknap Press of Harvard University Press, 1963), 172–73.

6. Ibid., 176–77, 186.

7. Robert Fogelson, *America's Armories: Architecture, Society, and Public Order* (Cambridge, MA: Harvard University Press, 1989).

8. Martin Ridge, *Ignatius Donnelly: Portrait of a Politician* (Chicago: University of Chicago Press, 1962); Frederick Jaher, *Doubters and Dissenters: Cataclysmic Thought in America, 1885–1914* (London: Free Press, 1964).

9. Google Ngrams suggest that the term "gridlock" dates to 1962, the same year as "Billennium," although use did not take off until the 1980s.

10. "That Population Explosion," magazine cover by Boris Chaliapin, *Time*, January 11, 1960, http://content.time.com/time/covers/0,16641,19600111,00.html.

11. Miles A. Powell, "Pestered with Inhabitants: Aldo Leopold, William Vogt, and More Trouble with Wilderness," *Pacific Historical Review* 84 (May 2015): 195–226.

12. Vivian Sobchack, "Cities on the Edge of Time: The Urban Science-Fiction Film," in *Alien Zone II: The Spaces of Science-Fiction Cinema*, ed. Annette Kuhn (New York: Verso, 1999), 133.

13. Donella Meadows et al., *The Limits to Growth: A Report for the Club of Rome's Project on the Predicament of Mankind* (New York: Universe Books, 1972).

14. Smith's story was later included in the multiauthor collection *Future Boston*, whose underlying premise is that a geological anomaly causes Boston and its immediate environs to sink and let in the ocean, while the rest of the United States is unaffected.

15. Watery cities are one of Robinson's favorite images. In addition to these examples, *The Wild Shore* (1984) includes a visit to San Diego's Mission Valley, where the towers of late twentieth-century hotels rise from impounded water like moated fortresses.

16. The windup girl of the title is a genetically engineered "new person," brought from Japan as a businessman's aid, then abandoned in Bangkok to a life of prostitution and sex shows. Under the extremes of degradation, she snaps her obedience conditioning to kill her tormenters. She is a fascinating character and a most sympathetic murderer who plays an inadvertent catalytic role in the plot and manages to survive the end of the city.

17. In *Shipbreaker* (2010) he also transposes the third world industry of ship disassembly to a future North America.

CHAPTER 7. KEEP OUT, YOU IDIOTS! THE DESERTED CITY

1. Mike Davis, *Ecology of Fear: Los Angeles and the Imagination of Disaster* (New York: Metropolitan Books, 1998); Max Page, *The City's End: Two Centuries of Fantasies, Fears, and Premonitions of New York's Destruction* (New Haven, CT: Yale University Press, 2010).

2. Nick Yablon, *Untimely Ruins: An Archaeology of American Urban Modernity, 1819–1919* (Chicago: University of Chicago Press, 2009).

CHAPTER 8. MARKET AND MOSAIC

1. Peter Langer, "Sociology-Four Images of Organized Diversity," in *Cities of the Mind: Images and Themes of the City in Social Science*, ed. Lloyd Rodwin and Rob Hollister (New York: Plenum, 1984), 100–101.

2. Brian Stableford, "Cities," in *The Encyclopedia of Science Fiction*, ed. John Clute and Peter Nichols (New York: St. Martin's, 1993); Vivian Sobchack, "Cities on the Edge of Time: The Urban Science Fiction Film," *East-West Film Journal* 3 (December 1988): 4–19; John Gold, "Under Darkened Skies: The City in Science Fiction Films," *Geography* 86 (October 2001): 337–45.

3. Ray Oldenburg, *The Great Good Place: Cafés, Coffee Shops, Bookstores, Hair Salons, and Other Hangouts at the Heart of a Community* (New York: Paragon, 1989).

4. Samuel R. Delany, "On *Triton* and Other Matters: An Interview with Samuel R. Delany," *Science Fiction Studies* 17 (November 1990): 307.

5. Ron Randall, *Trekker*, No. 1 (Milwaukie, OR: Dark Horse Comics, 1987), 8.

6. Science fiction readers are also familiar with more benign bars that provide the setting for a long series of tall tales and mind-puzzle stories: Arthur C. Clarke's White Hart Pub, Larry Niven's Draco Tavern, and Spider Robinson's Callahan's Place.

7. Andrew Milner, "Darker Cities: Urban Dystopia and Science Fiction Cinema," *International Journal of Cultural Studies* 7 (September 2004): 259–79.

8. Ibid., 268.

9. Norman Klein, "Building *Blade Runner*," *Social Text*, no. 28 (1991): 148; Robert Silverberg, "The Way the Future Looks: *THX 1138* and *Blade Runner*," in *Omni's Screen Flights / Screen Fantasies: The Future according to the Science Fiction Cinema*, ed. Danny Peary (Garden City, NY: Doubleday, 1984), 187; "Directing *Alien* and *Blade Runner*: An Interview with Ridley Scott by Danny Peary," in Peary, *Omni's Screen Flights / Screen Fantasies*, 189.

10. Interpretations of the *Blade Runner* city run both negative and positive. David Desser emphasizes the "mélange of swarming humanity" in which inequalities of race and class are inscribed in a dangerous cityscape, but Vivian Sobchack writes

that it is "a city experienced less as base and degraded than as dense, complex, and heterogeneous" and endlessly stimulating. David Desser, "Race, Space and Class: The Politics of Cityscape in Science Fiction Films," in *Alien Zone II: The Spaces of Science-Fiction Cinema*, ed. Annette Kuhn (New York: Verso, 1999), 93; Sobchack, "Cities on the Edge of Time," 136.

11. Stephen Rowley, "False LA: *Blade Runner* and the Nightmare City," in *The "Blade Runner" Experience: The Legacy of a Science Fiction Classic*, ed. Will Brooker (New York: Wallflower Press, 2005), 210; Klein, "Building *Blade Runner*."

12. Robert Neuwirth, *Shadow Cities: A Billion Squatters, a New Urban World* (New York: Routledge, 2004); Brodwyn Fisher, Bryan McCann, and Javier Auyero, eds., *Cities from Scratch: Poverty and Informality in Latin America* (Durham, NC: Duke University Press, 2014).

13. Robert E. Park, "The City: Suggestions for the Investigation of Human Behavior in the Urban Environment," *American Journal of Sociology* 20 (March 1915): 577–612.

14. Jacob Riis, *How the Other Half Lives: Studies among the Tenements of New York* (New York: Charles Scribner's Sons, 1890), 25.

15. Claude Fischer, *To Dwell among Friends: Personal Networks in Town and Country* (Chicago: University of Chicago Press, 1982).

16. The text references Turkish and Kurdish immigrants to the cities and references real nations in a way that would put the cities somewhere around Transylvania, but since the cities have a port, they may be nearer to Moldova. Or is the location to be interpreted as a seacoast in Bohemia to emphasize the element of fantasy?

17. Scott Bollens, *On Narrow Ground: Urban Policy and Conflict in Jerusalem and Belfast* (Albany, NY: SUNY Press, 2000).

18. Leonie Sandercock, *Cosmopolis II: Mongrel Cities in the 21st Century* (New York: Continuum, 2003), 1.

19. Richard Sennett, *The Fall of Public Man* (New York: Knopf, 1977), and *Together: The Rituals, Pleasures, and Politics of Cooperation* (New Haven, CT: Yale University Press, 2012); Michel de Certeau, *The Practice of Everyday Life*, trans. Steven Rendell (Berkeley: University of California Press, 1984).

20. Joan Gordon, "Hybridity, Heterotopia, and Mateship in China Miéville's *Perdido Street Station*," *Science Fiction Studies* 30 (November 2003): 467. Also see Mark C. Childs, "Learning from New Millennium Science Fiction Cities," *Journal of Urbanism* 8 (March 2014): 97–109.

21. Christopher Palmer, "Saving the City in China Miéville's Bas-Lag Novels," *Extrapolation* 50, no. 2 (2009): 224–38.

22. Joan Gordon and China Miéville, "Reveling in Genre: An Interview with China Miéville," *Science Fiction Studies* 30 (November 2003): 364.

23. Howard S. Becker, *Art Worlds* (Berkeley: University of California Press, 1982). My student Marianne Ryder has used the concept to understand the emergence of the Puget Sound region as a center for sophisticated glass sculpture, an art world that embraces artists, educational programs, exchanges of expertise across continents, specialized workplaces, patrons, galleries, and museums that legitimize the art outside its place of production. See Marianne Ryder, "Forming a New Art in the Pacific Northwest: Studio Glass in the Puget Sound Region, 1970–2003" (PhD diss., Portland State University, 2013).

24. Edward Glaeser, *The Triumph of the City: How Our Greatest Invention Makes Us Richer, Smarter, Greener, Healthier, and Happier* (New York: Penguin, 2011), 247.

25. Ibid., 1.

26. The novels expand on a setting that Gibson introduced in the short story "Skinner's Room," written as part of a 1990 museum exhibition on Visionary San Francisco.

27. Michael Beehler, "Architecture and the Virtual West in William Gibson's San Francisco," in *Postwestern Cultures: Literature, Theory, Space,* ed. Susan Kollin (Lincoln: University of Nebraska Press, 2007), 88.

28. Gary Westfahl, *William Gibson* (Urbana: University of Illinois Press, 2013), 121; James Thrall, "Love, Loss, and Utopian Community on William Gibson's Bridge," *Foundation* 91 (Summer 2004): 97–115.

29. For a quick suggestion along these lines see Neil Campbell, *The Cultures of the American New West* (Chicago: Fitzroy Dearborn, 2000), 160–61.

30. Graham Murphy, "Post/Humanity and the Interstitial: A Glorification of Possibility in Gibson's Bridge Sequence," *Science Fiction Studies* 30, no. 1 (March 2003): 74; Beehler, "Architecture and the Virtual West," 82–86.

31. Samuel R. Delany, "On *Triton* and Other Matters: An Interview with Samuel R. Delany," *Science Fiction Studies* 17 (November 1990): 303–4.

32. Salman Rushdie, *Imaginary Homelands* (London: Granta Books, 1992), 394. Italics in original.

AFTERWORD: CITIES THAT WILL WORK

1. George Tucker, *The Progress of the United States in Population and in Wealth in Fifty Years* (New York: n.p., 1843), 127.

2. Kevin Lynch, *Wasting Away: An Exploration of Waste; What It Is, How It Happens, Why We Fear It, How to Do It Well* (San Francisco: Sierra Club Books, 1992), 109.

3. Hull is Griffith's home city, re-created after her move to the United States. The locale is identified in Andrew M. Butler, "Thirteen Ways of Looking at the British Boom," *Science Fiction Studies* 30 (November 2003): 381.

4. Nicola Griffith, "Layered Cities," *ParaDoxa* 2, no. 1 (1996): 37.

5. Ibid., 40.

6. Michelle Reid, "Crossing the Boundaries of the 'Burn': Canadian Multiculturalism and Caribbean Hybridity in Nalo Hopkinson's *Brown Girl in the Ring*," *Extrapolation* 46, no. 3 (2005): 297–314; Sharon DeGraw, "*Brown Girl in the Ring* as Urban Policy," in *Blast, Corrupt, Dismantle, Erase: Contemporary North American Dystopian Literature*, ed. Brett Josef Grubisic, Gisele M. Baxter, and Tara Lee (Waterloo, ON: Wilfrid Laurier University Press, 2014), 193–215.

7. Robert Markley, "'How to Go Forward': Catastrophe and Comedy in Kim Stanley Robinson's Science in the Capital Trilogy," *Configurations* 20, nos. 1–2 (Winter–Spring 2012): 7–27.

8. Rebecca Solnit, *A Paradise Built in Hell: The Extraordinary Communities That Arise in Disaster* (New York: Viking, 2009).

9. Kathleen Ann Goonan, "Cities of the Future?," *ParaDoxa* 2, no. 1 (1996): 31.

NOTES ON SOURCES

Cities are one of the most common science fiction settings, along with spaceships and habitats and the surfaces of distant planets, but their role in speculative fiction has received relatively little sustained attention.

Efforts to define a typology of science fiction cities or to categorize their roles in literature and film include Brian Stableford, "Cities," in *The Encyclopedia of Science Fiction*, ed. John Clute and Peter Nicholls (New York: St. Martin's, 1993), 226–27; John Dean, "Science Fiction City," *Foundation* 23 (October 1981): 64–72; John Clute, "The City and Urban Fantasy," *ParaDoxa* 2, no. 1 (1996): 19–26; Vivian Sobchack, "Cities on the Edge of Time: The Urban Science-Fiction Film," in *Alien Zone II: The Spaces of Science-Fiction Cinema*, ed. Annette Kuhn (New York: Verso, 1999), 123–43; John Gold, "Under Darkened Skies: The City in Science Fiction Films," *Geography* 86 (October 2001): 337–45.

Treatments of the tension between depictions of utopias and dystopias often highlight cities in the course of their discussion. Examples are Tom Moylan, *Scraps of the Untainted Sky: Science Fiction, Utopia, Dystopia* (Boulder, CO: Westview, 2000), and Rob Latham and Jeff Hicks, "Urban Dystopias," in *The Cambridge Companion to the City in Literature*, ed. Kevin R. McNamarra (New York: Cambridge University Press, 2014).

A challenging analysis of the function of cities within the science fiction imagination is found in Gary K. Wolfe, *The Known and the Unknown: The Iconography of Science Fiction* (Kent, OH: Kent State University Press, 1979).

Scholars have gravitated to a number of individual science fiction cities as iconic or representative cases. Examples are the city of Fritz Lang's *Metropolis*, the Los Angeles of *Blade Runner*, China Miéville's New Crobuzon, Arthur C. Clarke's Diaspar, Samuel R. Delany's Tethys, and the urban settings in William Gibson's "Sprawl" and "Bridge" trilogies. Coruscant in the Star Wars universe has accreted a vast body of fan-sourced commentary and elaboration. Other science fiction cities, such as those depicted by C. J. Cherryh or Alastair Reynolds, have yet to acquire the same thickets of popular and critical consideration.

Much of the scholarship on science fiction comes from the fields of literature, media studies, and cultural studies (fifteen of the seventeen editors and contributors to the recent *Cambridge Companion to American Science Fiction* are from these fields, for example). In addition, sociologists, geographers, urban planners, and other social scientists are often interested in the intersections between science fiction, social theory, and political practice. For example, the specific category of cities in cyberpunk fiction has attracted comment from Mark C. Childs, "Learning from the New Millennium: Science Fiction Cities," *Journal of Urbanism* 8, no. 1 (2015): 97–109; Natalie Collie, "Cities of the Imagination: Science Fiction, Urban Space, and Community Engagement in Urban Planning," *Futures* 43 (May 2011): 424–31; Robert Warren, Stacy Warren, Samuel Nunn, and Colin Warren, "The Future of the Future in Planning: Appropriating Cyberpunk Visions of the City," *Journal of Planning Education and Research* 18 (Autumn 1998): 49–60; and others, including myself.

SCIENCE FICTION NOVELS AND STORIES

When a reprinted version has been quoted, the original publication data and reprint information are both given.

Aldiss, Brian. *Non-Stop*. London: Faber and Faber, 1958.

Asimov, Isaac. *Caves of Steel*. 1954. New York: Bantam Spectra, 1991.

———. *Foundation*. Garden City, NY: Doubleday, 1951.

———. *Foundation and Empire*. Garden City, NY: Doubleday, 1952.

———. *Lucky Starr and the Oceans of Venus*. Garden City, NY: Doubleday, 1954.

———. *Second Foundation*. Garden City, NY: Doubleday, 1953.

Bacigalupi, Paolo. *The Water Knife*. New York: Knopf, 2015.

———. *The Windup Girl*. San Francisco: Nightshade Books, 2009.

Ballard, J. G. "Billennium." 1962. In *Cities of Wonder*, edited by Damon Knight, 92–107. New York: Macfadden-Bartell, 1967.

———. "The Concentration City." 1957. In *The Complete Short Stories*. London: Flamingo/HarperCollins, 2001.

———. *High-Rise*. New York: Liveright, 1975.

Banks, Iain M. *Surface Detail*. New York: Orbit, 2010.

Barnes, John. *A Million Open Doors*. New York: Tor, 1992.

———. *Mother of Storms*. New York: Tor, 1994.

Baxter, Stephen. *Flood*. New York: ROC, 2009.

Bear, Elizabeth. "The Red in the Sky Is Our Blood." In *Metatropolis*, edited by John Scalzi, 121–58. Burton, MI: Subterranean, 2009.

Bear, Greg. *Moving Mars*. New York: Tor, 1993.

———. *Strength of Stones*. New York: Warner Books, 1988.

Benford, Gregory. *In the Ocean of Night*. New York: Dell, 1977.

Blish, James, *Cities in Flight*. New York: Avon, 1970.

Boyle, T. C. *The Tortilla Curtain*. New York: Viking, 1995.

Bradbury, Ray. *The Martian Chronicles*. 1950. New York: William Morrow, 1997.

Brin, David. *Existence*. New York: Tor, 2012.

Brunner, John. *The Sheep Look Up*. New York: Harper & Row, 1972.

———. *Stand on Zanzibar*. 1968. New York: Orb, 2011.

Buckell, Tobias. "Stochasti-City." In *Metatropolis*, edited by John Scalzi, 71–120. Burton, MI: Subterranean, 2009.

Butler, Octavia. *Parable of the Sower*. New York: Four Walls Eight Windows, 1993.

Cadigan, Pat. *Tea from an Empty Cup*. New York: Tor, 1998.

Cherryh, C. J. *Cyteen*. New York: Warner Books, 1988.

———. *Downbelow Station*. New York: DAW Books, 1981.

———. *Regenesis*. New York: DAW Books, 2009.

———. *Sunfall*. New York: DAW Books, 1981.

Christopher, John. *Wild Jack*. 1974. New York: Collier Books, 1991.

Clarke, Arthur C. *The City and the Stars*. 1956. Princess Anne, MD: Yestermore, n.d.

———. *The Sands of Mars*. 1951. In *Prelude to Mars*. New York: Harcourt Brace, 1965.

Cline, Ernest, *Ready Player One*. New York: Random House, 2001.

Collins, Suzanne. *Catching Fire*. New York: Scholastic, 2009.

———. *The Hunger Games*. New York: Scholastic, 2008.

———. *Mockingjay*. New York: Scholastic, 2010.

Coupland, Douglas. *Generation X*. New York: St. Martin's, 1991.

———. *Microserfs*. New York: HarperCollins, 1995.

———. *Shampoo Planet*. New York: Washington Square, 1992.

Cronin, Justin. *The Passage*. New York: Ballantine. 2009.

Delany, Samuel R. *Babel-17*. New York: Ace, 1966.

———. *Trouble on Triton: An Ambiguous Heterotopia*. 1976. Middletown, CT: Wesleyan University Press, 1996.

DeLillo, Don. *Cosmopolis*. New York: Scribner's, 2003.

Disch, Thomas. *334*. London: MacGibbon & Kee, 1972.

Donnelly, Ignatius. *Caesar's Column*. 1890. Cambridge, MA: Belknap Press of Harvard University Press, 1960.

DuPrau, Jeanne. *City of Ember*. New York: Random House, 2003.

Ellison, Harlan. "A Boy and His Dog." 1969. In *The Essential Ellison*, edited by Terry Dowling, 905–38. Omaha: Nemo, 1987.

England, George Allan. *Darkness and Dawn*. Boston: Small, Maynard & Co., 1914.

Forster, E. M. "The Machine Stops." 1909. In *The Science Fiction Hall of Fame*, vol. 2B, *The Greatest Science Fiction Novellas of All Time*, edited by Ben Bova, 248–79. New York: Avon, 1973.

Frank, Pat. *Alas, Babylon*. Philadelphia: Lippincott, 1959.

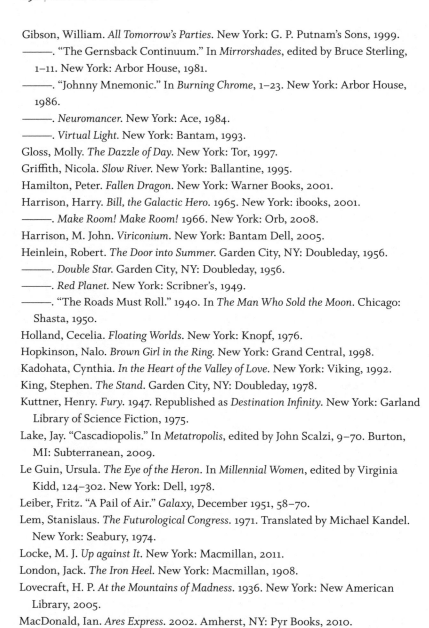

Gibson, William. *All Tomorrow's Parties*. New York: G. P. Putnam's Sons, 1999.

——. "The Gernsback Continuum." In *Mirrorshades*, edited by Bruce Sterling, 1–11. New York: Arbor House, 1981.

——. "Johnny Mnemonic." In *Burning Chrome*, 1–23. New York: Arbor House, 1986.

——. *Neuromancer*. New York: Ace, 1984.

——. *Virtual Light*. New York: Bantam, 1993.

Gloss, Molly. *The Dazzle of Day*. New York: Tor, 1997.

Griffith, Nicola. *Slow River*. New York: Ballantine, 1995.

Hamilton, Peter. *Fallen Dragon*. New York: Warner Books, 2001.

Harrison, Harry. *Bill, the Galactic Hero*. 1965. New York: ibooks, 2001.

——. *Make Room! Make Room!* 1966. New York: Orb, 2008.

Harrison, M. John. *Viriconium*. New York: Bantam Dell, 2005.

Heinlein, Robert. *The Door into Summer*. Garden City, NY: Doubleday, 1956.

——. *Double Star*. Garden City, NY: Doubleday, 1956.

——. *Red Planet*. New York: Scribner's, 1949.

——. "The Roads Must Roll." 1940. In *The Man Who Sold the Moon*. Chicago: Shasta, 1950.

Holland, Cecelia. *Floating Worlds*. New York: Knopf, 1976.

Hopkinson, Nalo. *Brown Girl in the Ring*. New York: Grand Central, 1998.

Kadohata, Cynthia. *In the Heart of the Valley of Love*. New York: Viking, 1992.

King, Stephen. *The Stand*. Garden City, NY: Doubleday, 1978.

Kuttner, Henry. *Fury*. 1947. Republished as *Destination Infinity*. New York: Garland Library of Science Fiction, 1975.

Lake, Jay. "Cascadiopolis." In *Metatropolis*, edited by John Scalzi, 9–70. Burton, MI: Subterranean, 2009.

Le Guin, Ursula. *The Eye of the Heron*. In *Millennial Women*, edited by Virginia Kidd, 124–302. New York: Dell, 1978.

Leiber, Fritz. "A Pail of Air." *Galaxy*, December 1951, 58–70.

Lem, Stanislaus. *The Futurological Congress*. 1971. Translated by Michael Kandel. New York: Seabury, 1974.

Locke, M. J. *Up against It*. New York: Macmillan, 2011.

London, Jack. *The Iron Heel*. New York: Macmillan, 1908.

Lovecraft, H. P. *At the Mountains of Madness*. 1936. New York: New American Library, 2005.

MacDonald, Ian. *Ares Express*. 2002. Amherst, NY: Pyr Books, 2010.

Martel, Suzanne, *The City under Ground*. New York: Viking, 1964.

Matheson, Richard. *I Am Legend*. New York: Gold Medal Books, 1954.

McHugh, Maureen. *Half the Day Is Night*. New York: Tor, 1994.

McMahon, Donna. *Dance of Knives*. New York: Tor, 2001.

Miéville, China. *The City and the City*. New York: Ballantine, 2009.

———. *Embassytown*. New York: Del Rey Books, 2011.

———. *Perdido Street Station*. New York: Ballantine, 2001.

———. *The Scar*. New York: Ballantine, 2002.

———. *Un Lun Dun*. New York: Macmillan, 2007.

Murphy, Pat. *The City Not Long After*. New York: Bantam Spectra, 1990.

Nagata, Linda. "Nahiku West." In *The Best Science Fiction and Fantasy of the Year*, edited by Jonathan Strahan, 543–63. San Francisco: Night Shade Books, 2013.

Niven, Larry. *The Patchwork Girl*. New York: Ace, 1980.

———. *Ringworld*. New York: Ballantine, 1970.

———. *The Ringworld Engineers*. 1980. New York: Ballantine, 1981.

Niven, Larry, and Jerry Pournelle. *Oath of Fealty*. 1981. New York: Pocket Books, 1982.

Norton, Andre. *Star Man's Son: 2250 A.D.* 1952. In *Darkness and Dawn*. New York: Baen Books, 2003.

———. *Star Rangers*. 1953. In *Star Soldiers*. New York: Baen Books, 2001.

Oliver, Chad. "The Wind Blows Free." *Magazine of Fantasy and Science Fiction*, July 1957.

Platt, Charles. *The Twilight of the City: A Novel of the Near Future*. New York: Macmillan, 1977.

Pohl, Frederik. *The Years of the City*. New York: Timescape Books / Simon & Schuster, 1975.

Pohl, Frederik, and Cyril Kornbluth, *Gladiator-at-Law*. 1955. New York: Bantam, 1977.

Priest, Christopher. *Inverted World*. 1974. New York: New York Review Books, 2008.

Randall, Ron. *Trekker*. Milwaukie, OR: Dark Horse Comics, 1987.

Reeve, Philip. *Mortal Engines*. New York: Scholastic Books, 2001.

———. *Predator's Gold*. New York: Scholastic Books, 2003.

Reynolds, Alastair. *Chasm City*. 2001. New York: Ace Books, 2003.

———. *Terminal World*. New York: Ace Books, 2010.

Richerson, Carrie. "The City in Morning." In *Bending the Landscape: Original Gay and Lesbian Science Fiction*, edited by Nicola Griffith and Stephen Paget, 232–41. Woodstock, NY: Overlook, 1999.

Robinson, Kim Stanley. *Fifty Degrees Below*. New York: Bantam, 2005.

———. *Forty Signs of Rain*. New York: Bantam, 2004.

———. *The Gold Coast*. New York: Tor, 1988.

———. *Green Mars*. New York: Bantam, 1994.

———. *Red Mars.* New York: Bantam, 1993.

———. *Sixty Days and Counting.* New York: Bantam, 2006.

———. *2312.* New York: Orbit, 2012.

———. "Venice Drowned." 1981. In *Remaking History and Other Stories.* New York: Tom Doherty Associates, 1994.

———. *The Wild Shore.* New York: Ace, 1984.

Rusch, Kristine Kathryn. *Anniversary Day.* Lincoln City, OR: WMG Publishing, 2011.

———. *City of Ruins.* Amherst, NY: Prometheus Books, 2011.

Sargent, Pamela. *Cloned Lives.* Greenwich, CT: Fawcett, 1976.

Sawyer, Robert. *Red Planet Blues.* New York: Ace, 2013.

Scalzi, John. "Utere Nihil Non Extra Quiritationem Suis." In *Metatropolis*, edited by John Scalzi, 159–210. Burton, MI: Subterranean, 2009.

Scott, Melissa. *Burning Bright.* New York: Tor, 1993.

Shirley, John. *City Come A-Walkin'.* 1980. New York: Four Walls, Eight Windows, 2000.

Silverberg, Robert. *The World Inside.* 1971. New York: Tom Doherty Associates, 2010.

Simak, Clifford, *City.* 1952. Baltimore: Old Earth Books, 2004.

Smith, Cordwainer. "The Ballad of Lost C'Mell." 1962. In *The Best of Cordwainer Smith*, 227–306. Garden City, NY: Nelson Doubleday, 1975.

———. "The Dead Lady of Clown Town." 1964. In *The Best of Cordwainer Smith*, 117–92. Garden City, NY: Nelson Doubleday, 1975.

———. "Under Old Earth." 1966. In *The Best of Cordwainer Smith*, 193–234. Garden City, NY: Nelson Doubleday, 1975.

Smith, David Alexander. "Dying in Hull." 1988. In *Future Boston: The History of a City, 1990–2100*, edited by David Alexander Smith, 71–82. New York: Tor, 1994.

Steele, Allen. *Lunar Descent.* New York: Ace, 1991.

Stephenson, Neal. *The Diamond Age.* New York: Bantam, 1995.

———. *Snow Crash.* New York: Bantam Spectra, 1992.

Sterling, Bruce. *Islands in the Net.* New York: Ace, 1989.

Varley, John. *Dark Lightning.* New York: Ace, 2014.

Whates, Ian. *City of Dreams and Nightmares.* Nottingham, UK: Angry Robot, 2010.

Zahn, Timothy, *Heir to the Empire.* 1991. New York: Ballantine, 2011.

FILMS AND TELEVISION PROGRAMS

The Abyss. Dir. James Cameron. 1989.

Akira. Dir. Katsuhiro Otomo. 1988.

Alphaville. Dir. Jean-Luc Godard. 1965.

Babylon 5. 1994–98.

Battlestar Galactica. 2004–9.

Blade Runner. Dir. Ridley Scott. 1982.

A Boy and His Dog. Dir. L. Q. Jones. 1975.

Captain Nemo and the Underwater City. Dir. James Hill. 1969.

City of Ember. Dir. Gil Kenan. 2008.

Demolition Man. Dir. Marco Brambilla. 1983.

Escape from New York. Dir. John Carpenter. 1981.

Futurama. 1999–2013.

I Am Legend. Dir. Francis Lawrence. 2007.

In Time. Dir. Francis Nicol. 2011.

Just Imagine. Dir. David Butler. 1930.

The Last Man on Earth. Dir. Ubaldo Ragona and Sidney Salkow. 1966.

Logan's Run. Dir. Michael Anderson. 1976.

Metropolis. Dir. Fritz Lang. 1927.

Minority Report. Dir. Steven Spielberg. 2002.

The Omega Man. Dir. Boris Sagal. 1971.

Snowpiercer. Dir. Joon-Ho Bong. 2013.

Soylent Green. Dir. Richard Fleischer. 1973.

Star Trek: Deep Space Nine. 1993–99.

Star Wars, Episode I: The Phantom Menace. Dir. George Lucas. 1999.

Star Wars, Episode II: Attack of the Clones. Dir. George Lucas. 2002.

Star Wars, Episode III: Revenge of the Sith. Dir. George Lucas. 2005.

THX 1138. Dir. George Lucas. 1971.

Total Recall. Dir. Paul Verhoeven. 1990.

WALL-E. Dir. Andrew Stanton. 2008.

INDEX

Note: page numbers in *italics* refer to figures

CARL ABBOTT is a professor emeritus at Portland State University, having taught urban studies and planning since the late 1970s. He is the author of the prize-winning books *The Metropolitan Frontier: Cities in the Modern American West* and *Political Terrain: Washington, D.C., from Tidewater Town to Global Metropolis.* He has also written several feature articles for the journal *Science Fiction Studies* and the book *Frontiers Past and Future: Science Fiction and the American West.*